Richard III : His Life & Character

By Sir Clements E. Markham

Copyright © 2013 Alex Struik.

Alex Struik retains sole copyright to the cover design of this edition of this book.

All rights reserved. No part of this publication may be reproduced, stored in a retrieval system, or transmitted, in any form or by any means, electronic, mechanical, photocopying, recording or otherwise, without the prior permission of the copyright owner.

The right of Alex Struik to be identified as the author of the cover design of this work has been asserted in accordance with the Copyright, Designs and Patents Act 1988.

Cover Design by Alex Struik.

ISBN-13: 978-1482373103

ISBN-10: 1482373106

Contents

PREFACE 5
PART I 9
   CHAPTER I BIRTH AND CHILDHOOD 9
   CHAPTER II DEATH OF RICHARD'S FATHER AND BROTHER AT THE BATTLE OF WAKEFIELD.......18
   CHAPTER III THE CROWNING VICTORY OF TOWTON 29
   CHAPTER IV THE CROWN LOST AND WON— BATTLE OF BARNET 47
   CHAPTER V MARGARET OF ANJOU AND HER SON EDWARD 62
   CHAPTER VI THE BATTLE OF TEWKESBURY 78
   CHAPTER VII MARRIED LIFE AND PUBLIC SERVICES OF RICHARD DUKE OF GLOUCESTER 89
   CHAPTER VIII ACCESSION OF RICHARD III 98
   CHAPTER IX CONDITION OF THE PEOPLE 115
      Peerage of Richard III 121
   CHAPTER X REIGN OF KING RICHARD III 138
      CORONATION PROCESSION OF KING RICHARD III. 141
      PEERAGE OF RICHARD III. 155
   CHAPTER XI THE BATTLE OF BOSWORTH 170
      CONTEMPORARY SOVEREIGNS 184
PART II 190
   CHAPTER I THE AUTHORITIES............................190
   CHAPTER II EXAMINATION OF THE CHARGES AGAINST RICHARD III...208

CHAPTER III FURTHER CHARGES AGAINST RICHARD III 230
CHAPTER IV THE MAIN CHARGE AGAINST RICHARD III 258
CHAPTER V HENRY TUDOR IN THE DOCK 271
   LOYAL MEN WITH THE KING AT BOSWORTH 276
CHAPTER VI MR. GAIRDNER'S RICHARD III 308

PREFACE

There are periods of history when the greatest caution is called for in accepting statements put forward by a dominant faction. Very early in my life I came to the conclusion that the period which witnessed the change of dynasties from Plantagenet to Tudor was one of these. The caricature of the last Plantagenet King was too grotesque, and too grossly opposed to his character derived from official records. The stories were an outrage on common-sense. I studied the subject at intervals for many years, and in the course of my researches I found that I more or less shared my doubts with every author of repute who had studied the subject for the last three centuries, except Hume and Lingard. My own conclusions are that Richard III. must be acquitted on all the counts of the indictment. The present work is divided into two parts, the first narrating the events of his life and times, and the second examining the various accusations against him. I did not contemplate publication because I thought that in these days prejudices were too strong to make it possible that a fair and candid hearing should be given to the arguments. But I determined to consult some historical friends, and I was pleased to find that to a great extent I was mistaken.

In the first place, I wrote a full abstract of my arguments, for publication in the 'Historical Review,' acting under the advice of my old schoolfellow, Professor Freeman, to whom I sent it in the first instance. It so happened that Mr. Freeman had given attention to part of the subject. He upset some odious fabrications of the chroniclers affecting the character of Margaret of Anjou, by proving that she was in Scotland at the time when the battle of Wakefield was fought. Freeman seldom wrote on so late a period of our history, and we owe this modern excursion to a visit to Mr. Milnes Gaskell at Thornes.

After reading what I sent him, Professor Freeman wrote on August 13, 1890: 'Your abstract has set me a-thinking. It is only a Robert of Bellême who does that kind of thing. On your main point I will talk to Gardiner and Stubbs. Meanwhile, I have shown your manuscript to Sidney Owen, who read it and held it to be what lawyers would call considerable. Owen had been at those times, and holds Henry VII. to be at least capable of it.

'It would be a self-denying ordinance in Gairdner if he accepted your view, for he has gone more straight at that time than anybody else. Gardiner has written to him, and he is a little fierce, as was to be expected, but if you are like me, no man's fierceness will hinder you from dining and sleeping as well as usual. The matter is at all events worth discussing.'

Professor York Powell read my manuscript, and wrote: 'I have read the manuscript and think there is something worth looking into. Henry's conduct to Tyrrell is exceedingly suspicious. Either Richard or Henry might have put the boys to death, but it would be interesting for many reasons to know which it was. I am not convinced by Markham, but I do not think Gairdner has the right to be cocksure. The Morton suggestive idea is very ingenious and pretty, and quite probable. It has interested me much to read Markham's letter, for I remember my difficulties in the matter and the point I got to, that the great men did not, for a time, hold the now vulgate view of the murder of the princes. I should rejoice should Markham light upon additional evidence in favour of his thesis, which à priori is by no means unlikely. There is something about Richard's character, ability, and reign which, I think, attracts every real student of history, and gives one a feeling that he has been unfairly dealt with.'

In 1891, the abstract of my work was published in the 'Historical Review,' and Bishop Creighton, who was then the editor, wrote: 'Thank you for your paper, which I have read with great interest. It certainly makes out a strong case.'

There were two rejoinders from Mr. Gairdner, which enabled me to recast and improve parts of my work by the light of his criticism.

I lost my adviser, Mr. Freeman, in 1892. One of the last things he did was to warn me of an objection taken by Miss Edith Thompson, which enabled me to meet it.[1]

After careful revision I showed my manuscript to the late Sir Archibald Milman, who had given close attention to those times. On December 27, 1897, he wrote: 'It is your bounden duty to tell your story of Richard III., giving the date for every fact. It is only by sticking to dates that you get at truth in criminal causes, and the same method must be followed at the bar of history. It would be a pleasure to think that the last Plantagenet was not a cruel scoundrel. By giving dates and authorities for them, you render a great service. Richard's loyalty and able administration in the north seem inconsistent with such ferocity. I was much interested in one of your facts, that, according to the story put forward by Henry VII., the bodies of the little princes were taken up from the place of hasty interment and placed in consecrated ground. But lo! they remained under the staircase, where they were found in Charles II.'s reign.'

In consequence of Sir A. Milman's letter I made another close scrutiny of dates given by various authorities for the same events with important results. I also went very carefully over the ground of the battlefields of Wakefield, Towton, Barnet, Tewkesbury, and Bosworth; and I added some chapters to the work.

The correspondence to which I have referred has led me to the conclusion that students of history are not, as I once believed, unwilling to reconsider the questions which form the subject of the present work, when they are presented from new points of view; and that the well-known arguments which were supposed to suffice for the defence of the Tudor stories in the past are in these days insufficient. The numerous points now raised and submitted for the judgment of students are at all events worth discussing. The present work is about as complete as very frequent revision can make it.

[1] She pointed out that the titles of Norfolk and Nottingham, granted by Edward IV. to his second son Richard, were given by Richard III. to Lords Howard and Berkeley, and that, therefore, young Richard must have been dead. The answer is that the grants to Lords Howard and Berkeley were made on June 28, 1483, before it was even pretended that young Richard had been murdered.

PART I

CHAPTER I BIRTH AND CHILDHOOD

The castle of Fotheringhay[1] was the birthplace of our last Plantagenet king. This venerable pile stood on the banks of the river Nen, in Northamptonshire, amidst 'marvellous fair corn ground and pasture.' From its battlements there was an extensive view, bounded to the westward by the forest of Rockingham, while on the other side the abbey church of Peterborough and the woods of Milton intercepted the distant expanse of fen country. Originally built by bold Simon de St. Liz in the twelfth century, the castle had fallen into ruin when it reverted to the crown, and was granted by Edward III. to his son Edmund of Langley.

Edmund, who was created Duke of York by his nephew Richard II., rebuilt the castle and founded a college hard by. Fotheringhay was surrounded by a double moat with drawbridges, the river Nen serving as the outer moat on the south side, and the Mill Brook, flowing between the castle yard and the little park, to the east. The walls were of stone, and the great gate in the north front was adorned with the arms of England, as differenced for Edmund of Langley, impaling the arms of Castille and Leon.[2] The keep, built in the shape of a fetterlock, was on a mount in the northwest angle of the castle; and below there was a great courtyard surrounded by stately buildings, a chapel, and 'very fair lodgings,' as Leland tells us. The great hall was seventy feet long, with a deep oriel window at one end.[3]

Here dwelt Edmund the first Duke of York, his son Edward the second Duke, who fell at Agincourt, and his grandson Richard, the third Duke. Edmund projected the foundation of a college near the parish church, to consist of a master, eight clerks, and thirteen choristers. He commenced the choir, while his son and grandson completed and richly endowed this religious house. The church was a fine specimen of the Perpendicular architecture of the time, and the cloisters had numerous windows filled with stained glass.

The third Duke of York resided at Fotheringhay during part of every year when he was in England, with his beautiful wife the Lady Cicely Nevill, the 'Rose of Raby,' and their troop of fair children. But he also held vast estates elsewhere. In Yorkshire the castles of Sandal and Conisborough were part of his paternal inheritance. On the Welsh borders he had succeeded to all the possessions of the Mortimers, including Ludlow and Wigmore. For his mother was the heiress of Edmund Mortimer, Earl of March, and also of Lionel Duke of Clarence, the second surviving son of King Edward III. Baynard's Castle, in the City of London, was the Duke's town house.

The 'Rose of Raby' bore her husband twelve children, and they came of a right noble English stock. In their veins flowed the blood of Plantagenet and Holland, Mortimer and FitzAlan, Nevill and Percy, Clifford and Audley. Five of these fair branches died in infancy. Ann, the eldest of those who survived early childhood, was born at Fotheringhay in 1439. The three next, Edward, Edmund and Elizabeth, first saw the light at Rouen, when their father was making a last gallant stand for English dominion in France, from 1442 to 1444. Margaret was born at Fotheringhay. The Duke and Duchess were ruling in Ireland when George was born at Dublin Castle. The three last births were at Fotheringhay, but of these only Richard, the eleventh child, survived infancy.

Richard Plantagenet was born at Fotheringhay Castle on October 2, 1452. He probably passed the first five years of his life there with George and Margaret. The elder sisters, Anne and Elizabeth, were married to 'Lancastrian' noblemen, the Dukes of Exeter and Suffolk, when Richard was still in infancy. His elder brothers, Edward Earl of March and Edmund Earl of Rutland, were separated from him by an interval of ten years, and lived with their tutor Richard Croft at Ludlow or Wigmore. So that Richard's childhood must have been passed with his brother George and his sister Margaret, the future Duchess of Burgundy. But both were a few years older than little Richard.

We obtain a glimpse of the home life of the two elder boys, Edward and Edmund, from a letter to their father which has been preserved.[4]

'Right high and right mighty prince, our full redoubted and right noble lord and father.

'As lowly with all our hearts as we, your true and natural sons can or may, we recommend us unto your noble grace, humbly beseeching your noble and worthy fatherhood daily to give us your hearty blessing; through which we trust much the rather to increase and grow to virtue, and to speed the better in all matters and things that we shall use, occupy, and exercise.

'Right high and right mighty prince, our full redoubted lord and father—

'We thank our blessed Lord, not only of your honourable conduct and good speed in all your matters and business, of your gracious prevail against the intent and malice of your evil willers, but also of the knowledge that it pleased your nobleness to let us now late have of the same by relation of Sir Walter Devereux Kt.[5] and John Milwater Esq.,[6] and John at Nokes, yeoman of your honourable chamber. Also we thank your noble and good fatherhood for our green gowns now late sent unto us to our great comfort, beseeching your good lordship to remember our porteux,[7] and that we might have some fine bonnets sent unto us by the next sure messenger, for necessity so requireth. Over this, right noble lord and father, please it your highness to wit that we have charged your servant, William Smyth, bearer of these, for to declare unto your nobility certain things on our behalf, namely concerning and touching the odious rule and demeaning of Richard Croft and of his brother. Wherefore we beseech your gracious lordship and full noble fatherhood to hear him in exposition of the same, and to his relation to give full faith and credence. Right high and right mighty prince, our full redoubted and right noble lord and father, we beseech Almighty Jesus give you as good life and long, with as much continual perfect prosperity as your princely heart can best desire. Written at your castle of Ludlow on Saturday in Easter week.

'your humble sons
  'Edward (Earl of March)
  'Edmund (Earl of Rutland).'

The boys evidently did not like their tutor, declaring him to be tyrannical and disagreeable.[8]

CHILDREN OF RICHARD, DUKE OF YORK

1. Anne. Born at Fotheringhay, August 11, 1439. (Duchess of Exeter.)

2. Henry. Born at Hatfield, February 10,1441. (Died in infancy.)

3. Edward. Born at Rouen,[9] April 28, 1442. (Earl of March. King.)

4. Edmund. Born at Rouen, May 17, 1443. (Earl of Rutland.)

5. Elizabeth. Born at Rouen, April 22,1444. (Duchess of Suffolk.)

6. Margaret. Born at Fotheringhay, May 3, 1446. (Duchess of Burgundy. Died 1503.)

7. William. Born at Fotheringhay, July 7, 1447. (Died young.)

8. John. Born at Neath, November 7, 1448. (Died in infancy.)

9. George. Born at Dublin, October 21, 1449. (Duke of Clarence.)

10. Thomas. Born at Fotheringhay, 1450. (Died in infancy.)

11. Richard. Born at Fotheringhay, October 2, 1452.[10] (Duke of Gloucester. King.)

12. Ursula. Born at Fotheringhay, July 20,1455. (Died in infancy.)

W. WYRCESTER, Annales, 460-477.

Their father, the Duke of York, first Prince of the blood royal, was the most powerful and wealthy, as well as one of the ablest noblemen in the kingdom. He was moderate and prudent, and was unwillingly driven into resistance to the misgovernment of the corrupt faction which misused the powers they had seized, owing to the imbecility of Henry VI. His original object was not to assert his own undoubted title to the throne, but to obtain just and reasonable government by the removal of corrupt and incapable ministers. 'After repeated experience of bad faith, and after fruitlessly endeavouring to bind Henry by pledges, the Duke was at length forced into advancing his own claim.'[11]

Disaster followed the first attempt of the Duke of York at open resistance. He was overpowered by the Lancastrian forces at Ludlow, in October 1459, and his followers were scattered. The Duke himself, with his son Edmund, fled to Ireland. His eldest son, Edward Earl of March, escaped to Calais with the Earl of Warwick. The Duchess of York, and her three young children, Margaret, George and Richard, were taken prisoners at Wigmore. They were sent to Tunbridge Castle in the custody of their mother's sister, the Duchess of Buckingham, who had married a Lancastrian husband.

Little Richard was only seven years of age when he became a prisoner of war. The detention was of short duration. His eldest brother landed in Kent and marched to London. Troops flocked to the standard of the gallant youth, and he advanced northwards against his enemies. The Duchess of York then escaped from Tunbridge, and found an asylum for her little children at the chambers of John Paston, in the Temple.[12]

Meanwhile Edward, Earl of March, won a great victory at Northampton, and Henry VI. became his prisoner. He returned to London, but the children had not been two days in John Paston's chambers before their mother was summoned to meet her husband at Hereford, who was returning from Ireland. The children were left with servants. Young Edward, however, while busily engaged in preparing for the defence of the city, found time to visit his little brothers and sister every day.[13]

[1] 'Fodringeia' in Domesday. 'Fodering' is part of a forest separated from the rest, for producing hay.

[2] He married Isabella of Castille and Leon.

[3] Mary Queen of Scots was tried and beheaded in the great hall of Fotheringhay. But it is untrue that the castle was destroyed by James I. on that account. James granted it to Lord Mountjoy, and it was intact, though out of repair, when it was surveyed in 1625. It began to be dismantled soon after this survey; but the work of demolition was very gradual. The college buildings had been desecrated and destroyed by John Dudley, Duke of Northumberland, to whom they were granted by the government of Edward VI. The last remains of the castle were demolished in the middle of the last century. See Historic Notices in reference to Fotheringhay, by the Rev. H. K. Bonney (Oundle, 1821).

[4] MS. Cotton, Vesp., F. iii., fol. 9. Printed in the first series of Ellis's original letters, i. 9, letter v.

[5] This Sir Walter Devereux, son of Walter Chancellor of Ireland 1449, when the Duke of York was Lord Deputy, was born in 1432. He married Anne, heiress of Lord Ferrers of Chartley, and was summoned to Parliament by that title jure uxoris. Sir Walter Devereux, Lord Ferrers of Chartley, fell gloriously at Bosworth, fighting for his King, Richard III., the younger brother of his two young friends Edward and Edmund. He was ancestor of the Devereux, Earls of Essex.

[6] Afterwards esquire to Richard Duke of Gloucester. He fell at the battle of Barnet, fighting by his young master's side.

[7] Breviary.

[8] Richard Croft of Croft Castle, in Herefordshire, is the odious ruler mentioned by the young princes. He was faithful to King Edward during the Tewkesbury campaign; but the boys had some insight into character. For Croft appears to have been a time-server. He got made Treasurer of the Household to Henry Tudor, and fought for him at Stoke. To please his new patron he appears to have told some story, disparaging to Edward IV., which, in a garbled form, appeared in Hall's Chronicle.

[9] Edwardus quartus Rothomagi natus. Rous, p. 210.

[10] Rous says that Richard was born on the feast of the eleven thousand virgins, October 21. But this was really George's birthday, in 1449.

[11] Gairdner. The Duke's mother, Anne Mortimer, was grand-daughter of Philippa Countess of March, the only child of Lionel Duke of Clarence, second son of King Edward III. Henry VI. was great-grandson of John Duke of Lancaster, third son of Edward III.

[12] Paston Letters, i. 525. Christopher Hansson to John Paston.

[13] 'And sythe y left here bothe the sunys and the dowztyr, and the Lord of Marche comyth every day to se them.'—Paston Letters.

CHAPTER II DEATH OF RICHARD'S FATHER AND BROTHER AT THE BATTLE OF WAKEFIELD

In October 1460, the Duke and Duchess of York, with young Edmund Earl of Rutland, reached London. The Duke's superior right to the crown, as representative of the second son of Edward III. while Henry VI. only derived from the third son, was recognised and declared by Act of Parliament. But, in consideration of the reverence felt for his father and of his own long tenure, it was enacted that Henry should retain the throne for life, provided that he acknowledged the Duke as heir-apparent. This Act of Settlement received the royal assent and became law, all opposing statutes being repealed. On November 9, the Duke of York was solemnly declared Heir-Apparent and Lord Protector during Henry's life.

But Queen Margaret and her partisans refused to be bound by the acts of the King, her husband, in Parliament. She fled to Scotland, and the Lancastrians raised a formidable army in Yorkshire. It is probable that the Duke of York was not fully aware of the numbers opposed to him, though he may have foreseen that the Lancastrian army would become larger if time was allowed to slip away. There was also some danger from the machinations of the Tudors[1] in Wales. Arrangements to counteract these evils were promptly made. The Duke assembled a small force to advance northwards and confront the Lancastrian army. The Duke of Norfolk, who was warmly attached to the House of York, and the Earl of Warwick were to remain in London until Christmas, and then to follow with reinforcements. The young Earl of March advanced to the Welsh borders to collect forces, disperse the Tudor rising, and then join his father in Yorkshire.

On December 1, 1460, the Duke of York was with his wife and children at Baynard's Castle for the last time. He bade farewell to his loving Duchess and the children; little Richard was a child of eight, Margaret and George a few years older. The gallant young Edmund Earl of Rutland was nearly eighteen, well able to fight by his father's side, and he accompanied the Duke. On December 2, the Duke of York set out with his brother-in-law the Earl of Salisbury and the Earl of Rutland. Salisbury had with him his son, Sir Thomas Nevill, and the force, barely numbering 5,000 men, was led by other experienced captains. Chief among them was old Sir David Hall, the Duke's faithful friend and adviser in all military affairs. Sir John and Sir Hugh Mortimer, illegitimate brothers of the ill-fated Earl of March, rallied to their nephew's standard with many Yorkist knights, such as Sir Thomas Parr, Sir Edward Bourchier, and Sir James Pickering. The force included a company of Londoners under the command of the Warden of the Mercers' Company, stout John Harrow.

The Duke of York advanced by easy marches, for he did not reach his castle of Sandal, about a mile south of Wakefield, until Christmas Eve. Here he halted while a summons was sent out to assemble his Yorkshire tenants and adherents. It is said that Lord Nevill, a kinsman of the Duchess of York, came to Sandal as a friend of the Duke, and induced him to grant a commission to raise men; and that when he had raised about 8,000, he treacherously brought them to swell the ranks of the Lancastrian army.[2]

At this time the Duke's eldest son Edward was at Shrewsbury. The poor Duchess and her young children anxiously waited for news at Baynard's Castle. Henry VI., with the Duke of Norfolk and the Earl of Warwick, observed the festival of Christmas in the palace of the Bishop of London, in St. Paul's Churchyard. Afterwards the

King went to enjoy a few days' hunting at Greenwich and Eltham. Queen Margaret and her son were in Scotland. The Lancastrian leaders were assembled with a great army at Pomfret.

Edward III. had granted Sandal and Conisborough Castles to his son Edmund, the Duke's grandfather. The Duke himself had frequently resided at Sandal, sometimes with his wife and family. The castle stood on a grassy knoll, steep on one side, with a gentle slope to the south. It is a little less than a mile from the bridge which spans the river Calder at the town of Wakefield, the intervening space sloping gently from Sandal. It was then partly wooded. Leland tells us the bridge was of stone, with nine arches, and that it had on it 'a right goodly chapel of our Lady.' It led to the market place whence two streets, called Norgate and Wrengate,[3] formed communications with gates on the northern side of the town. The houses were then nearly all of timber, but there was a handsome parish church consecrated in 1322, with a tower and spire 228 feet high. From the bridge one road went south by Sandal to Barnsley and Sheffield; another branched off to the eastward, and divided again into two, one leading to Doncaster, the other to Pomfret. To the westward the river Calder flanked the fields between Sandal and Wakefield Bridge. Near the castle is the fine cruciform church of Sandal Magna, where there was a chantry belonging to the castle.

There are scarcely any remains of Sandal Castle, which was razed by order of the Long Parliament in 1648. But fortunately a drawing was made in 1560 and preserved in the office of the Duchy of Lancaster. It is engraved in the 'Vetusta Monumenta.' A lofty donjon, with flanking round towers, stood on the verge of the steep descent to the north-east, and two smaller square towers, connected by a wall, formed the western face. The principal gate, protected by a barbican, was in the centre of the southern face; and on this side the enceinte consisted merely of a wall without towers. An arcade or cloister led from the gate to the main entrance of the donjon, and the roofs of various buildings appear above the parapet of the southern wall. On the northwestern side of the inner courtyard a flight of steps led to a covered archway opening on a semicircular stone pulpit supported by a single pillar. The castle was surrounded by a moat, and the ground it covered was about forty yards square. We gather these details from the drawing. The existing ruins consist of part of the gatehouse, three arches of the arcade leading to the keep, bits of wall on the west side, and the great mound covering the ruins of the keep.

Sandal Castle was built on a natural hill of sandstone, and in those days it must have presented an imposing appearance from Wakefield Bridge, with its lofty towers rising over the trees. There were extensive views in every direction from the castle walls. Northward is Wakefield and the rich valley of the Calder. To the west were the woods stretching away until the view is bounded by Woolley Edge. The woods and lake of Chevet are to the south, and a wide extent of country was visible to the east, with Nostell Priory and Walton Manor hidden among the trees. But, although Sandal commanded extensive views, yet, owing to the wooded character of the country, an enemy might approach without his force being fully known to the garrison.

The Duke of York kept his Christmas in Sandal Castle, with his son Edmund Earl of Rutland, his brother-in-law the Earl of Salisbury, old Sir David Hall his trusty military adviser, many other captains, and 5,000 men. Sir David knew that the enemy was near in overwhelming numbers. He anticipated a siege until relief could come from the south, and he, therefore, sent out foraging parties to bring in supplies.

The Lancastrian chiefs at Pomfret received news of the arrival of the Duke at Sandal on Christmas Day. They were engaged for three days in collecting their forces. On the 30th they began their march from Pomfret, a distance of eight miles. Lord Clifford, with his Yorkshire friends, led the van, so as to become the right wing in forming the battle, resting on the river Calder. The Dukes of Somerset and Exeter and Earls of Devon and Northumberland were in the centre. The rear, which would form the left wing in wheeling into line, was under the command of the Earl of Wiltshire. Sir Andrew Trollope was the principal military adviser and chief of the staff.

On the last day of the year the division under Lord Clifford came in sight of the towers of Sandal, and attacked a foraging party which appears to have been returning from Wakefield. This was seen from the castle. The Duke determined to come to the rescue with his whole force. He probably believed that Clifford was considerably in advance of the main body of the enemy. Sir David Hall thought otherwise, and strongly represented the danger of running such a risk. But the chivalrous Duke spurned the idea of leaving his foraging party to be destroyed without making an effort at their rescue.

The Lancastrians under Clifford were between the castle and Wakefield Bridge, and the great gate faced to the south. It was, therefore, necessary for the Yorkist force, barely 5,000 strong, to march out with their backs to the enemy, and to deploy round the castle hill, before forming line to attack. This was done, and a brilliant charge was made on the field between Sandal and Wakefield—a Balaclava charge. The Duke himself, rightful heir to the throne, and his trusty brother-in-law, the Earl of Salisbury, led this forlorn hope. Near them was the gallant young Prince Edmund in the flower of his age, about to flesh his maiden sword. There, too, was old David Hall, knowing that all was lost, but resolved to fight for his beloved master to the end. Success must have attended on the reckless bravery which Hall deplored, if Clifford's force, about equal in numbers, had been unsupported. But the main body of the Lancastrians arrived during the thick of the fight with overwhelming numbers, while their left wing, under the Earl of Wiltshire, cut off the retreat to the castle. There was nothing left but to die bravely. The Duke of York fell, fighting to the last. Camden says that there was a small space hedged round enclosing a stone cross, on the spot where the Duke fell. His faithful knights fell around him. Among them were his uncles John and Hugh Mortimer, Sir David Hall the tried and trusty councillor, his wife's nephew Sir Thomas Nevill, Sir Edward Bourchier, Sir Eustace Wentworth, Sir James Pickering, Sir John Gedding, Sir Thomas Harington, Sir Hugh Hastings, Captains Fitzjames, Baume, Digby and Ratford. Two gallant brothers, William and Thomas Parr, fought steadily beside their master. William was slain, but Thomas escaped, surviving to be the grandsire of Queen Catherine Parr. Sir Walter Lymbricke, Sir Ralph Stanley, Captain Hanson and John Harrow, the loyal mercer of London, were wounded and taken prisoners.

When all hope was gone young Prince Edmund, with a few followers, perhaps with the Harry Lovedeyne whose service was 'right agreeable' to him and his brother in the happy days of their childhood, fought his way through the encircling foe and reached Wakefield Bridge. But they were closely pursued by some of Clifford's men, perhaps by Clifford himself. Leland tells us that the prince 'was overtaken a little above the bars beyond the bridge, going up a clyming ground'; that is in the street leading up to the market place from the bridge. He and his few followers turned at bay, and we may be sure that young Edmund Plantagenet did not die before his enemies had been made to pay dearly for his life.[4]

No quarter was given to the defeated soldiers by the Lancastrians, 2,000 were slaughtered in the field or during the flight, and the prisoners were all killed. The Earl of Salisbury escaped from the battle, but was taken prisoner the same night by a servant of Sir Andrew Trollope and conveyed to Pomfret, where he was put to death.

The Lancastrian leaders took counsel after the battle, and decided on the perpetration of an inhuman piece of folly. The bodies of the Duke of York and of the Earls of Rutland and Salisbury were buried at Pomfret. But their heads were ordered to be stuck on the gates of York. The Duke's head was placed upon Micklegate Bar, with a paper crown on it by way of insult. The heads of the Earls of Salisbury and Rutland, of Sir Thomas Nevill, Sir Edward Bourchier, Sir Thomas Harington, Sir William Parr, Sir James Pickering and John Harrow were also ordered to be stuck on the different gates of York.

As soon as Queen Margaret received the news in Scotland, she came to York and joined the victorious army. It was resolved to march direct to London, and the northern soldiers were bribed by permission to pillage the whole country. This they did for fifteen miles on either side of their track; attacking churches, taking away vessels, books and vestments, and even the sacramental pyx after shaking out the eucharist, and killing the priests who resisted. Reaching St. Albans they continued the work of pillage, and defeated the troops sent out from London to oppose them. They even recovered the person of Henry VI. But here their successes ended. The gates of London were closed, provisions ran short, and the Lancastrian marauders retreated into Yorkshire.[5]

When the dreadful news of the battle of Wakefield reached London, the Duchess of York was plunged into grief at the loss of her noble husband and gallant young son, and she was terrified for the safety of her children. The two little boys, George and Richard, were put on board a vessel in the Thames and sent to Holland. There, under the protection of Philip the Good, Duke of Burgundy, they were established at Utrecht with suitable tutors. The Duchess of York, with her little daughter Margaret, remained in London awaiting events.

The age of Edward Earl of March was then only eighteen years and eight months. He was at Shrewsbury when the terrible blow fell upon him. It spurred him into resolute action. He had collected a good force, with which he turned upon the Tudors and crushed them at Mortimer's Cross. There was a parhelion when the victory was decided. Edward adopted the sun in splendour as his special cognizance. He then advanced to London by rapid marches, and was proclaimed king as Edward IV.

Richard was thus hurried away to Holland. He was but eight years old when he saw his father and brother Edmund mount their horses at the gate of Baynard's Castle; and when the sad news came that they were slain, and that he would see them no more. In after years Richard took part in the pious act of the children of the Duke of York. They re-endowed the beautiful chapel on Wakefield Bridge, which was built in the reign of Edward III.,[6] and dedicated it to the memory of their brother Edmund.

[1] Owen Tudor, a Welsh squire, had three sons by Catharine, the widow of Henry V.; Edmund and Jasper created by Henry VI. Earls of Richmond and Pembroke, and Owen a monk at Westminster. They were half-brothers of Henry VI.

[2] Stow's Chronicle, p. 412.

[3] An abbreviation of Warenne-gate. The Earls of Warenne and Surrey were Lords of Wakefield for more than two centuries.

[4] Of all the baseless fabrications of the Tudor chroniclers, Hall's story of the death of Edmund Earl of Rutland is the most absurd. Hall says that the prince was scarcely twelve years of age, that his tutor and schoolmaster, named Robert Apsall, secretly conveyed the little boy out of the field, that they were espied and taken by Lord Clifford, that the child knelt on his knees demanding mercy; that the schoolmaster made a speech; that Clifford gave a truculent reply; and that Clifford then struck the child to the heart with a dagger.

This fable rests on there being a child. If there was no child nothing of the sort happened.

The contemporary evidence is simply that after the battle Lord Clifford killed the Earl of Rutland on or near Wakefield Bridge. William of Worcester says:—'et in fugiendo post campum super pontem apud Wakefelde Dominus de Clyfforde occidit Dominum Edmondum comitem de Rutlande, filium Ducis Eborum.' William of Worcester also gives the birthdays of all the children of the Duke of York. Edmund was born at Rouen on May 17, 1443. He was in his eighteenth year, and not a child. It was George, born on October 21, 1449, in Ireland, who was in his twelfth year when the battle of Wakefield was fought;

but he was left in London with his mother, as any child of that age was sure to have been. Even if the Duke had brought a child to Sandal, he would have been left in the castle, not taken into the thick of a desperate battle. Edmund was old enough to accompany his father, and doubtless acquitted himself manfully. These facts also relieve the gallant Clifford's name from a vile calumny. Holinshed and Shakespeare follow Hall, and all later historians have continued to repeat the absurd story without taking the trouble to ascertain Rutland's age at the time of the battle of Wakefield.

[5] The weight of authority is decisively against the Duke of York having been taken prisoner, and in favour of his having been killed in the battle. William of Worcester says: 'Ubi occubuerunt in campo Dux Eborum, Thomas Nevill,' &c. The Croyland chronicler, Fabyan, Polydore Virgil, Hall, and Stow concur. Hall says, 'He, manfully fighting, within half an hour was slain and dead.' But Whethamstede states that the Duke was taken prisoner and grossly insulted: that he was set upon an ant-hill, a crown of woven grass was put on his head, and that the soldiers bowed their heads before him, saying in derision: 'Hail, King without a kingdom!' Whethamstede adds, 'non aliter quam Judæi coram Domino.' But this John Bostock of Whethamstede was Abbot of St. Albans, and violently prejudiced against the Lancastrians for their marauding and pillaging in his neighbourhood. It is generally stated that Queen Margaret took part in the barbarities of her adherents. Stow, for instance, says that Lord Clifford cut off the Duke's head, put a paper crown on it, stuck it on a pole, and presented it to the Queen, who 'was not lying far from the field.' But there is clear proof that the Queen was actually in Scotland when the battle of Wakefield was fought. William of Worcester says: 'Dicto bello finito Regina Margareta venit ab Scotia Eboraco.' This is confirmed by the Croyland

chronicler, who says, 'Inpartibus borealibus morabatur.' Margaret had nothing to do with the Lancastrian barbarities, except that she allowed the heads to remain on the gates of York. She was forced to tolerate the deeds of her savage adherents.

[6] See The Chapel of Edward III. on Wakefield Bridge, by N. Scatcherd (1843).

CHAPTER III THE CROWNING VICTORY OF TOWTON

When the Lancastrians, after their success at St. Albans, had failed before London, they retreated northwards with the person of Henry VI., and proceeded to collect forces in Yorkshire for one more great effort, making their headquarters in the city of York. Meanwhile the young Earl of March, after his victory at Mortimer's Cross on February 2, 1461, advanced to London with his Welsh and border tenantry. He was joined on the road by the Earl of Warwick, whose incapacity as a military commander had been the cause of the disaster at St. Albans on the 17th of the same month.

Edward was only in his nineteenth year when he entered London and succeeded to his father's rights, and to the duty of avenging the cowardly insults heaped upon that father's body. He found his mother, the widowed Duchess, with his little sister Margaret, at Baynard's Castle.

Edward was tall and eminently handsome, with a fair complexion and flaxen hair, 'the goodliest personage,' says Comines, 'that ever mine eyes beheld.' His capacity for command, his fortitude, and prudence were far beyond his years, and he had already acquired experience in two pitched battles.

On his arrival in London Edward called together a great Council of Lords, spiritual and temporal, and declared to them his title to the Crown. The assembled Lords determined that, as King Henry had, contrary to the solemn agreement made with the Duke of York and the Parliament which met in October 1460, violated his word, and as he was useless to the Commonwealth, he should be deprived of all sovereignty. Edward was elected and acknowledged as King.

That night the young King was once more at home with his mother and sister; but it was a melancholy home-coming. Two months before, the whole family was united at Baynard's Castle, now the father was slain and his head fixed on Micklegate Bar at York. The beloved brother, Edward's companion from earliest infancy, also dead; the two younger brothers sent abroad for safety; his uncle, Salisbury, killed, with Sir David Hall, the trusted friend of the family, and many more. Yet a feeling of pride must have mingled with the bereaved mother's grief as she gazed on the superb young warrior who was the last hope and prop of her house.

Next day the citizens of London assembled at their muster in St. John's Fields, just outside the city, where they were reviewed by Lord Fauconberg, the King's uncle, an experienced warrior who had seen much service in France. As Sir William Nevill, he was at the siege of Orleans, and since 1429 he had been summoned to Parliament jure uxoris, for he had married Joan, the heiress of the last Baron Fauconberg. As soon as he had completed the muster, his nephew, George Nevill, Bishop of Exeter, made a speech to the people. He explained to them how King Henry had broken the agreement solemnly made with the Duke of York only four short months before; he demanded of them whether they would have a forsworn king any longer to rule over them; and he called upon them to serve and obey the Earl of March as their earthly sovereign lord. The multitude cried 'Yea! Yea!' with great shouts and clapping of hands. 'I was there,' says William of Worcester, 'I heard them, and I returned with them into the city.'

On the same evening the Lords and Commons went to Baynard's Castle to report what had taken place to young Edward, and he was persuaded to assume the kingly office by the Archbishop of Canterbury and the Bishop of Exeter. Next day, being March 4, he rode to St. Paul's as King Edward IV. and made an offering. After Te Deum he was conveyed to Westminster, where he sat in the Hall while his title was declared to the people as son and heir of Richard, Duke of York, and by authority of Parliament. Henry VI. was deposed quod non stetisset pacto, neque paruisset senatûs consulti decreto. Edward then entered the Abbey under a canopy in solemn procession, and received homage from the lords, returning by water to London, where he was lodged in the Bishop's palace. On the 5th he was proclaimed King through the city as Edward IV; but there was to be no coronation until he was victorious over his enemies.

No time was lost. On Saturday, March 7, the Earl of Warwick left London for the north, with what Fabyan calls 'a great puissance of people.' Four days afterwards the King's infantry followed, consisting of borderers from the Welsh marches, Kentish men, and Londoners. On Friday, March 13, Edward himself rode through Bishopsgate with a great body of men, and attended by many lords and knights. Since the death of Sir David Hall, Edward's uncle Fauconberg was the most able and experienced general on the Yorkist side, and he was now the King's chief adviser. A powerful adherent was John Mowbray, Duke of Norfolk, who is so frequently mentioned in the 'Paston Letters.' Representative of Thomas de Brotherton, the youngest son of Edward I., the Duke had vast wealth and great influence in the eastern counties, but he was in failing health. Sir John Ratcliffe, K.G., called Lord Fitzwalter jure uxoris, Sir Henry Ratcliffe, Lord Scrope of Bolton, Sir Walter Blount, Sir John Wenlock, Sir John Dynham, Sir Roger

Wolferstone, William Hastings, Robert Home of Kent, the King's cousins Humphry and John Stafford, were the principal captains.

The marches were made in a leisurely way to give time for followers to join from various directions, and it was a fortnight before Edward formed a junction with the Earl of Warwick, and mustered his army between Pomfret Castle and Ferrybridge, about forty thousand strong. Reinforcements had flocked to him during the march, especially in Nottinghamshire. Sir John Ratcliffe, with a young illegitimate son of the Earl of Salisbury, was stationed with a small force at Ferrybridge, to guard the passage of the river Aire.

Meanwhile, the nobles who had rallied round the proud Margaret of Anjou were collecting their strength at York. The Duke of Somerset, although he was only in his twenty-fourth year, was the chief commander in the Queen's army. The son of her favourite, who had been slain in the first battle of St. Albans, and the head of a powerful connection, Margaret placed great reliance on the prowess and influence of the young Duke. His first cousin was Thomas Courtenay, Earl of Devonshire, a lad of twenty, who came to York with the Fulfords, Fortescues, and other west-country squires. His sister Eleanor was married to James Butler, Earl of Ormonde and Wiltshire, K.G., a more mature nobleman who had reached his fortieth year, but who was more noted for running away than for fighting. His brother, Sir John Butler, accompanied him. Next to Somerset the most influential leader was Henry Percy, Earl of Northumberland, who was also in his fortieth year. His family had fought and bled in the Lancastrian cause. His father was slain at St. Albans, his brother, Lord Egremont, at Northampton. Another brother, Sir Richard Percy, now rode by the Earl's side at the head of a numerous body of retainers. Lord Clifford, Lord Dacre of Gillesland, Lord FitzHugh, and Sir John Nevill came with a great muster of West Riding and Westmoreland yeomen; while Lord Welles and Sir William Talboys rallied the Lincolnshire yeomen round their standards. Lord Roos, Sir Ralph Eure, and Sir John Bigot of Musgrave Castle, joined the army with their Yorkshire tenantry; and the Duke of Exeter, Lord Hungerford, and Lord Beaumont swelled the throng with their levies.

Nor were lawyers and churchmen wanting to prop the falling cause. Sir John Fortescue, the Lord Chief Justice, was at York, for he believed the parliamentary title of King Henry to be good, and would not desert him in his need. There too, in attendance on poor Henry, was Dr. Morton, the parson of Bloxworth and Master in Chancery—a treble-dyed traitor and falsifier of history, who afterwards flourished like a green bay tree, and died Cardinal Archbishop of Canterbury at the age of ninety.

So far as experience and military training were concerned, the reliance of the Lancastrians was on Lord Welles, Lord Hungerford, and Sir Andrew Trollope. Lionel Lord Welles, now in his fifty-fifth year, had seen much service in France, and had filled the important posts of Lieutenant in Ireland and Captain of Calais. Lord Hungerford had served under the great Talbot, and was present at the fatal battle of Chastillon, where he was taken prisoner. At that time, during his father's life, he was known as Lord Molines, in right of his wife. Trollope was a veteran of the French wars, and seems to have been looked to as the officer who would marshal the army and select positions. He had been a trusted Yorkist captain, and was long in command of the Calais garrison. But when the two rival armies were confronted near Ludlow, in October 1459, he had secretly deserted with a large part of the best soldiers from Calais and gone over to Queen Margaret. This had given her a temporary triumph; and Trollope had since been her most trusted military adviser.

The force collected at York numbered 60,000; and the largest bodies of men that have ever tried conclusions on English ground were thus gathered together between York and Pomfret.

A distance of twenty-five miles separated the towers of Pomfret Castle, under whose shadows young Edward was marshalling his avenging army, from Micklegate Bar, over which the head of his beloved father was withering in the chilling gales of that bitter month of March 1461. Nine of those miles covered the distance from York to Tadcaster on the river Wharfe, and the rest of the distance, from the Wharfe to the Aire, was the scene of the momentous campaign.

The tract of country between the Wharfe and the Aire is a portion of that magnesian limestone formation which extends in a narrow zone across Yorkshire. It is crossed by the principal streams flowing to the Humber, the Ure, the Nidd, the Wharfe, the Aire, the Went, and the Don; and they all form picturesque gorges, with overhanging limestone cliffs and crags, before they enter the great alluvial plain of York. This hilly limestone region, between the Wharfe and the Aire, was once a great forest of elm trees. It was the Elmet of remote times. When the forest was cleared the name remained, and the people called the limestone country 'Elmet lands.' The little river Cock rises on Bramham Moor, flows through this limestone country in a winding course among the undulating hills, and falls into the Wharfe below Tadcaster. Passing the village of Barwick-in-Elmet, it winds along the skirts of 'Becca Banks,' so famous for rare wild flowers, flows under the bridge at Aberford, and westward to Lead Hall, a farmhouse in a great meadow about half a mile short of the village of Saxton. Thence it takes a northerly course to its junction with the Wharfe. Here the winding little brook has hills on either side, covered with woods, with Towton on the right bank, and Hazlewood, the ancient seat of the Vavasours, to the left. It passes through extensive willow garths, and by the village of Stutton, entering the Wharfe, near Tadcaster, after a course of about ten miles.

At present the road from York to Pomfret turns south at the end of Tadcaster Street, and goes direct to Towton and Sherburn, passing the lodge gate at Grimston. But in those days it continued along the left bank of the Cock to beyond Stutton, crossed the little brook by Renshaw Wood, and led up a gentle slope to the hamlet of Towton. By this route the Lancastrian army advanced from Tadcaster, and encamped on the fields between Towton and Saxton. The main road leads direct from Towton to Sherburn, leaving Saxton on the right, and Scarthingwell, with its mere and heronry, on the left. From Sherburn to Ferrybridge the distance is six miles due south. The distance from Ferrybridge, by Sherburn and Saxton, to the battlefield of Towton is nine miles.

On March 26, 1461, the great army of the Lancastrians was encamped round the hamlet of Towton. King Edward's headquarters were at Pomfret, and he had an advanced post to defend the passage of the river Aire in his front, at Ferrybridge, under the command of the titular Lord Fitzwalter, an experienced veteran of the French wars. The object of the Lancastrian leader in advancing across the Wharfe was to oppose the passage of Edward's army over the river Aire at Ferrybridge. The deposed King and Queen, with Lord Roos and Dr. Morton, awaited the event at York. But the Lancastrians were too late. Lord Clifford and Sir

John Nevill, however, did press forward in advance, in hopes of surprising the outlying post of Yorkists at Ferrybridge. In this they were successful. The guard at the bridge was taken completely by surprise before the dawn of March 28, and slaughtered by Lord Clifford's men. Lord Fitzwalter, hearing the noise, thought it was merely a disturbance among his own soldiers. He jumped out of bed, ran down with a battle-axe in his hand, and was slain as he came into the street. The brave young bastard of Salisbury fell with him.

This unexpected onslaught caused a panic in the Yorkist camp, which was increased by the conduct of the excitable Earl of Warwick. He lost his head, galloped up to the King's tent, dismounted and killed his horse, crying out, 'Let him fly that will, for surely by this cross I will tarry with him who will tarry with me, fall back fall edge!'[1] The conduct of young Edward was very different. Perfectly cool and collected, his firmness restored order among the soldiers. He soon saw that the attack had been made by a small force which would as rapidly retreat. He, therefore, gave prompt orders to his uncle, Lord Fauconberg, to cross the river Aire at Castleford, about three miles to the left, with troops led by Sir Walter Blount and Robert Home of Kent. His object was to intercept the retreat of Lord Clifford. This judicious order was ably carried out by the veteran general. Fauconberg overtook the enemy, and a complete rout of the Lancastrians followed. The chase was continued through Sherburn to a little dell or valley called Dittingdale,[2] between Scarthingwell and Towton. Here there was a rally, close to the outposts of the main army of the Lancastrians. Lord Clifford, while taking off his gorget, owing to its having chafed his neck, was struck by an arrow and killed. Sir John Nevill was also slain, and there was a great slaughter among the flying troops. The Yorkist pursuers fell back on their supports without serious loss.

Lord Clifford was only in his twenty-sixth year. His father was slain at the first battle of St. Albans, and he had naturally joined the same cause with enthusiasm. But, as has already been pointed out, the story of his having assassinated a defenceless little boy on Wakefield Bridge is a fiction. There is no reason to believe that Clifford was such a base caitiff. He was evidently an active and enterprising leader. It is the tradition of the family that he was buried, with a heap of undistinguished dead, on the battlefield. Sir John Nevill, a younger brother of the second Earl of Westmoreland, and father of the third Earl, was probably buried within Saxton Church.[3] The loss of these two gallant and influential young leaders, whose scattered fugitives brought in the news on that Friday night, must have cast a gloom over the Lancastrian army.

King Edward now resolved to advance with his whole force and attack the enemy where he was encamped. He believed that the main body could not have been very far distant when Lord Clifford was detached to make the attack at Ferrybridge. The van division of the Yorkist army, led by Lord Fauconberg and Sir Walter Blount, was already across the river Aire, and orders were given to them to march northwards by Sherburn and Saxton. The King himself, with the Earl of Warwick, was to follow at the head of the main body. The Duke of Norfolk should have led the van, but he was taken ill, and it was arranged that he should remain behind at Pomfret, with Sir John Wenlock and Sir John Dynham, and follow next day with the rear division and any reinforcements that might have arrived.[4]

During March 28, the Eve of Palm Sunday, the Yorkist army was marching northwards in two divisions. It must have been late in the afternoon when the division of Lord Fauconberg passed through Sherburn-in-Elmet, a long street with the old Norman church on an isolated hill to the westward. Two miles more brought him to Saxton late in the evening. Saxton was a small village, with the manor house of the Hungates, and a very old church of Norman times. Thence a steep ascent leads northward to the battlefield. To the east is the high road from York to Pomfret, passing over elevated ground. To the west is a ravine with sides sloping down to the valley of the Cock. The latter brook is seen winding through the green valley, with roads on either side. Northwards there was high undulating ground, and the hamlet of Towton is two miles north of Saxton.

On the ground between Towton and Saxton the Lancastrian army was encamped. The centre, led by the Earl of Northumberland and Sir Richard Percy, with Lord Welles and Sir Andrew Trollope, was formed across the road leading up from Saxton. To the east, forming the Lancastrian left, Lord Dacre and his brother-in-law Lord FitzHugh were encamped on some land called 'North Acres.' To the west, forming the right wing, were the Earls of Devonshire and Wiltshire, and Lords Hungerford and Beaumont. The Dukes of Somerset and Exeter commanded a reserve at Towton village.

When Lord Fauconberg arrived at Saxton he ascertained the position of the enemy and sent intelligence to the King. Edward had probably reached Sherburn by that time, and he at once pushed forward to the neighbourhood of Saxton. The whole Yorkist force numbered 48,640 men, including the reserves, which were still at Pomfret under the Duke of Norfolk.

Palm Sunday dawned and found the host of young Edward facing the long array of Lancastrians. It was bitterly cold. The advance up the hillside from Saxton village was made between eight and nine o'clock in the forenoon, and when the hostile forces came in sight there was a great shouting. At the same time snow began to fall. The wind was northerly in the early morning, but it veered round, became fresher, and by nine o'clock it was driving the snow full into the faces of the Lancastrian troops. The two armies, just before they closed, were separated by an undulating depression which marks the exact position.

Lord Fauconberg caused every archer under his standard to shoot one flight of arrows and then halt. The enemy felt the volley, but could not judge of distances on account of the blinding snow. Their arrows fell short. As soon as the quivers of the enemy were nearly empty, Lord Fauconberg gave the order for his archers to advance, shooting as they came on, and they not only shot off their own arrows, but gathered those of the enemy and sent many of them back whence they came. Then the Earl of Northumberland ordered his men to close, and the battle became a fierce hand-to-hand combat all along the line. For several hours the desperate conflict continued, ebbing and flowing with doubtful result, the snow still falling. King Edward was everywhere, exhorting and encouraging the men, leading them on when they wavered, and helping the wounded out of the fray. The struggle was obstinate and long doubtful. Men were falling fast on both sides. Lord Scrope of Bolton was severely wounded. Robert Home, the valiant captain of Kent, who came from Appledore on the Rother, fell dead.

Messengers had been sent in hot haste to hurry up the Duke of Norfolk with the reserves. He arrived at about noon. With his trusty lieutenants Wenlock and Dynham, he led his men up the road from Sherburn, keeping well to the east of Saxton, and ailing upon the Lancastrian left flank at 'North Acres.'

This was the turning point of the battle. The Lancastrians were disheartened at the arrival of fresh foes. The fighting continued until late in the afternoon, and the slaughter was prodigious, but gradually the Lancastrian left wing was doubled up on the centre; the confusion increased, and there was a complete rout. Lord Dacre had fallen early in the day. He was killed by a boy who shot him from a 'bur' tree,[5] when he had unclasped his helmet to drink a cup of wine. The lad thus avenged his father's death, who had been slain by the northern baron. Lord Caere's friends, Sir John and Sir Thomas Crakenthorpe, from the banks of the Eden, fell with him. The Earl of Northumberland, Sir Richard Percy, Lord Welles, and Sir Andrew Trollope were slain in the thick of the fight, with many more. The retreat to the eastward being cut off by the Duke of Norfolk, the defeated army fled down the steep slopes into the valley of the Cock closely pursued.

The well-mounted noblemen, Somerset and Exeter, Devonshire and Wiltshire, Beaumont, Hungerford, and FitzHugh, with many knights, effected their escape. But the footmen were cut down by hundreds in the pursuit. The little Cock beck is not very wide, but it is deep, and many fugitives were drowned in it. The country people declared that the pursuers crossed the brook on dead bodies, and that the river Wharfe was coloured with blood. The Croyland monk relates that the blood of the slain lay caked with snow, which then covered the ground, and that afterwards, when the snow melted, the blood flowed along the furrows and ditches for a distance of two or three miles. The chase continued all night and part of next day.

Fully 10,000 were stated to have been wounded or made prisoners, and Polydore Virgil says that some were cured and some died. This disposes of the statement of Hall, which is adopted by modern writers, that no quarter was given. Edward always gave quarter to the men and junior officers of a defeated army.

The fugitive nobles only had time to ride through York, calling upon Henry and Margaret, with their child, to mount and ride as hard as their horses would carry them. Away they went out of Bootham, and through the dark forest of Galtres, to take refuge in Scotland.

King Edward advanced to York on Monday, March 30, 1461, where he was received with great solemnity by the mayor and commons of the city, in procession. They obtained grace through the intercession of Lords Montagu and Berners. The heads of the Duke of York, the Earl of Rutland, and the Earl of Salisbury were removed from the gates of York, and placed with the bodies at Pomfret, preparatory to the subsequent magnificent obsequies at Fotheringhay and Bisham.

Only four executions took place at York, of the Earl of Devonshire, Sir Baldwin Fulford, Sir William Talboys, and Sir William Hill. The Earl of Wiltshire was captured by William Salkeld at Cockermouth. For this prominent actor in the barbarous deeds after Wakefield fight there could be no forgiveness. He was beheaded at Newcastle on May 1.

The Earl of Northumberland, a first cousin of King Edward, was buried in the north choir of St. Denis church at York, probably with his brother Sir Richard Percy. The body of Lord Welles was taken to Methley, and buried in the Waterton Chapel. Lord Dacre was buried, with his horse, in Saxton churchyard, on the north side of the church, where there is a monument to his memory. The undistinguished dead were at first buried in five great pits on the battlefield, and in separate graves in the valley. It was a tradition that red and white roses grew and flourished on the battlefield, and it is true that there are many rose bushes in the meadows. Leland tells us that Master Hungate of Saxton caused the dead bodies to be brought from the pits on the battlefield, and buried in consecrated ground, in a trench running the whole length of Saxton churchyard.

King Edward kept his Easter at York, which fell that year on April 5. He then advanced as far as Durham, whence he returned southwards, leaving the pacification of the north to the Earl of Warwick and his brother Lord Montagu. Early in June Edward was at the manor of Sheen, and on the 26th of that month he came from Sheen to the Tower of London. On the 27th he created thirty Knights of the Bath, and on Sunday the 28th he was solemnly crowned in Westminster Abbey by Cardinal Bourchier, Archbishop of Canterbury.

The King liberally rewarded his supporters. The Duke of Norfolk died in November 1461, and was buried before the high altar at Thetford. But Lord Fauconberg was created Earl of Kent and Lord High Admiral. He died in 1463. Sir Walter Blount was created Lord Mountjoy and a Knight of the Garter. Sir John Dynham, a valued adherent, was created Lord Dynham; and Sir John Wenlock, already a Knight of the Garter, was created Lord Wenlock. Many Yorkists were knighted, either on the field or afterwards at the coronation. Young William Hastings, the King's most faithful follower, was knighted on the field, and created Lord Hastings, in July 1461. Among the Knights of the Bath were the gentlemen of Nottinghamshire who had joined the King on the march northward, Sir Robert Clifton, Sir Nicholas Byron, and Sir Robert and Sir John Markham.

Edward IV. was 'a King who, with many faults, was most honourably anxious from the first to do justice even to the meanest of his subjects.'[6] After the first heat of battle had passed he was placable and forgiving. He had strong and justifiable cause for resentment against his opponents at Towton. In the white heat of his indignation, with the sight of his father's head over Micklegate Bar fresh in his recollection, he stayed his avenging hand after four executions. The bill of attainder passed by his first Parliament included 150 names, but many were afterwards granted full pardons, and all who submitted received back portions of their estates. The Duke of Somerset made his peace, and was taken into favour. The son of the Earl of Northumberland was restored to all his father's honours. The brother of the Earl of Wiltshire, though he was also at Towton, was restored to all his estates, was taken into favour, and succeeded as sixth Earl of Ormond. Similar forgiveness was extended to the Courtenays, and to the brother of Lord Dacre. Although Lord Hungerford continued in rebellion, Edward IV. treated his wife and young children with kindness and generosity, making an ample provision for them out of their father's forfeited lands. The son of Lord Welles was taken into favour, and had a grant of all his father's forfeited property. Lord FitzHugh was forgiven and employed in positions of importance. Mr. Thorold Rogers says:—'I entirely discredit the stories told of the tyranny and suspiciousness of Edward IV. He never refused a petition for pardon.'[7]

All historians unite in the statement that the old nobility of England was nearly annihilated by the battles and executions during the Wars of the Roses. But facts are opposed to this theory. Scarcely a single peerage became extinct owing to the Wars of the Roses.[8]

The battles of Wakefield and Towton made a deep impression on the mind of Prince Richard, although he was but eight years old. The fate of his father and brother in a battle which drove him into exile, and then the crowning victory following so rapidly, could not fail to do so. In later years he erected a memorial chapel at Towton, where prayers were to be offered up for the souls of the fallen. It was standing in Leland's time, but there is now no vestige of this pious work of King Richard III.[9]

[1] Mr. Green, in his History of the English People, places the time of Warwick's killing his horse 'at one critical moment' during the battle of Towton. But the evidence that this act of folly was perpetrated owing to the panic after the surprise at Ferrybridge is quite conclusive.

[2] Hall has Dintingdale, Habington spells it Dindingdale, Baker has Dandingdale. There is no such place on the maps. But Whitaker, in his History of Craven, says that the Rev. F. Wilkinson, Vicar of Bordsey, discovered the almost forgotten name of Dittingdale, as that of a dell or small valley in Scarthingwell Park.

[3] Leland says that the Earl of Westmoreland was killed, and buried within Saxton Church. Hall also includes the Earl of Westmoreland among the slain. They mistook him for Sir John Nevill. The Earl himself did not die until 1485. Sharon Turner and later writers repeat the blunder. The Earl of Westmoreland was not in the battle.

[4] Mr. Green says that 'the Duke of Norfolk came with a fresh force from the eastern counties.' The Duke came from Pomfret, having left London with the King. Sharon Turner says: 'We owe the remarkable fact of the battle beginning at four o'clock in the afternoon and continuing through the night, and of Norfolk's coming up the next clay at noon to Hearne's fragment.' This fragment was transcribed by Hearne from an old manuscript, but not older than Hall's Chronicle. The statement that the battle began at four on Saturday afternoon and went on through the night, not only contradicts Hall and Stow, but is also impossible. Edward's army could not have got over the ground in time to begin the battle at four in the afternoon. Possibly the mistake of the anonymous writer of Hearne's fragment arose from having been told that Lord Fauconberg came in sight of the Lancastrian army at twilight. It was not the twilight of

Saturday afternoon, but of Palm Sunday morning, as Hall explains.

[5] Loidis and Elmete, p. 156. Dr. Whitaker says that the word 'bur' is very distinct in Glover's manuscript. It means an alder tree, from the old Norse 'bur' or 'baurr.'

[6] Gairdner. Introduction to the Paston Letters, ii. p. xii.

[7] Work and Wages, ii. 316.

[8] The Duke of Exeter was separated from his wife, and had no children. The Duke of Somerset, who was beheaded, had six daughters, and another was unmarried. But the House of Somerset was perpetuated in that of Beaufort. A few new peerages became extinct because their recipients did not marry, such as Egremont and Wenlock. But Lord Egremont was a Percy, and the family of Percy continued to flourish. No more peerages became extinct owing to the Wars of the Roses than would have done so in a time of profound peace.

[9] There is a warrant for 40l. to be given for building the chapel at Towton, dated November 28, 1483 (Harl. MSS., No. 413). In July 1488, an indulgence of forty days was granted ad speciosam capellam in villa de Toughton (per Saxton) de novo a fundamentis sumptuose et nobiliter erectam, super quodam loco seu fondo ubi corpora procerum et magnatum ac aliorum hominum multitudine copiosa in quodam bello in campis circumjacentibus inito interfectorum sepeliuntur. In December 1502 another indulgence of forty days was granted. The exact site of the chapel is the garden behind Mr. Kendall's house.

CHAPTER IV THE CROWN LOST AND WON— BATTLE OF BARNET

The young princes, George and Richard, were in Holland for about six months, under the protection of the Duke of Burgundy. They resided at Utrecht. Then the news came of Edward's accession, and the crowning victory of Towton. The two boys were brought home again, and were soon under their mother's immediate care, with their sister Margaret.

Immediately after the coronation, George was created Duke of Clarence; and Richard Duke of Gloucester, Earl of Carlisle, and Earl of Richmond,[1] a title which had merged in the crown after the attainder of Edmund Tudor. Richard was created a Knight of the Garter in 1465. In February 1466 his sword and helmet were placed in St. George's Chapel, and he took possession of his stall in the following April. His stall plate is now in the ninth stall on the south side of the choir, in St. George's Chapel at Windsor. The arms are France and England quarterly, with a silver label of three points, each ermine with a canton gules. The crest is a crowned leopard gold, on a cap of estate, with a label as in the arms, round his neck. The helm is barred as used in the mêlée, the only one on the early plates, the rest all being tilting helms.

The first public appearance of young Richard was on the occasion of his father's solemn obsequies. The Duke of York's body, and that of his son Edmund Earl of Rutland, had to be conveyed from Pomfret to Fotheringhay, and the Duke of Gloucester, then in his fourteenth year, was appointed by the King to be chief mourner. On July 22, 1466, the bodies of Richard Duke of York, and of his son, Edmund Earl of Rutland, were taken from their temporary resting place at Pomfret, and placed in a chariot covered with black velvet, richly embroidered with cloth of gold. At the feet of the Duke stood the figure of an angel clothed in white, bearing a crown of gold, to signify that of right he was a king. The chariot was drawn by four horses trapped to the ground. Every horse carried a man, and upon the foremost rode Sir John Skipwith, who bore the Duke's banner displayed. Bishops and abbots, in their robes, went two or three miles in front, to prepare the churches for the reception of the bodies.'[2] The boy Duke of Gloucester followed next after the chariot, accompanied by noblemen and heralds. In this order they left Pomfret and rested that night at Doncaster. Thence they proceeded by easy stages to Blythe, Tuxford, Newark, Grantham, and Stamford. On Monday, July 27, the procession arrived at Fotheringhay. The bodies were carried into the church by servants of the deceased, and received by the King and his Court in deep mourning.

Edward IV. built a magnificent shrine in the choir, over the tombs of his father and brother, and completed the works of the college, including the cloister.[3]

There is reason to believe that the young Duke of Gloucester received his knightly training in the use of arms from the age of fourteen, in the household of his cousin the Earl of Warwick. There are payments to the Earl for costs and expenses incurred by him on account of Richard, the King's brother. Here he was the companion of Francis Lovel and Robert Percy, for both of whom he formed a friendship which ended only with death. Here too he was the playfellow of his cousin Anne Nevill, and an attachment was probably then formed between them, which was destined to bear fruit in after years. We find Richard and Anne sitting together at the installation feast of her uncle the Archbishop of York in 1467.

Richard was short in stature, with a delicate fragile frame, the right shoulder being slightly higher than the left. But he had been inured to warlike exercises, and was fond of hunting and all manly sports. He had light brown hair and a very handsome face, full of energy and decision, yet with a gentle and even melancholy expression when the features were at rest.[4]

While Richard was receiving a knightly education in the north, his brother Edward was conducting his own and the country's affairs recklessly and without wisdom. The secret marriage ceremony he went through with the widow of Lord Grey of Groby, and her subsequent coronation, had estranged the nobles, and their disgust was increased by the promotion and enrichment of her Woodville relations. The Earl of Warwick, the cousin and formerly the supporter of Edward, became the chief among the malcontents. He married his daughter Isabella to the Duke of Clarence, without the King's consent or knowledge, and afterwards fostered and encouraged disturbances and insurrections. At last he went to France with Clarence, and made an agreement with Margaret of Anjou to restore Henry VI. to the throne. Finally he returned to England, with the Duke of Clarence, as an open enemy of King Edward. Troops rapidly flocked to his standard, and the country was lost and won as if by magic.

Warwick had used all his arts of persuasion to induce the younger brothers of the King to be false to their allegiance. With Clarence he succeeded; but Richard never wavered for a moment. His loyalty to his brother was not to be shaken. There is something very touching in the unalterable affection between Edward and Richard. In Edward, from the time when he used to visit his little brother every day in Paston's chambers, to the hour of his death, there was a loving protection and a solicitude for the lad's welfare which was shown in many ways. On the part of Richard there was loyalty and zeal for his elder brother's service as well as warm affection. His motto was

'LOYAULTÉ ME LIE.'[5]
(Loyalty bindeth me.)

From the moment that Warwick became a traitor, Richard was constantly by his brother's side, sharing his long marches,[6] his dangers and hardships. When Warwick landed and proclaimed the restoration of Henry VI., King Edward summoned his forces to assemble at Doncaster, particularly relying on the Marquis Montagu, Warwick's brother, in whose loyalty he implicitly believed. Edward related to the historian Comines the events immediately preceding his flight from the kingdom. He was in a fortified house with his friends, to which the only access was a bridge, and the troops were quartered in the villages near. Suddenly news arrived that Montagu and others were riding among his soldiers shouting for Henry. Edward hastily put on his armour and sent a body of faithful adherents to defend the bridge. There was nothing left but flight. Accompanied by his brother Richard and a few loyal friends the King galloped off, leaving Lord Hastings to gain time by defending the bridge. Hastings made some terms for his followers with Montagu, and then followed his master. Reaching Lynn, in Norfolk, the fugitives found two Dutch vessels on the point of sailing. They immediately went on board without other clothes than leurs habillemens de guerre.[7] The brothers were accompanied in their flight by Lords Hastings, Rivers, and Saye, and a few faithful knights. Narrowly escaping capture by an Easterling ship, they landed near Alkmaar in North Holland. A gown lined with martens was the only thing of value wherewith King Edward could pay his passage; and he was saved from capture by the Easterlings through the intervention of the Sieur Louis de Bruges, Lord of Gruthuus, who received the fugitives with generous hospitality and conducted them to The Hague. King Edward and his host were brother Knights of the Golden Fleece, an obligation which the lord of Gruthuus most fully recognised. He gave up his great house at Bruges for the use of the exiled princes, who resided there during the ensuing winter, and he also lent them his château of Oostcamp. From Bruges, King Edward and his brother proceeded to the court of the Duke of Burgundy at St. Pol, to seek for aid in recovering the crown of England. Charles the Bold publicly declined to interfere, and the Lancastrian Duke of Somerset hurried to London with the good news. But Charles had been married, in 1468, to the Princess Margaret of York, who was devotedly attached to her brothers. She opened a correspondence with the Duke of Clarence in England, to induce him to return to his allegiance. Through her influence, the aid which had been withheld publicly was given in secret. She smoothed all difficulties, and enabled her brothers to undertake their romantic enterprise. For Edward was resolved to recover his crown, and Richard, from this time, was his efficient lieutenant.

Richard's services in Flanders, and especially in fitting out the expedition, secured for him the full confidence of his brother. The ships had to be equipped very secretly and with great care. The Duchess Margaret had procured a grant of 15,000 florins, and permission to get ready four ships of Flanders and thirteen hired Easterlings[8] which were to be at Edward's service until he should land in England, and for fifteen days afterwards. The next step was the selection of a seaport where the expedition could be quietly fitted out. The Lord of Gruthuus again proved a friend in need. He had married Margaret, the sister of Henry van Borselle, Lord of the island of Walcheren. The traditions of the family of Borselle were adverse to the House of Lancaster, for Francis van Borselle was the lover, and eventually the husband, of that unfortunate Jacoba of Holland who was treated so shamefully by Humphrey Duke of Gloucester. The excellent ports of Veere and Flushing were, therefore, placed at Edward's disposal.

The expedition was fitted out in the port of Veere, under the protection of Henry van Borselle. Besides the King and young Richard, Lords Hastings, Rivers, and Saye were the principal leaders. The expeditionary force consisted of 900 men, in addition to the crews of the ships. A select body of 300 Flemish gunners, armed with hand-guns, formed part of the little army; and this is nearly the first time that these new weapons are mentioned in English warfare. The men carried slow matches, and are called 'smoky gunners' by Fabyan. Richard actively helped in the preparation of this daring little expedition at Veere; for by this time the King had learned to appreciate his brother's remarkable ability and fitness for command.

By the end of February 1471, the ships were ready. They were brought down the Channel from Veere to Flushing and the troops were embarked. But they had to wait nine days in Flushing Roads for a fair wind, and it was not until Monday, March 11, that the gallant adventurers sailed for the Norfolk coast. Edward was in one ship with Lord Hastings, while his brother had a separate command in another vessel, each being followed by a squadron of transports. It is probable that the exiled King shaped a course for the coast of Norfolk in the hope that the influence of the Duke, who was faithful to his cause, would ensure him a cordial reception. But he was disappointed. Two knights, named Sir Robert Chamberlain and Sir Gilbert Debenham, went on shore at Cromer and found the country occupied by Warwick's adherents. Edward, therefore, steered for Yorkshire, and encountered a gale of wind which lasted from March 12 to 14, scattering his little squadron. When Edward and Hastings anchored off Ravenspur,[9] on the Holderness coast, no other vessel was in sight. The King landed and burnt his ship, resolved to regain his crown or perish in the attempt.

Edward stood on that dreary waste of sand with 500 followers. The look-out was black indeed. He had seen nothing of the other ships since they were separated by the gale off Cromer. He sent scouts to the adjacent villages, but not a man ventured to join his standard. While hesitating what should be the next step, horsemen appeared over the brow of a rising ground. The adventurers stood to their arms, but a few minutes turned anxiety into joy. The young Duke of Gloucester was seen to be at the head of a little force of 300 men. He had effected a landing at a point about four miles from Ravenspur, and hurried to join his brother. Soon afterwards Lord Rivers, who had reached the shore at a place called Pole, fourteen miles away, made his appearance. Thus was the little force once more united. They marched to Beverley and thence to York, but although armed men were seen, no one either molested them or came to their assistance. There appears to have been no ill-will among the people, but fear of the power of the Earl of Warwick and a belief that Edward's cause was hopeless.

The authorities of York did not dare to receive Edward as King. It was thought advisable that, at this stage, he should only claim his hereditary dukedom.[10] This deceived no one, but it would enable the mayor and aldermen of York to defend their conduct in the event of Edward's overthrow. They received him into their town, gave him supplies, and next day he marched southwards to Tadcaster.

The campaign by which Edward regained the crown was one of the most brilliant that has ever been conducted by an English general. It elicited proofs of consummate military skill from the Yorkist princes, and displays of valour and presence of mind in action which were never surpassed by any of their race. Edward IV. is entitled to an equal place as a military commander with Edward III. or Henry V. His strategy and resource were superior to those of either. He never lost a battle, though he never declined a combat. In three short months from the time that he landed with a handful of men on the coast of Holderness, he had outwitted and out-manoeuvred his opponents, had won two pitched battles, and had recovered his crown. Richard deserves scarcely less credit. He was only eighteen, yet he contributed largely to the success of the campaign, while in battle his brother entrusted the young prince with important separate commands.

Edward's little band of adventurers was opposed by the whole resources of England in the hands of the Earl of Warwick. The Earl himself was posted with a strong force at Coventry. His brother Montagu occupied an advanced position at Pomfret to intercept the invaders on their southward march. The Earl of Oxford was advancing from the Eastern counties, and Clarence from London. By a masterly flank march the King passed to the westward of Pomfret and reached Nottingham, leaving Montagu in his rear baffled and outwitted. At Nottingham loyal men began to flock to the King's standard. The Earl of Oxford and Duke of Exeter had advanced against him from the Eastern counties, but the rumoured increase of his forces made them halt at Newark. The King pressed onwards to Leicester, and marching thence to Coventry, offered battle to the Earl of Warwick, who was behind the walls with 7,000 men. Warwick declined. He was taken completely by surprise. This was on March 29, only a fortnight after

Edward had landed. Without losing a moment the royal army marched on to Warwick, and on the approach of Clarence from London, his brothers encamped in a field three miles on the road to Banbury.

The negotiations between King Edward and Clarence were conducted throughout by their younger brother Richard, and to him is due the credit of the reconciliation which took place. He thus restored one brother to his throne, and reclaimed the other from dishonour. The defection of Clarence left no enemy between the King and his capital. Edward reached Daventry on the night of April 6, attending divine service there on Palm Sunday. On the 9th he was at Northampton, and on the 11th he entered London, where he was joyfully received by the citizens.

Warwick was outwitted like his brother. There was nothing left for him but to follow the King, who could give him battle or not as he chose. So the baffled Earl concentrated his army, calling up Montagu from Pomfret, Vere and Exeter from Newark, and Somerset from the west. Having united his forces he marched towards London, reaching St. Albans on the 12th, and encamping on Gladmore Heath to the north of Barnet, and about ten miles from London, on the afternoon of April 13.

The King only had one full day in London, in which to organise his little army, now increased to 9,000 men, and to rest the faithful few who had marched with him from Ravenspur. He entered London on the 11th, and in the forenoon of the 13th he marched out to encounter his enemies. Advancing to Barnet his scouts drove out the scouts of Warwick and chased them for half a mile. The King then marched through the town, and reached Gladmore Heath when it was dusk. He encamped much nearer the enemy than he intended, and by reason of the darkness his line was not formed directly in front of the opposing force. The King's right extended beyond Warwick's left, while his left was similarly overlapped by Warwick's right. In one respect this was fortunate, for Warwick's artillery was in his right wing, and he kept up a fire all through the night[11] without doing any damage to his adversaries, because their left wing was not posted in front of the rebel right wing; but somewhat to the eastward of it.

Warwick had drawn up his army with his brother Montagu and John Vere, son of the attainted Earl of Oxford, in charge of the right wing consisting mainly of cavalry; the Duke of Somerset in the centre with archers and bill-men; and Warwick himself, with the Duke of Exeter, in command of the left wing. The opposing force of the King was inferior in numbers to that of the rebels. Edward, accompanied by Clarence and Henry VI., commanded the centre in person. On the left was Lord Hastings, while young Richard Duke of Gloucester, who was only eighteen years of age, had charge of the right wing. A strong body of infantry was kept in reserve. The King ordered strict silence to be observed throughout the night.

When the morning of Easter Sunday, April 14, at length dawned there was a dense fog, so that the two armies could barely distinguish each other. At half-past four the King advanced his standards, and sounded his trumpets for battle. There were flights of arrows, and then the opposing forces closed and encountered each other with hand strokes, in the thick mist. For a long time it was impossible for the leaders to know what was taking place in different parts of the field. Oxford found little to oppose him. He charged the followers of Lord Hastings and easily routed them, continuing the chase beyond Barnet. Then he returned to reinforce the main body; but here a fatal mistake occurred. The cognizance of King Edward was the sun in splendour, adopted after seeing the parhelion at Mortimer's Cross. The cognizance of the Veres was a star with rays.[12] When the soldiers of Warwick's centre, under Somerset, saw a fresh body of men approaching under the banner of the star, they mistook it for the King's cognizance and thought they were attacked in flank. A cry of treason ran through their ranks. Up to this time they had stubbornly resisted the onslaughts of King Edward and his men, but now they broke and fled. Somerset and Vere rode away with their men, and made good their escape.

Meanwhile the Duke of Gloucester had led his troops to a furious attack on the enemy's left wing which was commanded by Warwick in person. The Duke himself plunged into the thickest of the fight. His two esquires, John Milwater[13] and Thomas Parr, were slain by his side. At the moment when the fate of the battle was still uncertain, and when the King heard that his young brother was hard pressed, the reserves were brought into action, just as Somerset's division began to waver. Victory then ceased to be doubtful, and soon there was complete rout all along the rebel line. The Earl of Warwick and his brother Montagu fell either in the battle or in attempting to escape. The accounts vary. Though enemies and traitors to the royal brothers, they were cousins, and had once been devoted friends. The King sincerely mourned the death of Montagu, and the depth of Richard's sorrow is proved by his subsequent intercession for Montagu's heirs. The bodies, after being laid for two days in St. Paul's Cathedral, were honourably interred in the burial place of their mother's family at Bisham. The losses on the King's side included Lord Saye, who had shared Edward's exile, Humphrey Bourchier Lord Cromwell,[14] another Sir Humphrey Bourchier,[15] son of Lord Berners, and the son and heir of Lord Mountjoy. The losses, on both sides, amounted to about 1,500 men.[16] King Edward and the Duke of Gloucester returned to London the same day, while their army rested for the night on the battlefield.

[1] Rot. Parl. vol. vi. p. 227. Halsted, i. 432.

[2] Sandford, p. 391.

[3] The tombs were desecrated in the time of Edward VI., when the college was granted to John Dudley, Duke of Northumberland. Queen Elizabeth gave orders that they should be restored. The bones of Richard Duke of York, of the Duchess Cicely, and of Edmund Earl of Rutland, lapped in lead, were removed into the parish church. For the choir, where they rested under the beautiful shrine, had been destroyed. Mean monuments of plaster were then erected over them, and over the remains of Edward Duke of York, on either side of the altar. They are specimens of the taste of the Elizabethan age, fluted columns supporting a frieze and cornice, ornamented with the falcon and fetter-lock. In the inscriptions they have forgotten the name of young Edmund Earl of Rutland.

[4] Portrait at Windsor Castle. Dr. Parr, in a letter to Roscoe, speaking of the head of Lorenzo (the Magnificent) prefixed to Roscoe's biography, says: 'I am very much mistaken if, by invigorating a few traits, it would not make an excellent head of Richard III.'—Life of Roscoe, i. 178.

[5] Buck, p. 83.

[6] Paston Letters, ii. 357, 389.

[7] Comines.

[8] The ships of the towns belonging to the Hanseatic League, in the Baltic, and on the Elbe, were known in England by the name of Easterlings.

[9] Ravenspur appears, from the description of the writer in Fleetwood, to have been inside Spurn Head. He says: 'He landed within Humber on Holderness side, at a place called Ravenspoure.'

[10] The Tudor chroniclers, as is their wont, grossly exaggerate and misrepresent this incident: introducing imaginary details, including an oath before an altar, vows of allegiance to Henry VI., and other romances. These are the offspring of their zeal to please their Tudor paymasters, by traducing the House of York.

[11] Warkworth says that: 'each of them loosed guns at other all night.' Balls have been dug up weighing 1-½ lbs.

[12] The second Alberic de Vere, father of the first Earl of Oxford, was a crusader. In 1098 he was in a battle near Antioch when the infidels were defeated. During the chase, a silver star of five points was seen to descend from heaven and light on Alberic's shield, there shining excessively. It had ever since been borne in the first quarter of the Vere arms. This is the old tradition. Modern heralds suspect that the mullet was merely a mark of cadency adopted by the second brother of the second Earl, who retained it when he became third Earl.

[13] Mentioned in the letter of Edward and Edmund to their father.

[14] Ralph Cromwell, fourth Baron Cromwell, who was Lord Treasurer for Henry VI., and was the builder of Tattershall Castle, died childless in 1455. His sister Maud married Sir Richard Stanhope and had a daughter Maud, whose husband Sir Humphrey Bourchier, third son of Henry Bourchier Earl of Essex, by the Princess Isabel Plantagenet (aunt of Edward IV.), took the title of Lord

Cromwell jure uxoris. This Lord Cromwell seems to have been a student of law as well as a soldier. There is a manuscript copy of the statutes of Edward III. in the Hunterian Library of Glasgow University which once belonged to him. At the beginning there is the following entry: 'Eximii et preclari militis liber, Johannis Markham capitalis just, de B. Regis, Liber Humfredi Bourchier dmus Cromwell ex dono supradicti'; and at the end: 'This boke is mine Humphrey Bourchier Lord Cromwell by the gift of the right noble and famous judge Sir John Markham Chief Justice of the King's Bench.'

[15] Sir John Bourchier, fourth son of William Bourchier Earl of Eu, by Anne, daughter of Thomas Duke of Gloucester, married the heiress of Sir Richard Berners, and was summoned to Parliament as Lord Berners in 1455 to 1472. The second Humphrey Bourchier who was slain at Barnet was his son. Fabyan and Habington call him 'Lord Barnes.'

[16] Fabyan gives the number at 1,500. Habington says 4,600. Hall is unreliable as usual. He says 10,000 on both sides. Although some writers say that the King's army was superior in numbers, it is probable that, while Edward only had 9,000 men, the forces of Warwick were very much more numerous.

CHAPTER V MARGARET OF ANJOU AND HER SON EDWARD

It is necessary to look back a few years in order to consider the lives of the mother and son who now, for a time, come prominently into connection with the life story of Richard Duke of Gloucester.

Margaret, second daughter of René of Anjou and Isabelle of Lorraine, was born at Pont-à-Mousson on March 23, 1429, and baptized at Toul. As a child she went with her mother to Capua and Naples. Provence was also one of her homes, but she returned to Lorraine in her fifteenth year. She was only sixteen when the Duke and Duchess of Suffolk came to Nancy to demand her hand for Henry VI. of England, and in November 1444 she was married by proxy amidst great rejoicings; for the event secured a lasting peace with France. There was a great tournament in the Place de Carrière at Nancy to celebrate the event, at which Charles VII. and many of the chief nobles of France were present. Charles tilted with King René, bearing on his shield the serpent of the fairy Melusina. The daisy was young Margaret's cognizance, and Pierre de Brezé, Lord of Varenne, and Seneschal of Normandy, maintained the pre-eminence of the 'daisye flower' against all comers in the Place de Carrière.[1] This was no passing sentiment. Two at least in that brilliant throng remained true to the fair princess to the bitter end, Pierre de Brezé and the Duchess of Suffolk.

Margaret was not only very beautiful, she was endowed with rare gifts of intellect, which had been cultivated by travel in Italy and Provence, and through communion with her accomplished father. She set out for England attended by the Duke and Duchess of Suffolk and a train of nobles.

On her way she supped with the Duke of York at Mantes, and reached Honfleur on April 3, 1445. Thence she sailed across to Portsmouth, where she slept at the Maison Dieu. She was then taken in a row-boat to Southampton, but her marriage was delayed for some time by an illness. Henry VI., who was in his twenty-fourth year,[2] had been waiting for his bride at Southwick. The marriage took place at Titchfield Abbey on May 30.

Never was a young girl placed in a more wretched position. Married to a poor feeble creature who could be neither companion nor protector, surrounded by self-seeking intriguers, living in a foreign country with few to sympathise with or care for her; the years that followed her marriage could not fail to embitter the brave heart that no misfortune had power to crush. For years she lived on, the memories of the bright and happy court of her father gradually fading, while the cruel facts of her miserable position hardened round her.

It was in the eighth year after her marriage that Margaret became a mother. Her whole soul opened to the loving influence. All her pent-up womanly feelings found a vent. She at last had something to live for. Her brilliant intellect, her fortitude and devotion, her great powers of endurance, all she had, her whole being, became centred in this child— the one thing she had to love. For him she would face dangers, dare more than most men in perils and hardships, and, if need be, would become as a tigress at bay in defence of her young.

The prince was born at Westminster on October 13, 1453, being just one year younger than Richard. It was at a time when Henry VI. was in one of his fits of complete mental derangement which came upon him periodically, as they did upon his grandfather Charles VI. of France, from whom no doubt he inherited them. The Duke of York was administering the realm. The child was proclaimed Prince of Wales and Earl of Chester. His mother was just twenty-four, and Henry was in his thirty-third year. The Queen had lost her mother, to whom she was fondly attached, on the previous February 28. In hopes that the name would endear her boy to the people, Margaret gave him that of Edward. He was baptized by Cardinal Kemp, Archbishop of Canterbury, assisted by Waynflete of Winchester, the Duke of Somerset and Duchess of Buckingham[3] being sponsors. He was also created a Knight of the Garter.

From his very cradle the child was in the midst of war and turmoil. The misgovernment of the Beauforts had strengthened the legitimate claim of the Duke of York, which would never have had a chance against the parliamentary title of an able and popular king. But the Yorkists now had to reckon with the gifted and intrepid Queen, whose whole soul, and whose every gift of mind and body, were concentrated with fierce devotion on the defence of her child's birthright. Nothing but death could make her desist from efforts on his behalf.

Young Edward was only in his second year when the first battle of St. Albans was fought, on May 22, 1455. His mother had taken him to Greenwich, where she received the news of the death of Somerset and her other supporters, and of the wound received by Henry. During the following four years there were hollow reconciliations, but a death struggle was inevitable; and in June 1459 the court left London for Warwick, virtually to take the field. The child Edward was only five years old. He was destined never to see London again.

Margaret strove to make the child popular with the people, and to excite a feeling of loyalty for him. He was named

Edward to remind them of the king who added to the glory of England at Cressy and Poitiers. She adopted the badge of Edward III. as that of the Prince, and the pretty little boy, with long golden hair, distributed silver swans among the people wherever he went. The Queen could not bear him out of her sight, yet her dauntless eagerness would not allow her to be absent from scenes of strife, when her child's future depended on the result. Mother and child looked down on the battle of Blore Heath from the tower of Muccleston Church, and when Lord Audley was routed they fled to Eccleshall Castle. Then there were a few months of dawning hope, which was crushed at Northampton. Again Margaret watched the fortunes of the day with her child. She heard of the treachery of Grey, she saw the gallant young Edward of York leading his men over the trenches, and that the day was lost. The King fell into the hands of her enemies.

On the evening of that July 9, 1460, she rode away with her beloved child, a homeless fugitive. Between Eccleshall and Chester she was made prisoner by a party led by one John Cleger, a servant of Lord Stanley. Every instinct was on the alert when danger approached her child. She watched an opportunity while her captors were rifling the baggage, and escaped with little Edward in her arms. The adventures through which they passed are not recorded, but she was eventually joined by the Duke of Somerset, who conducted her to a safe refuge at Harlech Castle in Wales.

The Duke of York, with Henry in his power, induced the Parliament to alter the succession, and the claims of Henry's son were ignored. Henry VI. wrote a letter to his wife, ordering her to accept the new settlement, and to join him in London with her child. This must have been one of the bitterest moments of her unhappy life. But no reverse could daunt this romantic heroine. She went by sea from

Harlech to Scotland, and thence called upon all her supporters in the north to rally round the standard of King Henry. Margaret's appeal met with a prompt answer, and on the last day of the year 1460 the Duke of York lost his life at Wakefield, overwhelmed by superior numbers. The road was thus open to London, and Margaret made a vigorous effort to recover the birthright of her child. On February 17, 1461, she won the second battle of St. Albans and recovered the person of her husband; but she failed to induce the citizens of London to open their gates to her, and was obliged to retreat northwards. The Queen and her child appear to have been in the thick of the fight; and this was the third battle at which Edward had been present before he had reached his eighth year. The royal party retreated to York, while preparations were made for the final and decisive struggle between the two factions. On March 4, 1461, the young Earl of March was proclaimed King, and on the 29th he won the crowning victory of Towton.

Queen Margaret, with her husband and child, had remained at York, and there she received the news of the destruction of her hopes. There was nothing left for her but instant and rapid flight. The fugitives from Towton told her to mount at once, and the unhappy family, with a few faithful friends, galloped out of Bootham Bar, and plunged into the forest of Galtres. The Dukes of Somerset and Exeter and Lord Roos attended them. They escaped to Berwick and thence to Edinburgh, where Henry found a suitable abode with the Grey Friars. Margaret passed the following winter in Scotland, but in the spring, seeing no present hope from her English adherents, who appeared to be crushed, she resolved to seek help from abroad. Taking the little prince with her, she sailed from Kirkcudbright in April 1462, and landed in Brittany, whence she proceeded to the court of her cousin Louis XI., who was then at Chinon. It was resolved that some assistance should be given to the undaunted heroine in men and money. Her old champion Pierre de Brezé now flew to the succour of the forlorn Margaret in her distress. He organized an expedition, and in October 1462 he sailed to the coast of Northumberland with the Queen and her son. They landed at Tynemouth, but the foreign levies were repulsed and fled to their ships, abandoning de Brezé and the Queen. The fugitives were afterwards cut to pieces by troops under Sir Robert Ogle when they landed at Holy Island. De Brezé, with Margaret and her child, escaped from Tynemouth in a fishing boat and, after a perilous voyage, they landed safely at Berwick, which was then a Scottish port.

In Scotland there was but a cold welcome for Queen Margaret. It was necessary to make her way to Bamborough, which still held out for her, and there, abandoning present hope, the Queen and her child embarked to commence a life of exile in April 1463. They were accompanied by a band of faithful friends who would not desert them in their extremity. Chief among them was the Lord Chief Justice, Sir John Fortescue.

The Duke of Somerset, now a double-dyed traitor, with Sir Hugh Percy and others then rose in rebellion, and captured the castles of Alnwick and Bamborough. The Marquis Montagu, followed by Edward IV. in person, advanced rapidly from the south to put down the new insurrection. On April 25, 1464, the insurgents were defeated at Hedgley Moor, and soon afterwards the rest of Somerset's forces entrenched themselves near Hexham. Poor Henry was brought from Edinburgh, where he was quite contented with his Grey Friars, to the camp. The entrenchments were thrown up on Lyvel's plain, near Dowelwater, and Somerset awaited the attack. On May 8, 1464, Montagu came in sight, assaulted the position, and, after a desperate resistance, carried it with great slaughter. The Duke of

Somerset, Lords Roos and Hungerford were taken and beheaded, Henry galloped off on a swift horse in the direction of the Scottish Border. He concealed himself in the west of Yorkshire for a year, but was captured at Bolton Hall in June 1465 and taken to the Tower.[4]

Meanwhile, Queen Margaret encountered a furious gale of wind which lasted for twelve hours, but her vessel at length reached the Flemish port of Sluys. Thence she proceeded by Lille and Hesdin to the Court of the Duke of Burgundy at St. Pol. Here the exiles were hospitably received and supplied with money, and, after some stay, they went on to the castle of Koeur-la-Petite near St. Mihiel, on the Meuse. King René had assigned this castle as the residence of his daughter and grandson, with their followers.

No boy who had only reached his eleventh year ever went through such vicissitudes as Edward of Lancaster. He had been at four pitched battles, had ridden over hundreds of miles, had been seized by robbers, had wandered in trackless forests, had passed many nights on the bare ground, and in open boats. He had made hairbreadth escapes, and had suffered privations and hardships. Few children could have survived such a life. He must have had a robust frame combined with the high courage of his race. Through all, and protecting him at every step, he had his heroic mother as his companion; surrounding and pervading his life with her devoted love. Such experiences must have left a deep impression on the boy's character. It was a wild and turbulent opening for the young life, but now at last there was to be a brief interval of rest. For a few years he was to live more peaceably, receiving instruction and enjoying some pleasures, before destiny hurried him to a violent death.

St. Mihiel is a small town on the right bank of the Meuse, in the diocese of Verdun and Duchy of Bar. Near it there are enormous rocks overhanging the river, called Les Falaises de St. Mihiel. In the fifteenth century there was cultivation along the river banks, while extensive forests covered the Argonne mountains further back. Nearly opposite St. Mihiel, on the left bank of the river, was the old castle of Koeur-la-Petite, which René gave to his daughter Margaret[5]; and he contributed to her support as far as his narrow means would allow. Here she dwelt for the five succeeding years, watching the growth and education of her boy, and enjoying more happiness than she had known since her ill-fated marriage. She was within a few miles of Pont-à-Mousson, the place of her birth, and often saw her beloved father, and her sister Iolanthe.

Young Edward was devoted to field sports and martial exercises. His companions were the sons of knights and esquires who had remained faithful to his mother; and he loved to gallop with them over the valley, and to exercise with sword and lance. So much of his time was passed in these outdoor exercises that, as his years increased, the graver advisers of his mother began to think that he should give rather more of his attention to the acquisition of learning.

Among the exiles was the most learned and accomplished lawyer who sat on the English bench during the fifteenth century, and the young prince enjoyed the advantage of his companionship and instruction. John Fortescue of Ebrington was born in 1394, was educated at Exeter College, and became Lord Chief Justice in 1442. Considering the parliamentary title of the Lancastrian King not only good in itself, but even better than a merely hereditary title, he became a steady adherent of Margaret of Anjou. He wrote a treatise supporting the claim of the

Lancastrians on principles of constitutional law; while his presence in their camp gave judicial countenance to the appeal to arms. During his exile he mainly resided at St. Mihiel, in attendance on the little court of Koeur-la-Petite, and superintended the education of the prince. He was anxious to impart a knowledge of England and of English constitutional law to a prince who might some day have to rule over freedom-loving Englishmen, but who left his country when he was too young to recollect much about it. Fortescue has related the occasion of these studies being commenced, and the progress that was made.

'The Prince,' says the aged Chief Justice, 'as he grew up, applied himself wholly to martial exercises. He was often mounted on fiery and wild horses which he did not fear to urge on with the spur. Sometimes with his lance, sometimes with his sword, he made it his diversion to assault the young gentlemen, his attendants, according to the rules of military discipline.' In this Sir John Fortescue encouraged him, but he also urged him to study law, quoting Deuteronomy xvii. 18, 19. The boy replied that, although he ought to read the Divine law, it did not follow that he should study human laws. He said this thoughtfully, and looking very intently at the old judge. Fortescue answered that human laws were also sacred, that they were no other than rules whereby the perfect notion of justice could be determined, and that this justice must be the subject of the royal care. Quoting Wisdom i. 1, he said, 'Be instructed, ye judges of the earth. Love righteousness, ye judges of the earth. To love justice,' he concluded, 'you must acquire a competent knowledge of the laws.' Prince Edward was convinced by the discourse of his venerable tutor. He said, 'You have overcome me, good Chancellor, with your agreeable discourse, and have kindled within my breast a thirst for a knowledge of the law.' The boy candidly confessed that he did not wish to pass all his younger years in such studies. Then Sir John Fortescue explained to him the amount of legal knowledge that was necessary for a prince. In one year he could acquire sufficient acquaintance with the laws of England, and at the same time he could continue to inure himself to those martial exercises to which his natural inclination prompted him so much. 'Still make your diversion as it best please you, at your leisure,' said the tutor.

After this conversation, the aged judge of seventy-five and the young prince of fifteen devoted some hours of each day to a study of the English Constitution. These lectures, in the form of dialogues, were afterwards embodied by Fortescue in a treatise entitled 'De Laudibus legum Angliæ,' which was first printed in 1537. Edward began by asking his instructor to satisfy him that the laws of England were better adapted for the government of that kingdom than the civil law of the Holy Roman Empire. Fortescue proceeded to establish this point, specially dwelling on the fact that the English statutes were not made by the will of the Kings, but were enacted by the concurrent consent of the whole people, by their representatives in Parliament. He then explained the territorial division of England into counties, the duties of sheriffs, the method of empannelling juries, the procedure in civil and criminal causes. The boy approved highly of the system of trial by jury, the jurors being men chosen from among neighbours who knew the country and people. 'I know of myself,' he remarked, 'more certainly what is doing at this time in the Barrois where I reside, than what is doing in England.'

On another day the Chief Justice illustrated the good results of the English Constitution by comparing the condition of England with that of France ruled by a despotism. 'In the land of England,' he said, 'there are no wolves nor bears. The grazing lands are enclosed with hedgerows and ditches and planted with trees which fence the herds and flocks from bleak winds and sultry heat. There are many franklins and yeomen, of estates sufficient to make substantial juries, not a few spending 100l. a year and more. Other countries are not in such a happy situation, and not so well stored with inhabitants.' The prince then remarked that he could understand how the wealth and populousness of England had been caused by the superior excellence of her laws. But a doubt about the number of jurors had occurred to his youthful mind. He said, 'Although this method of sifting out the truth highly pleases me, yet there rests this doubt with me. Our blessed Saviour says: "It is written in your law that the testimony of two men is true" (John viii. 17), and again in Matthew xviii. 16.' Fortescue answered that our jury law did not contradict this, for if the testimony of two be true, a fortiori that of twelve ought to be presumed to be so. 'The more always contains in it that which is less.' Besides in England some cases may be proved before two only, such as facts occurring on the high seas, and proceedings before the Lord Constable and Earl Marshal.

On another occasion, having previously shown that the prosperity of England was due to laws agreed to by the people, Fortescue illustrated the evils of despotic power by the condition of France. 'You will remember,' he said, 'that you saw in France how the villages are so much oppressed by the King's soldiers that you could scarcely be accommodated in your travels. The troops pay for nothing, and treat the people barbarously if they are not satisfied. Thus the poor people are exposed to great calamities. The King of France will allow no one to use salt, but what is bought of himself at his own arbitrary price. All growers of vines must give a fourth to the King. All the towns pay the King great yearly sums for his men-at-arms; so that the peasants live in great hardships and misery. They wear no woollen. Their clothing consists of little short jerkins of sackcloth, no trowse but from the knees upwards, and legs exposed and naked. The women all go barefoot. The people eat not meat, except the fat of bacon in their soup. Nor are the gentry much better off. If an accusation is brought against them, they are examined in private, and perhaps never more heard of.

'In England it is very different. No one can abide in another man's house without his leave, or take his goods, except the King by his purveyors at a reasonable price. The King cannot put on taxes, nor alter the laws, nor make new ones. The English never drink water except for penance. They eat all sorts of flesh and fish. They are clothed throughout in good woollens; and are provided with all sorts of household goods. An Englishman cannot be sued except before the ordinary judge.' Having drawn this contrast between the French and English, the old judge continued: 'These advantages are due to the political mixed government which prevails in England. Those Kings who have wished to change it preferred ambition, luxury, and impotent passion to the good of the State. Remember that the king is given for the sake of the kingdom, not the kingdom for the sake of the king.'

Edward, although he frequently intervened with pertinent questions, showing that he was giving close attention to the subject, fully concurred in the arguments of his tutor, and must have derived great benefit from this course of studies. He was impressed with the duties of an English king, with the limited character of his power, and with the importance of a parliamentary title. Fortescue also began to occupy the young Prince in the active transaction of affairs of State. Edward himself wrote a despatch to Sir Thomas Butler, Earl of Ormonde, who was in Portugal representing the cause of the House of Lancaster to King Alfonso V.,[6] and he was acquainted with the proceedings of Sir John Fortescue when he made journeys to the court of Louis XI.

The residence at Koeur-la-Petite lasted for five years, 1465-69. The peaceful home was broken up through the treachery of the turbulent and self-seeking Earl of Warwick. Exasperated with Edward IV., owing to his marriage and connexion with the Woodville faction, Warwick had resolved to abandon the cause with which he was connected by ties of relationship and by life-long service. He had married his daughter Isabel to the Duke of Clarence without the King's consent, and had alienated that vacillating prince from his brother. He came to France with the Countess, his two daughters Isabel and Anne, and Clarence: and proposed to King Louis to espouse the cause of his cousin Margaret, and to restore Henry to the throne. The fear of an alliance between Edward IV. and the Duke of Burgundy caused Louis to entertain Warwick's scheme. But it was most distasteful to Margaret. Much as she longed for the restoration to her child of his birthright, she found it difficult to accept such aid. Warwick had not only been the most inveterate enemy of her family, he had also made himself personally odious to Margaret. He was now a double-dyed traitor. His motives were transparently selfish, and she believed neither in his new-born loyalty nor in his ability to help her. But the persuasions of Louis XI. and of her own relations at length induced her to come to the French court. The Queen and her son, attended by Sir John Fortescue and their other faithful adherents, left the happy home in the lovely valley of the Meuse in December 1469.

Margaret arrived at Tours, where the French court then was, accompanied by Prince Edward, King René, her brother John of Calabria, her sister Iolanthe, and her brother-in-law Ferry de Vaudemont. Warwick arrived soon afterwards, and with much reluctance Margaret consented to an interview. Negotiations were continued for several months; and on July 15 the court moved to Angers, where the Countess of Warwick and her daughter Anne were in attendance.

Warwick asked that Prince Edward should marry his daughter Anne, as the reward of his assistance. At first the Queen positively refused, but she at last gave a conditional and very unwilling assent, moved by the importunities of Louis XI. and her relations. The marriage was not to take place until after Henry VI. was restored to the throne and, if Warwick failed, the agreement was at an end. 'The said marriage shall not be perfyted until the Earl of Warwick has recovered the realm of England for King Henry.'[7] They were never married. They were, indeed, too young, Edward being seventeen, and Anne barely fourteen.[8] Knowing the dislike of his mother to such a union, and strongly prejudiced against it himself, it is not likely that Edward ever took more notice of Warwick's child than ordinary courtesy required, if indeed he ever saw her.

Queen Margaret made preparations for a voyage to England, where her supporters were expected to rise in the western counties and Wales. Warwick had preceded her by several months. Margaret was in her forty-second year, and she had lost some of her buoyancy and vigorous hopefulness with her youth. Still as determined as ever to assert the rights of her son, she trembled for his safety. She got ready to embark with feelings of deep anxiety and foreboding. Edward reached his seventeenth birthday in October 1470, and in November Queen Margaret and the Prince entered Paris, and were honoured with a grand official reception. Edward was now a handsome lad of seventeen, with a robust frame well seasoned by active outdoor life. He was tall for his age, with the features of his mother, and long golden hair. He was a good horseman and a practised man-at-arms. Well instructed in all the literary culture of the time, and doubtless inheriting some of his grandfather's love of poetry and romance, young Edward had also carefully studied the constitution and laws of England. He was fully convinced of the justice of his cause by the reasoning of one of the ablest lawyers of the time, and the hereditary bravery of his race now filled him with martial ardour. But he was still very young, and all these qualities of head and heart were as yet only budding towards maturity.

[1] Barante.

[2] Born in 1421.

[3] A Nevill. Sister of the Duchess of York.

[4] See Archæologia, 47 (ii), p. 265. Margaret was not at the battle of Hexham, and the robber story is a fabrication.

[5] Villeneuve, Vie de Roi René.

[6] Alfonso V. was a grandson of Queen Philippa, sister of Henry IV. of England, therefore a second cousin of Henry VI.

[7] Ellis, Original Letters, Second Series, i. 132.

[8] Born June 11, 1456.

CHAPTER VI THE BATTLE OF TEWKESBURY

There was long delay in the arrival of Queen Margaret in England with reinforcements. She was prevented from sailing by contrary winds at Harfleur. Three times the ships put to sea, and were forced to return. The Countess of Warwick, with her daughter Anne, arrived first at Portsmouth and, hearing of the death of her husband at Barnet soon afterwards, she took sanctuary in Beaulieu Abbey. Queen Margaret with her son Edward, Sir John Langstrother, Prior of St. John, Sir John Fortescue, and many exiled knights landed at Weymouth on April 14, the very day of the battle of Barnet.

Weymouth was then a small seaport with no suitable accommodation for so large a concourse. The Queen, therefore, passing through Dorchester, at once advanced fifteen miles northward from the sea coast, to the Abbey of Cerne. Dr. Morton, who accompanied her, had once been a monk at Cerne; and the Abbot was his old friend. This circumstance no doubt led to the decision of Queen Margaret to seek the hospitality of Abbot Roger Bemynster, and here she received tidings of the battle of Barnet, a disaster which seemed fatal to her cause. At first she was overwhelmed, and wished her boy to return to France. But in a few days she was joined by Edmund Beaufort, the last Duke of Somerset, and his brother John. Somerset had commanded the archers at Barnet, but had escaped and found his way to the Queen. Jasper Tudor,[1] the Earl of Devonshire, and Lord Wenlock followed closely on the heels of Somerset. They entreated her to persevere, assuring her that the west of England was ready to rise in her support, and that levies had actually been called out, with Exeter as the rendezvous. With some reluctance she consented, and her gallant son entered upon the last three weeks of his young life. Tudor was despatched to raise forces in Wales. Margaret, with the rest of her adherents, left Cerne Abbey after a stay of about ten days, marched to Exeter and thence, by Taunton, Glastonbury and Wells, to Bristol. Fresh levies joined and increased her forces as she advanced.

On April 16 King Edward heard that Queen Margaret had landed. He had returned to London two days before, after his victory at Barnet. On the 19th he went to Windsor and waited to collect men, celebrating the feast of St. George there on the 23rd. He saw at once that the enemy had only two courses: either to march on London and give him battle, or to go northwards and unite with Tudor's levies in Wales. His policy was to engage his adversaries as soon as possible, before they could be reinforced. He was not likely to receive more support until he had gained a decisive victory, and his position was established. Queen Margaret's generals tried to deceive him by sending detachments in several directions; but his final conclusion was that they intended to take a northerly direction, by crossing the Severn and marching into Wales. This it was his intention to prevent.

The King left Windsor on April 24, accompanied by his brothers Clarence and Gloucester, by Lords Hastings and Dorset, and by his old tutor Richard Croft. He had some artillery, which caused him to proceed by easy marches. A few reinforcements had arrived. Among them were forty soldiers paid and clothed by the city of Norwich. On the 27th Edward was at Abingdon, and on the 29th at Cirencester. He kept a somewhat northerly line, so as to fall on the enemy's flank if a rush was made at London. At Abingdon he heard that the Queen was at Wells. News came to Cirencester that she would be at Bath next day, and then advance to attack him. So he moved to meet her as far as Malmesbury. Then the news arrived that she had gone to

Bristol, and had resolved to give him battle at Chipping Sodbury. Lancastrian parties had even been sent to take ground on Sodbury Hill. On Thursday, May 2, the King marched to Chipping Sodbury, but found no enemy. It was a feint. The Lancastrians had gained a day on him, and were in full march to Gloucester. It was now a race to the Severn. It was life and death to the Lancastrian army to cross the river and join Tudor on the Welsh border. It was equally life and death for King Edward to prevent it. He encamped in a valley between the hill and Sodbury village on the night of the 2nd, anxiously waiting for correct intelligence. At three in the next morning he heard that the enemy was making a forced march on Gloucester. Luckily the castle was held by Richard, son of Lord Beauchamp of Powyke, for the King. Edward sent a trusty messenger, urging them to hold out, with the assurance that he was following rapidly. The messenger arrived in time.

The Lancastrian army had marched all through the night from Bristol, over the plain between the Cotswold Hills and the Severn. At ten in the forenoon of May 3, the Queen's forces came before the gates of Gloucester and summoned the place. Sir Richard Beauchamp manned the walls and refused to surrender. There was no time to spare. It was thought wiser to proceed to Tewkesbury without resting. They arrived at Tewkesbury at about four in the afternoon of the same day. But the troops had marched, during that day and the night before, a distance of thirty-six miles without rest. The men were exhausted, and could go no further. Margaret wanted them to pass over the Severn, but it was represented to her that if they could cross the river the King could follow, and attack them when they were worn out with fatigue. The Queen was right. It was resolved, however, that the troops should obtain some rest, and that a strong position should be taken up and entrenched, outside the town of Tewkesbury. There was a bridge over the Avon in those days, but none over the Severn at Tewkesbury.

Close to the first mile-post on the turnpike road, on the west side of Tewkesbury, there is a range of elevated ground called Holme Hill, where a castle once stood. The present workhouse is built on part of the site. Close behind it there is a field called 'the Gastons,'[2] and some ground laid out as a cemetery. On the east side of the road is Gupshill farm and gardens, and a field called 'Margaret's camp.' The Lancastrian position included the Gastons and Gupshill, with the abbey and the houses of the town immediately in the rear. It is described as 'a place right evil to approach.'[3] Strong entrenchments were thrown up in the front and both flanks, strengthened by muddy lanes and ditches.

On the same morning of May 3, at early dawn, King Edward marshalled his forces at Chipping Sodbury in three battalions, and prepared for a long march, with scouts in front and on the flanks. His infantry numbered 3,000 men. It was a very hot day and he took a direct line over the Cotswold Hills; rightly judging that the enemy, having failed before Gloucester, would make for Tewkesbury. Thither, therefore, he marched direct without a halt. The men found neither food nor even water, except at one small brook. But the King allowed no rest. He reached Cheltenham as the enemy got to Tewkesbury. At Cheltenham he served out the rations that had been brought, the men having marched 28 miles. Then he resumed the march, and at night he encamped within two miles of the enemy's position, having marched over thirty-four miles.

At dawn on Saturday, May 4, 1471, the army of Queen Margaret prepared to resist the assault of the King's forces.

The van was commanded by Edmund Duke of Somerset, and his brother Sir John Beaufort. Young Prince Edward was to lead the main battle, assisted by Lord Wenlock and the Prior of St. John. The rear division was under the Earl of Devonshire. Queen Margaret parted with her son that morning in deep anxiety, for the first and alas! the last time. She retired to a small religious house at Gupshill, with the Countess of Devonshire, the Lady Vaux and other ladies.

King Edward[4] arranged his army in three divisions. Young Richard of Gloucester[5] commanded the van guard with the artillery. The King himself led the centre. Hastings and Dorset conducted the rear. The King had observed a park with much wood to the right of the enemy's position, and he posted 300 spearmen there, to act as occasion might require. He then displayed his banners, blew his trumpets, and marched straight on the entrenchments.

Gloucester found so many hedges and deep dikes in front of him that he could not break into the enemy's line so as to come hand to hand. He ordered up the artillery and, also using arrows, opened on Somerset's division. Galled by the fire, Somerset then led his men down some lanes on the King's flank, which he had previously reconnoitred, and fell upon the troops of the Yorkist centre with great fury, driving them backwards. He charged Gloucester with the same impetuosity, and was in the full tide of success when, just as the King was rallying his men, the select 300 spearmen from the wood attacked Somerset's rear and caused a panic. This gave the King time to reform and resume the fight. Somerset's men now fell back, while the Duke of Gloucester made a desperate assault on the Lancastrian centre, behind the entrenchments. There was a short and gallant struggle, in which young Prince Edward fleshed his maiden sword, and then the Lancastrians broke in all directions. The rout was complete. The abbey water mills were in a meadow close to the town, and here many fugitives were drowned. There was a great slaughter in the 'Bloody Meadow' to the rear of the Lancastrian position, for it leads to a ford or ferry over the Severn called Lower Lode. But soon the King gave orders to spare the fugitives.

The brave young Prince, who led the main battle of the Lancastrians, bore himself valiantly, and played the man before his people in that supreme moment of his life. Of that we need have no doubt. Borne away in the rout, and followed closely by the victorious enemy, he was slain between Gastons and Tewkesbury. The closing scene is dimly shown to us. The horse is wounded and on its knees. Then the rider receives his death blow from behind. The helmet had been struck off. The bright golden locks sink down on the horse's mane,[6] and in another moment horse and rider fall and are ridden over. Thus ended the life of Sir Edward Plantagenet, K.G., Prince of Wales and Earl of Chester. His age was seventeen years and six months. He was a boy of great promise; courageous, intelligent, and affectionate. His short life must have embraced a large share of happiness. Even during all the dangers and hardships of his childhood, the loving arm of the devoted mother must have diverted those terrors which cause misery to unprotected children. The life at Koeur-la-Petite was a period of unclouded pleasure. Then came the excitement of the last campaign, and a glorious death on the battlefield. The body of Prince Edward was buried in Tewkesbury Abbey church.

The Earl of Devonshire, Lord Wenlock, Sir John Beaufort, Sir William Vaux, Sir Edmund Hampton, Sir E. Whittingham, Sir William Melding, Sir John Seymour, Mr. Henry, a captain of Bristol, and Sir William Roos were among the slain. Beaufort, Hampton, Vaux, Whittingham and Roos had shared the Queen's exile at Koeur-la-Petite.

The lords and knights who escaped from the battlefield took refuge in the abbey church, which, however, had no special privilege of sanctuary. They were tried for treason before the Earl Marshal and the Lord High Constable, a court which is recognised as legal by Chief Justice Fortescue. Thirteen[7] were condemned, and were beheaded in the market place of Tewkesbury on May 6, 1471. It must be remembered that the treason of which most of them were guilty was double-dyed, that is, they had been forgiven and had again become traitors.

Duke of Somerset

Prior of St. John
Sir Gervase Clifton
Sir Humphrey Audley
Sir Hugh Carey
Sir Thomas Tresham
Henry Tresham

Sir W. Newborough
Sir Walter Courtenay
James Gower
Lewis Miles
Robert Jackson
John Flory, of France

Gower was the young Prince's sword-bearer. Audley and Courtenay shared the Queen's exile. These might have been spared. Edward IV. was generous and forgiving after the first fury of the moment had passed. All inferior officers and soldiers were pardoned. Sir John Fortescue received pardon and died at a good old age at his seat at Ebrington in Gloucestershire. The intriguing Earl of Ormonde was also pardoned, as were many leading captains of the defeated army, Sir Henry Roos, Sir John Giles, Sir William Grimsby, Fulford, Parker, Basset, Throgmorton, Walleys and many more. Dr. Morton and Dr. Makerel, who were with the Queen, were also pardoned.

The King conferred knighthood on forty-three officers; including his old tutor Richard Croft, Sir John Pilkington, and Sir Thomas Strickland from Yorkshire; Sir Terry Robsart, Sir Edward Wodehouse, and Sir William Brandon from Norfolk; Sir John St. Lo, Sir E. Corbet and Lord Cobham. The names of Nevill, Courtenay, Berkeley, Hastings, Harington, Grey, Tyrrel, Pierpoint, Parr, Welby, Ratcliffe, Devereux also appear.

One turns with shuddering pity from the anguish beyond all power of utterance, from the black despair in the religious house at Gupshill where the Queen awaited the issue of the battle with her ladies.[8] They escaped across the Avon, and took refuge at Payne's Place in the parish of Bushley. Next day, continuing their journey towards Worcester, they found shelter in some religious house near that city. There they were captured by Sir William Stanley. It was reported that he announced the prince's death with callous brutality. It mattered little. The blow must have stunned the unhappy mother and nothing could add to its crushing effect. Her real life ended with that of her beloved child. Queen Margaret was brought to Edward IV. at Coventry, by Sir William Stanley, on May 11, and to the Tower of London on the 22nd.

Henry VI. died in the Tower on the 24th, at the comparatively early age of forty-nine. As Margaret arrived on the 22nd, she probably attended her husband during the last two days of his life. The Lancastrian leaning of the family of Lord Rivers, who was then Constable of the Tower, would ensure facilities being extended to her. Thence Margaret of Anjou was removed to Windsor, a ransom having been demanded for her. With thoughtful kindness King Edward finally entrusted the charge of the poor Queen to her old friend the Dowager Duchess of Suffolk at Ewelme.[9] The Duchess had come to Nancy for

Henry's bride, and had seen the beautiful young princess at the brilliant tournament. She now received her, after twenty-seven years, a childless and despairing widow, crushed to the earth by grief unspeakable. Margaret resided with the Duchess at Ewelme, and afterwards at Wallingford Castle until the ransom was paid by old King René.

On August 29,1475, the ransom, amounting to fifty thousand crowns, having been paid, Queen Margaret proceeded to embark at Sandwich, attended by three ladies and seven gentlemen, and escorted by Sir John Haute. She landed at Dieppe, and signed a renunciation of all rights derived from her marriage, at Rouen on January 29, 1476. Thence she went to Reculée, a league from Angers, where she lived with her old father until his death in 1480, aged seventy-two. The last sad years were passed at the château of Dampierre on the Loire, near Saumur, under the care of François de Vignolle, an old and faithful servant of her family. The brave and loving soul was at length released. Margaret of Anjou died at the age of fifty-two, on August 25, 1482, eleven years after the light went out of her life. She was buried in the cathedral of Angers.

[1] Jasper and Edmund Tudor were created Earls of Pembroke and Richmond by Henry VI. They were attainted and deprived of their earldoms by Edward's first Parliament. Subsequently Richard, Duke of Gloucester, was created Earl of Richmond; and the son of King Edward IV. became Earl of Pembroke.

[2] Leland says: 'intravit campum nomine Gastum,' and 'nomina occisorum in bello Gastriensis prope Theokesbury.' A place called 'the Vineyard' is mentioned. But 'vineyards' were merely apple orchards. Where manors were held of the King, the tenants were obliged to pay yearly a vessel of wine made of apples, or cider.

[3] 'In a close harde at the toune's end, having the toun and abbey at their backs, and before them defended by lanes and deep ditches and hedges.'—Holinshed.

[4] Then aged twenty-nine. Born April 28, 1442.

[5] Then aged eighteen and a half. Born October 2, 1452. He was just a year older than Prince Edward.

[6] So much is shown in a picture accompanying the narrative sent to Flanders by an eyewitness. It is in the public library at Ghent. See also Archæologia, xxi. 11-23.

[7] In the Pastern Letters there is a list of sixteen, Sir John Delves, Sir William 'Newbery' added, and Audley given twice, Jackson not being given (iii. 9).

[8] Speed, p. 684. See also a paper by the Rev. E. E. Dowdeswell on the 'Movements of Queen Margaret after the battle of Tewkesbury,' in the Transactions (x. 144) of the Bristol and Gloucestershire Archæological Society.

[9] 'As for Queen Margaret, I understand that she is removed from Windsor to Wallingford nigh to Ewelme, my Lady of Suffolk's place in Oxfordshire.'—Paston Letters, iii. 83.

Ewelme belonged to the Chaucer family, and Alice, the heiress of Geoffrey Chaucer, married William de la Pole, Duke of Suffolk. In 1424 the Duke and Duchess of Suffolk built a palace at Ewelme, rebuilt the church, and founded a hospital and a school there. Queen Margaret was received by the Duchess at Ewelme, and afterwards at Wallingford Castle.

CHAPTER VII MARRIED LIFE AND PUBLIC SERVICES OF RICHARD DUKE OF GLOUCESTER

While the King was engaged at Tewkesbury, the bastard of his uncle, Lord Fauconberg, made an attack on London Bridge, and when he was repulsed, he retreated to Sandwich. This disturbance hastened the return of Edward IV., who reached the Tower on May 21. To the Duke of Gloucester was entrusted the duty of following up the bastard, and early next morning he started for Kent. Arriving by forced marches at Sandwich, the rebel was taken by surprise and surrendered on the 26th. He was a first cousin of the King and of the Duke of Gloucester, though illegitimate; son of the general to whom, next to Edward, the victory of Towton was due. Richard took him to Middleham, and treated him kindly as a prisoner at large. But he escaped, was taken at Southampton, tried for his original treason, and beheaded.

Peace was once more restored to the land, and the Duke of Gloucester's great services were recognised by the country. The King and Parliament were soon afterwards occupied with Richard's marriage.

The estates of the Earl and Countess of Warwick were forfeited, and the Duke of Clarence, who had married the elder daughter, Isabella, desired to obtain the whole for himself. The Countess of Warwick, when she returned from France with her daughter, Anne, and received the news of her husband's death, took sanctuary in Beaulieu Abbey on the Southampton Water. After Tewkesbury, Clarence claimed the wardship of Anne, and tried to get her into his power.

The Duke of Clarence was grasping and selfish. He had no stability of character, was vacillating, and easily influenced by bad advisers. It is not clear how his sister-in-law escaped from his clutches; but his object was to prevent her from marrying and to seize her share of her parents' property, as well as that of his wife. It is certain that Anne left her mother at Beaulieu and placed herself under the protection of her uncle, George Nevill, Archbishop of York. But the circumstances are unrecorded. There is mention of a disguise as a cookmaid. The Archbishop placed her in sanctuary at St. Martin's-le-Grand: where her inclinations and wishes could in no way be influenced or overridden.

The young Duke of Gloucester sought the hand of his cousin Anne. They had been playfellows as children, and now the cousins formed an attachment which endured until death, Richard only surviving his wife for four months. Anne accepted the proposal of Richard, and his suit was approved by the King and by the Archbishop, the guardians of the two lovers. But Clarence made unreasonable difficulties about the settlement. From the 'Paston Letters' we learn that 'the King entreateth my Lord Clarence for my Lord Gloucester, and he answereth that he may well have my lady, his sister-in-law, but they shall part no livelihood.'

At length the marriage settlements were arranged by Parliament. Middleham was included in Gloucester's share of the Warwick inheritance. In 1472, Richard and Anne were happily married in Westminster Abbey by the Archbishop of York. His age was nineteen, that of his wife sixteen.

Their home was at Middleham, in beautiful Wensleydale, and Anne's mother, the Countess of Warwick, was taken from her sanctuary at Beaulieu, to live with them. Here the

Duke and Duchess passed several years, winning golden opinions from the people of the north, and acquiring great popularity in Yorkshire.

In 1475, the Duke of Gloucester was called from his home to accompany the King when he invaded France. Louis XI. offered a large sum of money if Edward IV. would abandon his ally, the Duke of Burgundy, and make peace. He also bribed Dr. Morton and Edward's principal courtiers. Under the evil influence of Morton and the Woodville faction, the King of England, after an interview with Louis, acceded to the disgraceful bargain. But the Duke of Gloucester also had an interview with King Louis and was not to be corrupted. He objected to the arrangement, and would have no part in it. His conduct was honourable and consistent. He maintained that faith ought to be kept with England's ally.

Richard Duke of Gloucester lived at Middleham Castle, with his wife and child, for ten years, from 1472 to 1482, from his twentieth to his thirtieth year. Here he had passed his early youth, had formed his most enduring friendships, and had first seen his cousin Anne. The ten years of peaceful married residence at Middleham was no doubt the happiest period of Richard's short but eventful life.

The ruins of the grand old pile, with the village and the church at their feet, still form a conspicuous object on the southern slope of Wensleydale. Middleham is about a mile and a half above the junction of the Ure and the Cover. In rear of the castle are the breezy downs, and in front the river Ure flows through rich pastures, with the town of Leybourne on the opposite slope. The castle consisted of a lofty Norman keep surrounded by an enceinte eighty yards long by sixty-five wide. The keep, which was built by Robert FitzRanulph in 1190, was fifty feet high, with walls nine feet thick, strengthened at the angles by buttresses rising into rectangular turrets. It was divided into two large rooms on each floor, the great hall having a lofty arched window, due to the taste of the Duke of Gloucester. In the north-east angle there was a curious mural chamber, twelve feet long by nine, opening on to the hall, and the east face of the keep was one side of the chapel. The outer walls were thirty feet high with square towers at the angles, and a gatehouse on the north face. The residential buildings stood against three sides of the enceinte, and seem to have communicated with the great hall in the keep by a covered passage.

The nearest neighbours of the Duke and Duchess of Gloucester were the Monks of Jervaux and Coverham, their cousin the Lord Scrope of Bolton,[1] and the Metcalfes of Nappa Hall.[2]

The manuscript volume No. 433 of the Harleian collection in the British Museum supplies a few glimpses of the home life at Middleham. We read of a pack of hounds and of the wages of a jester. There is the election of a king of rush bearing, and of a king of Middleham, evidently games for the amusement of the Duke's little son Edward, who was born about 1473.[3] The child's tutor was Richard Bernall, and the cost is recorded of his primer and psalter, and of satin to cover them. There are also payments for green cloth for my lord prince, and for a feather for my lord prince.

Though Middleham was Richard's home, his official residence, as Chief Seneschal of the Duchy of Lancaster in the north parts, was at Pomfret Castle. He also stayed occasionally at Sheriff Hutton, Skipton, and Barnard Castle. He was regarded as a trusted friend by his neighbours, and in September 1481 we find Lady Latimer showing her confidence in his integrity by appointing him supervisor of her will. She was a sister of his mother-in-law, the Countess of Warwick. The Duke of Gloucester bestowed great benefits on the city of York, where he was much beloved. During his frequent visits he was usually the guest of the Augustine friars,[4] and in their monastery he conferred with the authorities touching their local affairs. He was actively engaged in administrative work, and in giving his time to settle the affairs of his neighbours from 1472. In that year we find him writing about a robbery of cattle at Spofforth. In 1482 he was an arbitrator in the dispute between Robert Plumpton and his heirs-general.[5] He improved and beautified several Yorkshire churches, building an additional chapel at Sheriff Hutton, founding colleges at Middleham[6] and Barnard Castle, and a memorial chapel near the battlefield of Towton. Crosby Place, in Bishopsgate, became the town residence of the Duke and Duchess of Gloucester, after the death of its wealthy founder, Sir John Crosby, in 1475.

Richard, Duke of Gloucester, had been created Great Chamberlain and Admiral of England by his brother, and he was Lord Warden of the Cinque Ports. His little son Edward became Earl of Salisbury in 1478.[7] In 1480, when Richard had attained the age of twenty-eight, he was appointed Lieutenant-General of the North and Warden of the Marches. By his skill and energy he subdued part of the western border of Scotland for an extent of more than thirty miles, bringing portions under obedience to the King of England, 'to the great rest and ease of the inhabitants of the west marches.'[8] His administration was so able that it was remembered long after as a very model of efficiency.[9] In 1482 he received command of an army for the invasion of Scotland. In the summer of that year he entered Edinburgh, where he was received by the malcontent nobles rather as a friend than as an enemy. He reconciled King James III.

with his brother, enforced all the English demands, and captured the town and castle of Berwick after an obstinate resistance. This was a great achievement, and gave England an important advantage in case of future hostilities. Richard's services were cordially recognised by the Parliament which met in January, and no man stood in higher honour throughout the kingdom.

King Edward IV. died at Westminster on April 9, 1483, and was buried at Windsor. He had gone through a marriage ceremony with Elizabeth, daughter of Sir Richard Woodville of Grafton, and widow of Sir John Grey of Groby, on May 1, 1464. Besides the priest and his assistant, the only witnesses were Lady Grey's mother and two unnamed gentlewomen. Edward IV. had three sons and seven daughters by Lady Grey, of whom two sons and five daughters survived him.[10] He also had one son and one daughter by Elizabeth Lucy.[11] The Duke of Clarence had left a son Edward and a daughter[12] by Isabella, daughter of the Earl of Warwick.

[1] Lord Scrope was faithful to the end. His sister Agnes was married to Sir Richard Ratcliffe, one of the most loyal of Richard's friends.

[2] James Metcalfe of Nappa, near Aysgarth, served at the battle of Agincourt. He had two sons, Miles and Thomas. Immediately after his accession Richard III. appointed Miles Metcalfe one of the Judges of the County Palatine of Lancaster, and Thomas Metcalfe Chancellor of the Duchy (York Records, p. 58 n).

[3] According to Rous he was seven and a half in 1483, when he was made Prince of Wales. But the date in the text is more probable. See Sandford, p. 410.

[4] York Records, p. 125 n.

[5] Plumpton Correspondence.

[6] See the History of the Collegiate Church of Middleham, by the Rev. Wm. Atthill (Camden Society, 1847). The licence for erecting the church into a college was granted to the Duke of Gloucester on February 21, 1478, and he issued the Statutes on July 18, 1478. Miss Halsted, the laborious and conscientious biographer of Richard III., had a romantic attachment for Middleham, as the scene of the ill-fated young King's happy married life. She eventually married the Rector, and was buried in Middleham Church.

[7] Rot. Parl. 17 Ed. iv. p. 2, m. 16.

[8] Rot. Parl. vi. 204.

[9] Gairdner, p. 48, quoting Brewer's Letters and Papers of Henry VIII., vol. i. nos. 4518-5090, and vol. iv. no. 133.

[10] Elizabeth, born at Westminster on February 11, 1465. (Sandford says 1466, but Nicolas gives good reason for 1465 being the year.)

Cicely. The date of her birth is not recorded; but she came next to Elizabeth. Henry Tudor married her to his old uncle, Lord Welles, some time before December 1487. On his death in 1499, she married one Kyme of Lincolnshire. She died in about 1503.

Edward was born in sanctuary on November 14, 1470. On July 26, 1471, he was created Prince of Wales, and on June 20, 1475, Duke of Cornwall and Earl of Chester. He was also created Earl of March and Pembroke.

Richard was born at Shrewsbury in 1473, and was created Duke of York on May 28, 1474, Duke of Norfolk and Earl of Warren and Nottingham on Feb. 7, 1477. On January 15, 1478, he was married to Anne, daughter and heiress of John Mowbray Duke of Norfolk, she being then aged six. She died soon afterwards.

Anne was born in 1475, and in 1495 she married Thomas Howard Earl of Surrey; but no children survived infancy. She died before 1515.

Katherine, probably born in 1479, and in about 1495 she married William Courtenay Earl of Devon, and died in 1527.

Bridget, the youngest child, was born at Eltham on November 10, 1480. She became a nun at Dartford, where she died in 1517.

[11] Edward IV. had two children by Elizabeth Lucy. Arthur, who was created Viscount Lisle in 1524, and died in 1540; and Elizabeth, married to Lord Lumley.

[12] George Duke of Clarence, by his wife Isabella, daughter of Richard Nevill, Earl of Warwick, left two children:

Edward, born at Warwick Castle on February 21, 1475, and created Earl of Warwick by his uncle Edward IV., after his father's execution, in 1478.

Margaret, born at Farley Castle near Bath in 1473, created Countess of Salisbury in 1514, and married to a Tudor partisan named Richard Pole.

CHAPTER VIII ACCESSION OF RICHARD III

The Queen and her relations had acquired predominating influence in the counsels of Edward IV. Her brother Anthony was Earl Rivers, another brother Lionel was Bishop of Salisbury, her son Thomas Grey had been created Marquis of Dorset. Her sisters had been married to the Duke of Buckingham, the Earls of Kent, Arundel, Huntingdon and Lord Strange. Her brother-in-law, Edward Grey, had been made Viscount Lisle.

This Woodville faction had the design to monopolise all the powers of the state. The Woodvilles had received bribes from Louis XI., had caused the death of Clarence, and had shared his inheritance. They now looked to the minority of King Edward's son as an opportunity for still further gratifying their ambition. But they had never succeeded in alienating the affections of the King from his brother Richard.

At the time of the King's death his son Edward was residing at Ludlow in charge of his uncle Lord Rivers, his half brother Sir Richard Grey, his cousin Sir Richard Haute, Sir Thomas Vaughan and Dr. Alcock, Bishop of Worcester. The Marquis of Dorset, another half-brother of young Edward, was in possession of the Tower. The other chief councillors of the late King, including Bishops Rotherham and Morton, the Duke of Buckingham, Lords Hastings, Stanley and Howard, were in London. The Duke of Gloucester was far away in the marches of Scotland.

By his will King Edward IV. left the care of his son's person and the government of the kingdom during the minority to his brother Richard, without any colleague.[1] Richard Duke of Gloucester was a prince who had shown valour and generalship in the field, wisdom and ability in his civil administration. As a councillor he had upheld the honour of his country. He was beloved by the people of the north, and was deservedly popular throughout the land. He proceeded to York on hearing of his brother's death and attended the solemn obsequies in the minster. He then caused his nephew to be proclaimed, and began the journey to London, with 600 gentlemen of the north in attendance, all in deep mourning. He came to assume the responsibilities imposed upon him by his brother.

Very different was the conduct of the Woodvilles. They formed a conspiracy to set aside the late King's wishes, to exclude the Duke of Gloucester, and to retain by force the authority they had hitherto exercised through the Queen's influence. Rivers set out from Ludlow with 2,000 men, and a large supply of arms, on April 24.[2] Dorset seized the arms and treasure in the Tower, and fitted out a naval force to secure command of the Channel. Council Orders were issued in the names of Rivers—'Avunculus Regis,' and of Dorset—'Frater regis uterinus,' while that of the Duke of Gloucester was excluded. There can be no doubt of the treasonable designs of the Woodville faction, which are indeed proved by these overt acts; and which went the length of conspiring against Richard's life.[3]

The Duke of Buckingham hurried from London with 300 men, to warn Gloucester of his danger, and found him at Northampton on April 29, where he had expected to meet his nephew. They ascertained that Rivers had arrived that very morning with young Edward, and had pushed on to Stony Stratford, fourteen miles nearer London, to avoid a meeting between the boy and his uncle. This made his conduct still more suspicious. Rivers then, with Richard Grey and a portion of his force, returned to Northampton to give some plausible explanation to the two Dukes, while young Edward was to be hurried on to London. Gloucester acted with prompt decision. There was not a moment to lose. A Council was summoned, consisting of the nobles present, and it was resolved that Rivers and his fellow-conspirators should be arrested. The combined companies of Gloucester and Buckingham numbered 900 men. Rivers had a force of 2,000, but he had only brought a portion to Northampton, and his arrest, with his nephew Richard Grey, was effected without resistance. Gloucester then advanced rapidly to Stony Stratford, and was just in time. He found young Edward and his retinue on the point of starting for London. Vaughan and Haute were arrested; and the four prisoners were sent to Yorkshire to await their trials. Lord Rivers was taken to Sheriff Hutton, Grey to Middleham, Vaughan and Haute to Pomfret. Dr. Alcock was not suspected of complicity in the plot. He was a Yorkshireman and a staunch supporter of the White Rose. His subsequent conduct in welcoming King Richard at Oxford, accompanying him in his progress, and giving him the aid of his diplomatic services, proves that Bishop Alcock recognised the justice of that King's accession.[4]

The troops of Rivers, now without a leader, submitted to the Duke of Gloucester, who then resumed his journey, in company with his nephew. They reached London on May 4. As soon as the Queen Dowager heard that the plot was discovered, she went into sanctuary at Westminster[5] with her son Richard and five daughters. Here she was joined by her other son Dorset.

Young Edward took up his abode at the Bishop's Palace in St. Paul's Churchyard. Gloucester went to reside with his mother, the widowed Duchess of York, at Baynard's Castle. This edifice stood at the foot of St. Andrew's Hill, on the banks of the Thames, a little west of St. Paul's.[6] After the death of her noble husband at the battle of Wakefield, in 1460, the Duchess of York took little part in public affairs, although she survived for upwards of 33 years. A happy married life of 22 years was followed by a long and sorrowful widowhood. The wayward and lawless conduct of her eldest son with regard to his matrimonial affairs doubtless caused her constant anxiety, while the death of her son George by the hand of his brother added another pang to the widow's grief.

Richard, so far as appears, can have given his mother neither anxiety nor sorrow. Living happily at Middleham, married to his mother's grand-niece, and always gaining applause and approval whenever he took part in public affairs, he must have been the son from whom his mother derived most comfort. It was natural that, in this crisis of his fortunes, he should have sought counsel and support under that mother's roof, and we may fairly conclude that the subsequent proceedings, which led to Richard's assumption of the crown, had the sanction and approval of the Duchess of York.[7] The Duke of Gloucester had been recognised as Protector of the Realm before his arrival in London,[8] and on May 13 he summoned a Parliament to meet on the 25th of the following month. When the Duchess of Gloucester reached London on June 5, the Duke left Baynard's Castle, where he had resided with his mother for upwards of a month, and removed to Crosby Place[9] with his wife.

Up to this time affairs had gone smoothly. On June 5 the Protector had given detailed orders for his nephew's coronation on the 22nd, and had even caused letters of summons to be issued for the attendance of forty esquires who were to receive the knighthood of the Bath on the occasion.[10] But now there came a change. Dr. Robert Stillington, Bishop of Bath and Wells, apparently on June 8, revealed to the Council the long-concealed fact that Edward IV. was contracted to the Lady Eleanor Butler, widow of a son of Lord Butler of Sudeley, and daughter of the first Earl of Shrewsbury, before he went through a secret marriage ceremony with the Lady Grey.[11]

Dr. Stillington thus becomes a very important personage in the history of King Richard's accession; and it will be well to learn all that can be gleaned of his life. He first saw the light in an old brick manor house, which still stands on the right bank of the Ouse at Acaster Selby (then within the parish of Stillingfleet), about nine miles south of York.

The family of Stillington had long been established here, renting land from the Abbot of Selby, when two sons, Thomas and Robert, were born to Thomas Stillington and his wife Catherine, daughter of John Halthorp. Thomas succeeded to the paternal estate, while Robert was destined for the priesthood. He was sent to Oxford, and eventually took the degree of Doctor of Law with great distinction. He was a Fellow of All Souls, and became Rector of St. Michael's, Ouse Bridge, and a Canon of York in 1448 and 1451. Stillington was ever loyal to the cause of the White Rose. At some time in or before 1463, he witnessed the marriage contract which united Edward IV. to the Lady Eleanor Butler; the King strictly charging him not to reveal it. When Edward subsequently went through the same ceremony with the Lady Grey, his mother the Duchess of York, who was in the secret, remonstrated, but without avail. Edward was self-willed and headstrong. The Lady Eleanor retired to a convent in Norwich, where she died on July 30, 1466, and was buried in the Church of the Carmelites.[12]

In 1466 Dr. Stillington became Bishop of Bath and Wells, and in the same year Edward IV. made him Keeper of the Privy Seal. On June 8, 1467, he was installed in the high office of Lord Chancellor, in succession to Archbishop

Nevill. He delivered a very eloquent and statesmanlike speech at the opening of Parliament in May 1468, which made a deep impression. After holding the office of Chancellor, with dignity and credit, for six years, he resigned, owing to ill-health, in 1473. He was afterwards employed on an embassy to Brittany.

If the Queen Dowager and her relations had any knowledge of the first marriage, Bishop Stillington would be a source of anxiety and fear to them; while they could never be certain who else might know the secret besides the King's mother. We find that the Duke of Clarence was attainted on February 7, 1478, on a series of charges, most of them frivolous and none sufficiently grave to account for his death at the hands of his own brother. There must have been something behind. Mr. Gairdner has suggested that the execution of Clarence was due to his having discovered the secret.[13] Certainly that would satisfactorily account for it. The influence of the Woodvilles was paramount, and it would then be a necessity of their continuance in power that Clarence should cease to live. The character of Clarence made it impossible that a secret would be safe with him. His death was the only safe course for the Woodvilles. It is very significant that, at the very time of Clarence's attainder, Bishop Stillington was arrested and imprisoned[14] for 'uttering words prejudicial to the King and his State.' He was pardoned in the following June 1478. All this points clearly to the discovery of the first contract by Clarence, and to the utterance of some imprudent speech by the bishop, which was expiated by imprisonment followed by renewed promises of silence.

During the years following his imprisonment, Bishop Stillington appears to have devoted himself to the duties of his diocese. He always retained feelings of affection for the family at Acaster, and for the home of his childhood on the banks of the Ouse. Towards the close of his long and honourable career he founded a collegiate chapel on his brother's land at Acaster, dedicated to St. Andrew, for a provost and fellows, and for free education in grammar, music and writing. The grant was confirmed by King Richard III. in 1483. A fine collegiate church of brick, eighty-seven feet long and twenty-one broad, rose upon the banks of the Ouse, with twenty windows filled with stained glass. It was a memorial of the good bishop, and members of his family in later generations left in their wills that they wished to be buried at St. Andrew's college. The site is now marked by a few grassy mounds.[15]

Dr. Stillington was a good and pious bishop, an able statesman, and a most loyal and faithful adherent of the White Rose. His one fault was that he did not ensure his own destruction by proclaiming Edward's secret before that King's death. There was no urgent obligation to do so; but when the time arrived, he was bound to come forward, and he was probably urged by the Duchess of York to publish the truth. Richard had hitherto been ignorant of the early intrigues of his brother. He was only eleven and a half when the widow of Sir J. Grey was taken into favour, and the Butler contract was of a still earlier date.

The announcement must have fallen on Richard and the Council like a thunder clap. It was inevitable that the matter should be thoroughly sifted. There was a prolonged sitting of the Lords Spiritual and Temporal in the Council Chamber at Westminster, on June 9.[16] Bishop Stillington 'brought in instruments, authentic doctors, proctors, and notaries of the law, with depositions of divers witnesses.'[17] The majority of the Council must have seen at once that the illegitimate son of the late King could not succeed. Such a proceeding would inevitably be the precursor of innumerable troubles. The case was prepared to be laid before the Parliament which was summoned to meet on June 25.

There was, however, a small but powerful minority in the Council, led by Lord Hastings and Bishop Morton, to whom the prospect of losing the openings to their ambition offered by a minority was most distasteful. They commenced opposition[18] and began to meet apart, plotting against the Protector's government. This was soon followed by overt acts. Hitherto all orders and grants had been issued 'by the advice of our uncle, Richard Duke of Gloucester, Protector and Defender.' But on the 9th, and again on June 12, the conspirators issued orders without the Protector's name. They were preparing for open hostility. Hastings was intriguing with his former adversaries, the Woodvilles, both at Westminster and in Yorkshire. On June 10 the Duke of Gloucester became thoroughly alarmed. He despatched a letter to his faithful city of York, asking that troops might be sent up to protect and support him. It was delivered on the 15th. On the 11th a similar letter was sent to his cousin, Lord Nevill. Meanwhile, the Hastings faction was not idle. A supersedeas was secretly issued to the towns and counties, ordering the Parliament not to assemble.[19] It was received at York on June 21. This was done to delay or prevent the consideration of the question of illegitimacy, and of the evidence submitted by Bishop Stillington. Finally a plot was formed to seize the Protector and put him to death.[20]

The conspiracy was divulged to the Protector by Master William Catesby, who was in the confidence of Hastings. The danger was imminent. It was probably a question of hours. Richard acted with characteristic promptitude and vigour. On June 13 he proceeded in person to the Tower with a body of retainers, and arrested Lord Hastings at the council table on a charge of treason. The conspirators were caught, as it were, red-handed. A proclamation was then issued, giving the details of the plot, but unfortunately no copy remains. Hastings was condemned and executed on June 20, a week after his arrest.[21] The danger over, Richard mourned for the loss of his old companion in arms. 'Undoubtedly the Protector loved him well, and was loth to have lost him.'[22] A prominent feature in Richard's character was his generosity to the relations of his political opponents. In this respect the conduct which was habitual with him was almost unprecedented in his, and indeed in later times. In the case of Hastings, he at once restored the children in blood, and granted the forfeited estates to the widow. He also liberally rewarded the brother of Hastings for past services, and granted all his requests.

The conspirators in Yorkshire would probably have been pardoned, if they had not joined in this new treason with Hastings. But now an order was sent, through Sir Richard Ratcliffe, for a tribunal to assemble at Pomfret, to try Lord Rivers and his companions. The Earl of Northumberland was president of the court. They were found guilty. The accomplished Earl philosophically prepared for death. He had played for high stakes, had lost, and was ready to pay the penalty. He showed his confidence in the integrity and kindly feeling of the Duke of Gloucester by appointing him supervisor to the will which he made at Sheriff Hutton on June 23.[23] The trust was not misplaced. On the 25th, Rivers, Grey, Haute, and Vaughan were beheaded. Those arrested in London, with Hastings, were treated with unwise leniency. The treacherous Stanley was not only pardoned, but rewarded. Bishop Morton was merely taken into custody, and placed in charge of the Duke of Buckingham. Archbishop Rotherham, a weak tool in the hands of the others, after a brief detention, was allowed to return to his diocese.

Jane Shore, the mistress of Dorset, had been the medium of communication between Hastings and the Woodville faction. A penance was imposed upon her by the Church for her vicious life. But she was treated with considerate forbearance by Richard, whom she had tried to injure. He ordered her to be released, and consented, though reluctantly, to her marriage with his Solicitor-General.

The formidable coalition of the two malcontent parties was thus completely broken. The Woodvilles gave up all further resistance to the Protector's government. The Bishop of Salisbury, brother of the Queen-Dowager, and her brother-in-law, Viscount Lisle, came over to his side.[24] Elizabeth also, at the intercession of the Archbishop of Canterbury, sent her younger son Richard to join his brother Edward on June 16.[25] She herself remained in sanctuary with her daughters for a time, in order to make better terms.

In spite of the supersedeas which was treacherously sent out by the conspirators to prevent the meeting of Parliament,[26] the Lords Spiritual and Temporal and the Commons had assembled in London on the day appointed, June 25, and formed what in later times would have been called a Convention Parliament. The proofs of the previous contract of Edward IV. with Lady Eleanor Butler were laid before this assembly by Bishop Stillington and his witnesses, and it was decided by the three Estates of the Realm that the illegitimate son could not succeed to the throne. Owing to the attainder of the Duke of Clarence, his children were not in the succession. The Duke of Gloucester was, therefore, the legal heir: and it was resolved that he should be called upon to accept the high office of King. A statement of the royal title, styled 'Titulus Regius,' was prepared, in which it was set forth that the children of Edward IV. by the Lady Grey were illegitimate owing to that King's previous contract with the Lady

Eleanor Butler, that in consequence of the attainder of the Duke of Clarence, his two children were incapacitated; and that Richard, Duke of Gloucester, was the only true and rightful heir to the throne.

The children of Edward IV. being illegitimate, Richard was certainly the legal heir, because the children of Clarence were disabled by law. But their disability could be set aside at any time by a reversal of their father's attainder, or by the removal of any corruption in blood inherited in consequence of that attainder. Edward Earl of Warwick, son of George Duke of Clarence, was the rightful heir to the throne, when the children of Edward were proved to be illegitimate. He was born at Warwick Castle on February 21, 1475, and at this time his age was eight years and four months. But even if Richard had attempted to substitute this child for the son of the late King, it is very unlikely that the assembled notables would have consented. They dreaded, above all things, a long minority. When his own son died prematurely, King Richard showed his sense of the strong claim of his nephew by declaring young Warwick to be his heir.

It is alleged that on Sunday, June 22, 1483, an eminent preacher named Dr. Shaw had delivered a sermon at Paul's Cross, in which he explained the royal title to the people; and that a speech was made to the same effect, by the Duke of Buckingham, at the Guildhall on the 24th. This is not improbable.

On June 26,[27] the Lords Spiritual and Temporal and the Commons proceeded to Baynard's Castle with the Titulus Regius, to submit their resolution and to petition Richard to assume the crown. He consented. He was then aged thirty years and eight months. On the 27th he delivered the Great Seal to Dr. Russell, Bishop of Lincoln, a prelate celebrated for learning, piety, and wisdom.[28] On the 28th a letter was despatched to Lord Mountjoy at Calais, with instructions to acquaint the garrison of the new King's accession, and to secure their allegiance. Richard III. then organised his Council, and surrounded himself with able and upright advisers. There were only two false friends among them—the traitors Buckingham and Stanley.

[1] Bernard André, 23. Polydore Virgil, 530 (171, 173 Eng. trans.)

[2] Rous, 212. Croyland, 564.

[3] Rous says they had contrived the Duke's death, 213. Also the Croyland Monk, 565: 'Conspiratum est contra eos, quod ipsi contrivissent mortem ducis Protectoris Angliæ.'

[4] John Alcock was the son of a burgess of Hull, and was educated at the grammar school of Beverley. He graduated at Cambridge in 1461. He was Dean of St. Stephen's, Westminster, and one of the King's Council in 1470, and Bishop of Rochester in 1472. In 1476 he was translated to Worcester, and in 1483 was tutor to young Edward. He was at Oxford to welcome Richard III. after his coronation, and accompanied him on his progress to Warwick. In 1484 he was one of the Commissioners delegated to treat with the Scottish Ambassadors. In 1486 he was translated to Ely, where he built a tower of the Bishop's palace, and a beautiful chapel for his interment. His attachment to the house of York is shown by the ornaments in the vaulting of the basement of the tower, and in the chapel. The rebus on his name (two cocks with their feet on a globe) occurs alternately with the 'rose en soleil,' the badge of Edward IV. Bishop Alcock founded Jesus College at Cambridge. He died at Wisbeach in 1500.

[5] Croyland 565. Rous, 213.

[6] Baynard's Castle was so called from Baynard, one of the companions of the Conqueror, who had license to fortify his house on Thames bank within the city. It was fortified by his descendant in 1110 A.D. In 1428 it had become the property of the crown and, having been destroyed by fire, it was rebuilt by Humphrey Duke of

Gloucester. On his attainder it again reverted to the crown, and was granted to Richard Duke of York. It was long the residence of his widow, and here both Edward IV. and Richard III. accepted the crown. Baynard's Castle was gutted in the Great Fire of 1666. It had long been rented by the Earls of Pembroke, but seems to have been in a ruinous condition. It was probably pulled down during the clearance operations after the fire.

[7] One letter has been preserved from Richard III. to his mother, after his accession. It is written in most affectionate terms, and shows deference to her wishes. After her last surviving son's death at Bosworth the Duchess retired from the world entirely, living at her castle of Berkhampstead, under the rules of one of the monastic orders. She died in 1493, and was buried by the side of her husband at Fotheringhay.

[8] Mr. Gairdner has pointed out that he was styled Protector in two documents upon the Patent Rolls, dated April 21 and May 2.

[9] Crosby Place, in Bishopsgate Street, was built by Alderman Sir John Crosby, who died in 1475. The Duke of Gloucester had a lease of it from Sir John's widow. It must have been a princely residence, and the hall is still one of the finest examples of Perpendicular domestic architecture of the fifteenth century.

[10] Rymer, vol. xii. p. 186; Anstis, Obs.; Sir Harris Nicolas, History of the Orders of Knighthood, iii. ix.; Ellis, Original Letters, 2nd series.

[11] Comines says that the contract was made by the Bishop of Bath and Wells, who told Comines that he afterwards married Edward and Lady Eleanor. The King

charged him strictly not to reveal it. (Phil. de Comines, ii. 157.)

[12] Weever's Funeral Monuments.

[13] Gairdner's Richard III., p. 91.

[14] Rymer, xii. 66. In the papers of the Stonor family there is a letter from Elizabeth Stonor to her husband, dated March 6, 1478, in which she said that the Bishop of Bath had been brought into the Tower since her husband departed.

[15] All was destroyed and sold in the reign of Edward VI. (1552). But a view of the ruins, and of a monument of the founder of Acaster College, with a ground plot, is mentioned in Gough's Topography of Yorkshire, 1804, p. 469. Rents at the dissolution 27l. 13s. 4d. Worth 553l. 6s. 8d. Granted in 1552 to John Hulse and William Pendred.

The family of Stillington continued to flourish at Acaster and Kelfield, in the parish of Stillingfleet; greatly improving their estate by a marriage with the heiress of FitzHenry. In 1520 stained glass with the arms of Stillington impaling Bigod, was placed in one of the windows of Stillingfleet church. At that time Dr. Thomas Stillington was a man of great learning, and became Professor of Divinity at the University of Louvain. The Stillingtons continued to flourish at Kelfield Hall throughout the seventeenth century. The last male of the race was young in the days of Queen Anne. There is a portrait of him as a boy, in a classical costume, which was painted by Parmentier in 1708. It is now in the dining room at Moreby Hall. This Joseph Stillington of Kelfield died in 1742. His daughter Dorothy married William Peirse of Hutton Bonville.

[16] Stallworthe's letter to Sir W. Stonor. (Excerpt. Hist. p. 16.)

[17] Morton, in his account of a conversation with the Duke of Buckingham (Grafton, p. 126).

[18] Polydore Virgil, p. 540.

[19] Davies, York Records, p. 154. That this supersedeas was issued by the conspirators and not by the Protector's Council is proved by Dr. Russell having actually prepared a speech for the opening of Parliament on June 24. This speech has been preserved. The date of the supersedeas was probably before June 13.

[20] Rastell, p. 80,

[21] Stallworthe to Sir W. Stonor.

[22] Morton, p. 69, in Rastell. This is the evidence of a bitter enemy.

[23] The will is given in the Excerpta Historica, pp. 246-248. He also appointed William Catesby, another meritorious but shamefully maligned public servant, to be his executor.

[24] 'My Lord Lyle has come to my Lord Protector and waits on him.' Stallworthe's second letter (Excerpt. Hist. p. 16).

[25] Croyland, p. 566.

[26] Davies, York Records, p. 134.

[27] The date of Richard's accession is fixed by the Year Book. 'Les Reports des Cases.' See Davies, York Records, p. 157 n.

[28] 'A wise man and a good, and of much experience.'— Morton, in Rastell.

CHAPTER IX CONDITION OF THE PEOPLE

At Richard's accession we may pause to glance at the condition of the people of England 420 years ago, not in any minute detail, not probing the matter to any depth, but with the object of having the general surroundings in our minds, while contemplating the brief reign of our last Plantagenet.

The Lancastrian usurpation, effected by Henry of Bolingbroke (Duke of Lancaster), caused much ruthless slaughter, and led to the atrocious Act De heretico comburendo, passed to secure the support of the clergy for the usurper. His son, Henry of Monmouth, was a fanatic, but otherwise a man of a far nobler nature than his father. He secured his position by a popular but most unjust war with France, and by his own fascinating personality. From his landing at Havre to the death of Talbot at Châtillon, this war covered a period of thirty-eight years, from 1415 to 1453. It did not, however, exhaust the wealth of the country, nor did the other more odious policy of the Lancastrians in passing an Act for the burning of heretics, destroy all freedom of thought. But the war filled the country with lawless military adventurers, and the persecution unsettled men's minds.

The cause of the War of the Roses was the misgovernment of the faction which ruled in the name of Henry of Windsor, the feeble-minded grandson of Charles VI. of France, whose malady he inherited. Recognition during half a century had made the parliamentary title of the usurpers secure. Owing to the absence of an hereditary title, the House of Commons had never been more powerful. The Speakers were practically Chancellors of the Exchequer, and prepared the budgets. Speaker Tresham, who was murdered in 1450 by Lord Grey de Ruthyn, was the first to propose a graduated income tax, and was a great statesman. But the House was not strong enough to control an unprincipled executive. The usurpation would never have been challenged, after a Parliamentary recognition of sixty years, if the administration of the usurping faction had not been intolerably bad. The Duke of York was the rightful hereditary heir to the throne. His grandfather had been recognised as heir by a Parliament of Richard II. The Duke was a just and moderate statesman. Until a month before the battle of Wakefield his sole purpose had been the reform of abuses.

The war, however, was not a war of the people. Although London warmly supported the house of York, it was a war fought out by two parties of the nobles and their retainers, including some old veterans of the French war. The struggle did not in the least degree affect the ordinary life of England. Mr. Thorold Rogers tells us that, though he has read hundreds of documents compiled for private inspection only, chiefly manorial accounts, covering the whole period of the war, he has never met a single allusion to the troubles. 'The people,' he adds, 'were absolutely indifferent. Except the outrages of Margaret's army in 1461, no injury was done to neutrals. The war was as little injurious to the great mass of the people, in its immediate effects, as summer lightning. It had no bearing on work or wages.'

It is also a mistake, though a frequently reiterated one, that the English nobility, as a class, was almost destroyed by the War of the Roses. Nothing of the sort happened. Several noblemen fell in battle, others lost their lives on the scaffold. There are long lists of traitors in the bills of attainder. But the death of a nobleman did not include the deaths of his heirs; and most of those who were attainted eventually received pardons. After the heat of battle was over, Edward IV. was placable and good-natured. He never refused a petition for pardon.[1] Only two peerages became extinct from causes connected with the war. The Beauforts came to an end, and the Tiptoft peerage lapsed, the accomplished Earl of Worcester being childless. The lay peerage, including peers temporarily under attainder, numbered fifty-four on the accession of Richard III., quite as numerous as it was before the war.

We have not, therefore, to contemplate a devastated country and a decimated peerage at the time when our last Plantagenet King ascended the throne. England was fairly prosperous, and the numbers and wealth of the nobility had not been reduced. But how different was the whole face of the country! The outlines of the hills are alone the same. There were immense areas of forest and swamp where now the landscape consists of enclosed fields like a green chessboard. There were few enclosures,[2] but tracts of common land for each manor, and cultivation in long strips near the villages and manor houses. The beaten tracks, some following the lines of the old Roman roads leading to the towns and castles, were often almost impassable in winter. King Richard was the first to establish any kind of post. The scenery was very beautiful on the hills and in the forests, in the quiet valleys, and in the swampy fens. Wild animals, many now extinct, were then abundant, hunted occasionally, but, to a great extent, left in peace over vast areas of absolute solitude. It was a very beautiful England, but how utterly different from the England of the twentieth century!

The noble and gentle families passed most of their time in their counties, hawking and hunting, mustering their armed retainers, often disputing about their respective rights, sometimes trying to settle disputes by force regardless of law. Yet many were law-abiding and maintainers of the

King's peace, and a few were giving some attention to the new learning to which Caxton was now opening the door. Some of the elders had seen service in the French war which came to an end thirty years before. Only a great noble could raise or command a military force, but reliance was placed on the experience of some veteran, such as Hall or Trollope, to organise and direct as chief of the staff. In those troublous days the King might, at any time, have to send forth commissions of array.

Castles then studded the country, and the ruins of some of them still give a correct idea of their accommodation and general plan. Old Norman keeps reared their massive fronts, surrounded by lodgings and outworks of later construction. The keeps contained stately halls, guard rooms, and chapels. The more modern and more comfortable lodgings followed the lines of the outer defences, generally having covered communication with the keep. Such were King Richard's home at Middleham, the royal castles of Richmond, Conisborough and Tickhill. Hedingham, the home of the Veres in Essex, Rochester, the Tower of London, and a few others are still standing. Lord Bourchier, the Treasurer, had quite recently built a castle of brick at Tattershall in Lincolnshire, with a lofty keep still intact. The Treasurer's device of a purse frequently recurs there.

The castles of the later period were, however, generally built without the central keep. They consisted of square angle towers connected by curtains, one of which usually formed the great hall, as at Lumley. These were more numerous and probably more commodious. Bolton and Lumley are good examples. There was already a tendency to increase the conveniences and amenities of the old castles by the enlargement of windows and in other ways, as is shown by the fine oriel window at Barnard Castle, the work of Richard himself. The royal residences at Eltham, Sheen, and Windsor are believed to have been designed more for comfort and pleasure than for defence; although Windsor is a place of strength, with circular keep, and means to resist an enemy both in the upper and lower wards. The general tendency, during the last half of the fifteenth century, was to build for comfort rather than for defence.

In the courts and at the gates of the castles of noblemen there were guards wearing more or less of defensive armour, morions or bacinets on their heads, and brigandines of quilted linen or leather with small plates of iron sewn on them. Glaives or bills, crossbows with quarrels or darts, and bows and arrows were in the guard rooms.

The sons of the surrounding gentry were brought up and taught martial exercises and the other accomplishments of a gentleman of the time, at the castles of the lords their patrons, a custom which bound the nobility and lesser gentry together by common interests and common pursuits.

Much time was occupied in hunting and hawking, and the adherents of the House of York were more especially the votaries of the noble art of venery. The first English book of sport had the second Duke of York for its author, and was entitled 'The Master of Game.' The Duke declares that 'hunters live more joyfully than any other men,' and his work shows that he was a keen observer with a wonderfully accurate knowledge of natural history. With such a master and guide in their family the scions of the royal House of York were the leading sportsmen in the country, closely followed by their friends and numerous cousins among the nobility and gentry. The 'Book of St. Albans' by Juliana Berners the Prioress of Sopwell, treating of hawking, hunting, fishing, and the laws of arms, was also a work of that period, and was first printed at St. Albans Abbey by John Insomuch, the Schoolmaster, in 1481.[3] Jul ana divides the wild animals into beasts of venery—the wolf, wild boar, stag, hart and hare; beasts of the chase of the sweet foot—buck and doe and the roe—and of the stinking foot, wild cat, badger, fox, weasel, marten, squirrel, and others. She is particular in explaining the terms to be used in venery, that one must say a covey of partridges but a bevy of quails, and so forth. Closely allied to the arts of war and of venery was the law of arms, of which every gentleman of that day had some knowledge. Charges on shields and standards, on surcoats and liveries were regulated by the heralds, and after the ordinance of Henry V. were granted by the Sovereign. But in the most flourishing days of chivalry, those of Edward III., this was not essential. There was no Heralds' College,[4] and the only really interesting armorial bearings are those used in the days of the Plantagenets. With Tudors and Stuarts heraldry lost its chivalric significance, and coats of arms subsequently granted are unmeaning and vulgar.

Peerage of Richard III

PEERS

Relations of the Sovereign

* Duke of Suffolk (brother-in-law), K.G.
*+Earl of Lincoln (nephew), K.B.
*+Viscount Lovell (dearest friend),
   Lord Chamberlain, K.G.
*+Earl of Northumberland (1st cousin), K.G.
* Lord Greystoke (1st cousin).
* Lord Abergavenny, K.B.   }(cousins).
   Earl of Westmoreland   (sick) }

Minors

   Duke of Buckingham } (cousins)
   Earl of Essex   }
   Earl of Salisbury (son).
* Earl of Warwick (nephew).
   Earl of Pembroke (nephew).

Staunch and true

*+Duke of Norfolk, Ld. Admiral, K.G.
*+Earl of Surrey, K.G.
* Lord Audley, Ld. Treasurer.
*+Lord Zouch, K.B.
*+Lord Ferrers.

Marching to join the King
* Earl of Kent, K.B.
* Lord Dacre.
* Lord FitzHugh.
* Lord Lumley.

* Lord Ogle in the Marches,
* 2 Lords Scrope.

Other Peers

* Earl of Arundel, K.G.
* Lord Maltravers, K.G.
* Earl of Nottingham.
* Earl of Huntingdon.
* Earl of Wiltshire.
* Lord Grey of Wilton.
* Lord Grey of Codnor.
* Lord Grey of Powys.
* Lord Beauchamp.
* Lord Morley.
* Lord Stourton.
* Lord Cobham.
  Lord Mountjoy (at Calais).
  Lord de la Warre (abroad).
  Lord Dudley (very old).

Minors

  Earl of Shrewsbury.
  Lord Clifford.
  Lord Hastings.
  Lord Hungerford.

$$\begin{array}{r} \text{Peers } 42 \\ \text{Minors } 9 \\ \hline 33 \\ \hline \end{array}$$

Traitors
#John Vere, Earl of Oxford (under attainder).

  Courtenay, Earl of Devonshire.
  Grey, Marquis of Dorset.
  Woodville, Earl Rivers.
  Lord Beaumont.
  Lord Welles.
* Lord Lisle.
  Lord Dynham.
#Jasper Tudor (late Earl of Pembroke).
#Henry Tudor (calling himself Earl of Richmond).
*#Lord Stanley (turned traitor at the end).
*#Lord Strange.

* At the coronation.
+ At Bosworth for the King.
# At Bosworth for H. Tudor.

Attendance at the court or the Parliament led to a demand for lodgings in London. Baynard's Castle was the town residence of the Duke and Duchess of York. Crosby Place, which is still standing, was the home of the Duke and Duchess of Gloucester during the short protectorate. Cold Harbour, in Thames Street, alternately lodged the Earl of Salisbury (1453), Anne Duchess of Exeter, and her brother the Duke of Clarence. There were other houses of the nobility within the city, including Ely Place in Holborn, with large gardens behind them; and some of the richer citizens had handsome residences of which Crosby Place was an example. It was on the occasion of visits to the capital that opportunities were offered for those extravagant displays which were the fashion of that age, especially at the great tournaments.

The House of York was closely knit to the nobility by ties of kindred. Of the three Dukes, Suffolk was King Richard's brother-in-law, Buckingham and Norfolk were his cousins, as were the Earls of Northumberland, Westmoreland and Essex, and Lords Abergavenny and Greystoke. Lincoln was his nephew. Richard, moreover, had four first and several second cousins among the Barons; and the Archbishop of Canterbury was also his cousin. There must have been a feeling of kinship as well as of loyalty when the nobles gathered round the sovereign on state occasions.

Magnificence in dress was not a sign of ostentation and vanity, but of what was felt to be due to high rank and to ceremonial functions of state; and it was undoubtedly good for trade. Long gowns with high collars were the indoor and civil dresses, and they lent themselves to displays of great splendour. Thus, in the wardrobe accounts, we find among the materials for doublets and gowns, black velvet, crimson velvet, blue velvet figured with tawny, white velvet, white damask with flowers of divers colours, chequered motley velvet, cloth of gold, silks and satins, sarsenet, as well as embroidered shoes, and ostrich feathers. We find green, scarlet and white cloth, ermines, sables, fringes, gowns of blue velvet lined with white satin, golden aiglettes, and various furs. The keeper of the King's wardrobe also had in charge feather beds and bolsters, bed clothes, cushions, table cloths and napkins, and the King's carriage. Presents from the wardrobe are recorded as being given to the Duke of Norfolk, Lord Grey, Lord Stanley, Sir W. Parr, Sir J. Borough, Lord Audley and the College of Windsor. When the Duchess of Burgundy came to visit her brother, all her attendants were ordered to be clothed in cloth jackets of murrey and blue, while the knights appointed to attend upon her received gowns of velvet. The velvet was ten shillings a yard, the ostrich feathers ten shillings each. These wardrobe accounts of the last years of Edward IV. bear silent testimony to the lavish splendour of the court, and of court ceremonial in those days.

Increasing wealth resulted to the merchants and traders of the City, the Guilds flourished and increased in numbers, and there were periodical fairs in the country. At the Stourbridge fair, which was the chief mart of Lombard Exchange, glass, silks and velvets were sold by the Venetian and Genoese merchants, linen of Liège and Ghent by the Flemish weavers, hardware by Spaniards, tar and pitch by Norwegians, wine by Gascons, furs and amber by the Hanse Towns. Millstones came from Paris. Our own products were hides and woolpacks, the produce of the tin mines, and iron from Sussex. At Abingdon there was a cattle fair, at Winchester a wool and cloth fair. King Richard's Parliament gave much attention to the advancement of trade.

In London the wealthy merchants lived in handsome houses with gardens. The lawyers lived in the Inns of Court, and there were not wanting good inns and hostelries for passing travellers. We hear of the 'White Hart' in Southwark, the 'George' at Paul's Wharf, and several others.

The City Companies were acquiring great influence. The Skinners' Company founded the 'Brethren of the fraternity of Corpus Christi' of which the Duke of York and his sons Edward IV. and the Dukes of Clarence and Gloucester were members. Disputes between City Companies were amicably settled. There was one between the Skinners' and Merchant Taylors' with reference to precedence in City processions. In the reign of Richard III., 10 April, 1484, the two companies agreed to abide by the judgment of the Lord Mayor and Aldermen.

The award was that the Skinners should invite the Merchant Taylors to dinner every year, on the Vigil of Corpus Christi, and that the Merchant Taylors should invite the Skinners on the Feast of the Nativity of John the Baptist. On the first year after the arbitration the Skinners were to walk in all processions before the Merchant Taylors, on the next year the Merchant Taylors before the Skinners, and so on. Thus was arbitration established in the City during Richard's reign, a course always favoured and practised by the King himself.

The great glory of the Yorkist kings was the introduction of printing into England, in which their sister of Burgundy also took a liberal and enlightened part. Caxton tells us he was born in the Weald of Kent in 1422, and was apprenticed to Robert Large, a mercer of London and Lord Mayor in 1439. His house was in the north end of the Old Jewry, and here young Caxton lived until his master died in 1441, leaving him twenty marks. Caxton went to Bruges in 1441, and in 1453 he was admitted to the livery of the Mercers' Company. The Merchant Adventurers were an association of merchants trading to foreign countries, chiefly mercers. They had a 'domus Angliæ' at Bruges, and in 1464 Caxton was chosen 'Governor beyond seas.' In 1468 he attended the marriage of the young English Princess Margaret with Duke Charles of Burgundy, which was celebrated with great pomp. Caxton was not only a leading merchant at Bruges, he also took a great interest in literature and in the new art of printing. In 1469 he began the translation of 'Le Recueil des Histoires de Troyes,' and in the following year, when Duke Charles was invested with the Garter, Caxton made his first essay at printing, with the oration of Dr. Russell on that occasion. When, in October 1470, Edward IV. and his young brother Richard took refuge in Flanders, they received active assistance from the loyal merchant and printer, and in the same year Caxton entered the service of the Duchess Margaret and managed her trading in English wool for her. He was surrounded hy literary influences at Bruges, where there was a printing press encouraged by the Duchess.

In 1476 Caxton came to England, and in November 1477 he had established a printing press in his house at Westminster, under the shadow of the Abbey. It was in the Almonry near the old chapel of St. Anne, at the gate leading into Tothill Street. Caxton's house was the sign of the red pale.[5] John Esteney was then Abbot of Westminster (1474-98), but it is not recorded that Caxton received help or patronage from him. The first book printed in England was the 'Dictes and Sayings of Philosophes,' by Lord Rivers, in 1477. Then followed 'Cordyale' in 1479, and 'Chronicles of England' in 1480, 'Description of Britain' also in 1480. In that year the Duchess of Burgundy came to London to visit her brothers, and no doubt she then paid a visit to the printing press of her old friend Caxton. Five books came from that active press in 1481. 'The Mirrour of the World' was translated and printed for a citizen named

Hugh Brice as a present to Lord Hastings. 'Reynard the Fox' was translated by Caxton himself. The 'de senectute,' 'de amicitiâ,' and 'declamatio' of Cicero were translated by the ill-fated Earl of Worcester; as well as 'Godefroy de Boulogne.' A second edition of 'The game and play of Chess' completed the publications for 1481. During the whole of King Richard's reign, and under his enlightened patronage, Caxton's printing press showed great activity. The publications were 'Pilgrimage of the Soul' 'Liber Festivalis,' 'Quatuor Sermones,' the 'Confessio Amantis' of Gower, the 'Golden Legend,' 'Caton,' 'Knight of the Tower,' 'Æsop,' 'Paris and Vienna,' 'Life of Charles the Great,' the 'Canterbury Tales' of Chaucer, 'Life of our Lady,' 'King Arthur,' by Sir T. Mallory, who finished his work in 1470, and the 'Order of Chivalry' translated by Caxton and dedicated to his redoubted Lord King Richard.

Literature was beginning to receive attention from several members of the nobility, and the printing press gave this tendency very great encouragement. Among the books in the Wardrobe Account of Edward IV. which were ordered to be bound, were the 'Book of the Holy Trinity,' the Bible, 'Government of Kings and Princes,' 'Froissart,' Titus Livius, Josephus, 'Bible Historial,' 'La Forteresse de Foy'; and to this royal library his brother Richard added several books including the 'Romaunt of Tristram.'

Lord Rivers was an accomplished nobleman whose translations and original compositions are well known. But John Tiptoft, Earl of Worcester, was the most studious and learned, as well as the most accomplished, author and statesman of Yorkist times. Born at Everton, Cambridgeshire, Tiptoft was at Balliol College, and completed his education by a residence of three years in Italy. He was twice Lord High Treasurer, was Lord Deputy of Ireland, and was created Earl of Worcester. But he fell a victim to Lancastrian rancour during Warwick's brief usurpation. He was beheaded in 1470, and Caxton eloquently mourned his untimely death.

'This book,' Caxton wrote, 'was translated by the virtuous and noble Earl of Worcester into our English tongue, son and heir to the Lord Tiptoft, which in his time flowered in virtue and cunning, to whom I know none like among the lords of the temporality in science and moral virtue. I beseech Almighty God to have mercy on his soul, and pray all them that shall read this little treatise, likewise of your charity to remember his soul among your prayers. The right virtuous and noble Earl of Worcester, which late piteously lost his life, whose soul I recommend to your special prayers, also in his time made many other virtuous works which I have heard of. O God, blessed Lord, what great loss was it of that noble, virtuous and well disposed lord, when I remember and advertise his life, his science and his virtue. Methinketh God displeased over so great a loss of such a man, considering his estate and cunning, and also the exercise of the same with the great labours in going on pilgrimage unto Jerusalem, visiting there the holy places, and what worship had he in Rome in the presence of our holy father the Pope, and so in all other places until his death, at which death every man that was there might learn to die, and take his death patiently.'

Rivers and Worcester were not the only men of their day with literary tastes. The colleges at Oxford and Cambridge numbered among their alumni laymen as well as churchmen. The three great public schools of England already existed. The grammar school of Westminster, afterwards to become St. Peter's College under Queen Elizabeth, had a continuous existence from the time of Edward I. Winchester College had been founded by William of Wykeham. Eton College was a foundation due to Henry of Windsor. All three were flourishing. Boys went very young to the universities, and parents showed anxiety for their advancement in learning as well as for their due supply of clothing. Mrs. Paston desired a tutor named Grenefeld to send her word how her son Clement is doing his duty as regards his lessons. If he does not do well, and will not amend, Grenefeld is to lash him until he does amend, as his former tutor did, who was the best that ever he had at Cambridge. She is no less particular about his clothes, which were to be looked to. Clement had a short green gown, a short musterdevelers (gown of grey woollen cloth), a short blue gown, and a russet gown furred with beaver: a pretty good supply.

Later there was a Paston boy at Eton, one of whose letters has come down to us (1478). He desires hose clothes to be sent to him, one pair of some colour for holidays, and one for working days. It does not matter how coarse the one for common use is. He also asks for a stomacher, two shirts, and a pair of slippers. 'But,' adds the Eton boy, 'if it lyke you that I may come by water, and sport me with you in London a day or two this term time, then you may let all this be till the time that I come; and then I shall tell you when I shall be ready to come from Eton.' He wanted a holiday in the middle of term time, and he wanted the fun of boating down the river. So it was with many hundreds of other boys then as it is now; liking play better than work, but still learning, with or without the lash which Mrs. Agnes Paston believed to be so efficacious. The Etonian was about ten years younger than King Richard.

The Church, in the Yorkist days, had deteriorated. The devil's compact between Archbishop Arundel and Henry of Bolingbroke, by which Bishops were to be allowed to burn heretics on condition that the usurpation was upheld by the Church, had alienated the people. The Act De heretico comburendo was not a dead letter. There were many innocent sufferers. Henry of Monmouth was a fanatic. He argued with heretics and would gladly pardon on recantation, but if his victim did not recant he was actually present at executions and witnessed the cruel tortures. Caxton, some years after Henry's death (1439), saw with horror the burning on Tower Hill of the good Vicar of Deptford, whose love and charity had endeared him to the poor. Such scenes would not endear the Bishops to the people. The prelates were self-seeking politicians for the most part, and occasionally the people made short work of them. When Bishop de Moleyns, then Lord Privy Seal, came down to Portsmouth to pay the sailors and kept back some of their dues, he was seized by the mob and hanged in front of God's House. Bishop Ayscough of Salisbury met a similar fate. Mr. Thorold Rogers formed a very bad opinion of the clergy of the fifteenth century. He says 'the Bishops were on the whole bad men, parochial clergy not much better, monks worst of all. People deserted them for the secret but stirring exhortations of the Bible men.' But there were exceptions. Dr. Russell of Lincoln, King Richard's Chancellor, was a prelate and statesman of the highest integrity, so were Stillington of Bath and Wells, Alcock of Worcester, and Langton of St. David's.

The great monasteries still stood, in all their glorious architectural beauty, among the woodlands and by the trout streams; and charity was dispensed by their inmates. Religious foundations like Middleham College by King Richard, and Acaster College by Bishop Stillington, attest the piety of the age; and religious buildings proceeded apace. The beautiful chapel of St. George at Windsor was approaching completion in King Richard's time, and many fine church towers, especially in Suffolk, date from this period.

There were superstitious pilgrimages to shrines such as those of St. Thomas at Canterbury and of Our Lady at Walsingham, while obits and saints' days were scrupulously observed. Letters were almost always referred to saints' days, scarcely ever to the days of the month. In the 'Paston Letters' we have 'Monday next after St. Edmund the King,' 'the day next after St. Kateryn,' 'St. Pernall,' 'St. Leonard's Eve,' 'St. Erkenwald's,' and so on: even, in one instance, the date is fixed by the collect of the preceding Sunday. 'Wednesday next after Deus qui errantibus.' This seems to show that religion, or at least its rites and ceremonies, was really part of the actual life of the people. Miracle plays, such as those performed by the Corpus Christi guild at York, served to keep alive an interest in religion. There were also allegorical plays, and it seems that 'Every Man,' which has interested so many in these modern times, may have been acted before, and have impressed audiences in the days of the Yorkist kings.

The law was presided over by conscientious and learned judges. Old Fuller says of Markham and Fortescue that they were the 'Chief Justices of the Chief Justices.' Markham boldly resisted any attempt to intimidate him, and by his firm stand against King Edward established an important maxim in constitutional law. He did not confine his judgments to the bench, but upbraided evil-doers when he met them in the street. John Heydon, Recorder of Norwich, was stopped by the judge and brought to book in public, for putting away his wife and living with another; and also for his unjust conduct towards John Paston, in enforcing the doubtful claim of Lord Moleyns.

But the country was in a lawless state. Upright judgments were pronounced, but they could not always be enforced. Noblemen, like Lord Moleyns, occasionally acted in defiance of the law, and often there was no redress. We hear of 'a great multitude of misruled people at the house of Robert Ledeham who issue at their pleasure, sometimes thirty and more, armed in steel caps and jackets, with bows and bills, overriding the country, oppressing the people, and doing many horrible and abominable deeds.' There is a letter from Paston's wife reporting that 'they have made bars to bar the doors crossways, and wickets at every corner of the house to shoot out at, both with bows and hand guns.' This sounds like an expected siege. For she adds—'My worshipful husband, I pray you to get some cross bows and wyndacs with quarrels, for your holes have been made so low that my men cannot shoot out with a long bow, though we had ever so much need. Also get two or three short pole axes to keep the doors.' Then we are told of Robert Letham killing John Wilson's bullocks for arrears of rent, eating them, and then beating Wilson himself in Plumstead churchyard until he was in doubt of his life, besides beating John Coke's mother. When Sir Philip Wentford wants to settle a dispute, instead of going to law, he rides to Colchester with a hundred armed men. These were not altogether peaceful times. They were exciting, full of adventure, and there was much fun to be got out of them. Different, more eventful, perhaps less safe, than our days of policemen and penitentiaries, but far from unendurable.

These were trifles, and on the whole the country gentry of the fifteenth century lived in comfort on their manors. These manors included the lord's domain cultivated by his bailiff, the small estates of freeholders paying quit rents, the tenements and lands of the labourers held for services, and the waste or common on which all tenants had right of pasture. The manor house was usually built of stone, though brick was beginning to come into use. The house was generally divided into three principal rooms: the hall, the dormitories, and the solar or parlour with a southern aspect. In the hall the family and household dined. It was also used for the manor courts, for levying fines, and passing judicial sentences. The table was on trestles, there were a few stools and benches, and some chests for linen. Here would also be seen a pot of brass, several dishes, platters, and trenchers, iron or lateen candlesticks, a brass ewer and basin, and a box of salt. The walls were hung with mattocks, scythes, reaping hooks, buckets and corn measures. In the dairy were the pails, pans, churn, and cheese press. In the grange were the sacks of corn.

The manor land was ploughed twice, but half the arable remained fallow. When harvest was over pigs and geese were turned into the stubble. The means of supporting the stock in winter depended upon the supply of hay, for there were no root crops. The rest of the stock had to be killed down for salting on St. Martin's day (November 11). In the garden and orchard were apples and pears, damsons, cherries, currants, strawberries, kitchen herbs, onions and leeks, mustard, peas and beans, and cabbage. Crab apples were collected to make verjuice.

We are informed of the commissions John Paston received from his wife, in her numerous letters. Besides weapons of offence and defence she writes for ginger and almonds and sugar, also for frieze for their growing child with a note of the best and cheapest shop. Next she wants two dozen trenchers, syrup, quince preserve, oil for salads. As regards luggage John Paston writes to his brother, who was at an inn—the sign of the 'George' in Paul's Wharf—to put up in the mail his tawny gown furred with black, the doublet of purple satin, the doublet of black satin, and his writing box of cypress. These commissions give a little insight into the domestic arrangements of the time. But for a complete outfit of one of the lesser gentry equipped for war we must read over the contents of Mr. Payn's luggage, robbed from him by Jack Cade and his rabble at the sign of the 'White Hart' near London Bridge.

There was a fine gown of mixed grey woollen cloth trimmed with fine beavers. A pair of 'bregandyns,' which were coats of leather or cotton quilted, having small iron plates sewn over them; also leg harness. A bluish grey gown furred with martens. Two gowns furred with budge (lamb skin). Lastly, a gown lined with frieze. But the greatest loss was a set of Milan harness (armour). They forced Mr. Payn into the battle on London Bridge, where he was wounded; and robbed his wife in Kent of all but kirtle and smock. Those were exciting times, and luggage was not always safe, but on the whole they were times of plenty.

The fifteenth century was the golden age of the labourer. At no time were wages relatively so high. The people ate wheaten bread, drank barley beer, and had plenty of cheap, though perhaps coarse, meat at a farthing a pound (equal to 3d. now). If a labourer had to undertake a journey, there were houses as well as monasteries where doles were given to all wayfarers. The cottages of the poor were built of wattle and daub, but skilled labourers were fed at the table of the lord of the manor below the salt; and some of them lodged in the out-buildings. It is said that scurvy, in a virulent form, was a common disorder; as all the poor, except the numerous class of poachers, had to live on salt meat for six months, onions and cabbages being the only esculents. But the prevalence of this disorder has been exaggerated.

We have the evidence of Chief Justice Fortescue that the labouring class in England was far better off as regards lodging, clothing, and food than the peasantry of France and other countries of Europe.

PRICES--1484

Wheat, 5s. 3-¾d. the quarter.　| Hen, 2d.
Barley, 4s. 1-¼d.　| Swan, 2s. 6d.
Oats, 2s. 2-½d.　| Duck, 2d.
Beans, 3s. 8d.　| Charcoal, 6s. 5d. the load.
Oatmeal, 7d.　| Firewood, 1s. 10-½d. the load.
Malt, 3s. 10-¼d.　| Hurdles, 2s. the dozen.
Hay, 2s. 2d. the load.　| Salt, 4s. 8d. the quarter.
Wool, 5s. 4d. the ton.　| Tiles, 6s. 10d. the 1,000.
Ox, 10s.　| Bricks, 6s. 8d. the 1,000.
Calf, 3s.　|Gascony wine, 9s. 8-½d. the dozen
Sheep, 1s. 4d.　| gallons.
Pig, 5s. 4d.　| Sugar, 19s. the dozen pounds.
Horse, 60s.　| Pepper, 15s.　"　"
Capon, 3d.　| urrants, 2s. 4d. "　"
Goose, 1d.　|

Wages--Carpenter　6d. per day, 3s. a week, £9 2s. 6d. a year.
　　　　Tiler　　　6d.　"
　　　　Unskilled　4d.　"　　2s.　"

[1] Thorold Rogers.

[2] The enclosure grievance was just beginning to be felt.

[3] The second edition was brought out by Wynkyn de Worde in 1496.

[4] It was created by Richard III. in 1484.

[5] The 'pale' in heraldry.

CHAPTER X REIGN OF KING RICHARD III

King Richard was a young man in his thirtieth year when he came to the throne. During the previous ten years he had acquired considerable administrative experience, and had shown himself to possess ability, powers of application, and resolution. He was extremely popular in the north of England, where he had generally resided.

Young Richard was not tall, of slight build, with one shoulder a little higher than the other, but not so much as to be noticeable or to cause weakness. He was a formidable adversary in battle. The portrait at Windsor is so remarkable that it must have been taken from life. The eyes are a little closed, and give a thoughtful, almost dreamy look. The other features are regular. The lips thin and firm, the chin prominent. The whole expression is that of a thoughtful and earnest man, firm, resolute, and fearless. Dr. Parr remarked on the strong likeness between Richard III. and Lorenzo de' Medici, the Magnificent. His wife Anne inherited great beauty from the Nevills and Beauchamps, but she was fragile and delicate.

On July 4, 1483, King Richard III. and Queen Anne removed to the royal lodgings in the Tower, where their nephews Edward and Richard were residing. Owing to his illegitimacy the eldest boy, who had been proclaimed King and soon afterwards set aside, could not retain the titles of Wales and Cornwall, nor could the younger one continue to have the royal title of York. The younger boy had also lost his claim to the Mowbray titles of Norfolk and Nottingham by the death of the little Mowbray heiress to whom he had been betrothed. Those titles justly passed to the representatives of the aunts who succeeded Anne Mowbray as the heirs of that family, the Ladies Howard and Berkeley. Their sons were created Duke of Norfolk and

Earl of Nottingham respectively, on June 28. But Edward, the eldest boy, retained the earldoms separately conferred on him by his father, of Pembroke and March.

It was the King's intention to bring his nephews up and provide for them as became their rank and their near relationship to himself. 'He promised that he would so provide for them, and so maintain them in honourable estate, as that all the realm ought and should be content.'[1] The allegation that they never left the Tower is derived from the insinuations of very unscrupulous enemies.

It is much more likely that they resided in the royal household, and were the companions of the King's other nephew, the Earl of Warwick; at least until it became necessary to place them in safe keeping on the invasion of the realm by Henry Tudor. In the regulations for King Richard's household, dated July 23, 1484, it is ordained that 'the children are to be together at one breakfast.' Who were these children, if not the King's nephews? They were evidently children of high rank,[2] and Richard's little son Edward had died in the previous April.

Before the coronation, the King created eighteen Knights of the Bath, four of them sons or brothers of peers.

The coronation of King Richard III. and Queen Anne took place on Sunday, July 6, 1483. Its splendour was greater than had ever been known before. The Cardinal Archbishop placed the crowns on the heads of the new sovereign and his consort. He was surrounded by bishops, and nearly the whole peerage was present. Never was accession received with such unanimous consent by all ranks of the people. The attendance of a Woodville bishop and a Grey viscount gave grounds for the hope that even faction was at an end. On scarcely any other occasion was the aristocracy of

England so fully represented. The Duchess of Suffolk, as sister of the King, walked alone in state, in the procession. The intriguing wife of Stanley, mother of Henry Tudor, had the privilege of bearing the Queen's train.

CORONATION PROCESSION OF KING RICHARD III.

Serjeants of Arms
Heralds
Trumpets and Clarions
The Cross
Priests in grey amices
Bishops, with mitres and croziers
Abbots, with mitres

BISHOP OF ROCHESTER, bearing a cross

THE CARDINAL ARCHBISHOP

THE EARL OF NORTHUMBERLAND, bearing the
pointless sword of mercy

LORD STANLEY,   DUKE OF SUFFOLK,
EARL OF LINCOLN
bearing the mace of   bearing the sceptre   bearing the
orb
Constable

DUKE OF NORFOLK, bearing the crown

EARL OF SURREY, bearing the sword of state in scabbard

VISCOUNT LOVELL,   B C   B C EARL OF
KENT
bearing the sword   a i   a i bearing the sword
(civil) of justice   r n   r n (ecclesiastical)
                     o q   o q of justice
                         n u   n u
                         s e   s e
THE KING

141

                    Pair   Pair
                    of   of
                    porters   porters

BISHOP OF BATH AND   t   t BISHOP OF
                                       DURHAM
      WELLS   staves   staves

         DUKE OF BUCKINGHAM, bearing the King's train

                           Earls
                           Barons

       EARL OF HUNTINGDON,   EARL OF WILTSHIRE,
                      VISCOUNT LYLE,
      bearing the Queen's   bearing the Queen's   bearing the
                                rod
         sceptre   crown   with dove

            BISHOP OF EXETER   THE QUEEN
            BISHOP OF NORWICH

         LADY STANLEY, bearing the Queen's train

      DUCHESS OF SUFFOLK (King's sister), in state, alone

                     Twenty peeresses

142

The Duke of Buckingham put forward an important claim, soon after the coronation, and its success was an example of the lavish generosity of Richard III. Humphrey de Bohun, Earl of Hereford and Essex, died in the year 1372, leaving his two daughters co-heiresses of his vast estates. Alianore, the eldest, married Thomas of Woodstock, Duke of Gloucester, the youngest son of Edward III. Their daughter and eventual heiress Anne married Edmund Earl of Stafford, great-grandfather of the Duke of Buckingham. Mary, the second daughter, married Henry of Bolingbroke, Earl of Derby, who became Earl of Hereford by right of his wife, and eventually usurped the crown as Henry IV. His male descendants ended with his grandson Henry VI. The Duke of Buckingham claimed that the moiety of the Bohun estates which Mary brought to Henry IV. and which had merged in the crown, should now revert to him as the male heir of both sisters. Legally, the claim was untenable, and it had been rejected by Edward IV. Richard, however, generously conceded all that Buckingham asked, making a formal grant of the lands in question under his own sign manual.

On his accession the generous young King was anxious to be reconciled with all his subjects with whom he had ever had differences. Among these was a certain Sir John Fogge, a low intriguer, with whom the King condescended to shake hands. This treacherous fellow soon afterwards joined in Buckingham's rebellion. Like Louis XII. of France King Richard forgot and forgave all offences against the Duke of Gloucester.

The Royal Progress
The King set out on a progress through England,[3] a fortnight after the coronation, accompanied by the Duke of Buckingham and a large retinue. The young Earl of Warwick, Richard's nephew, was also with him, having

been liberated from durance in the Tower, where he had been kept by the Marquis of Dorset as his ward, ever since the death of his father Clarence. Young Warwick was also at his uncle's coronation.

The King left Windsor for Reading on the 23rd, arriving at Oxford on July 24, where he was received by old Dr. Waynflete, Bishop of Winchester, and the Bishops of Worcester, St. Asaph, and St. David's. He was lodged in Magdalen College, and on his departure the aged Dr. Waynflete caused to be entered in the College register—

VIVAT REX IN AETERNUM.

On August 1 the King was at Gloucester, and here the Duke of Buckingham took his leave and proceeded to his estates in Wales, accompanied by his intriguing prisoner Bishop Morton. Passing on to Tewkesbury on August 4, Richard arrived at Warwick on the 8th, where he was joined by the Queen, who came direct from Windsor.[4] The court remained a week at Warwick, and comprised the young Earl of Warwick, five Bishops,[5] the Earls of Lincoln, Surrey, and Huntingdon, Lords Stanley, Dudley, Morley, Scrope, and Lovell, the Chief Justice, the Scottish Duke of Albany, and the Spanish Ambassador. On the 10th the royal party was at Coventry, on the 17th at Leicester, on the 22nd at Nottingham. The King and Queen arrived at Pomfret on the 27th, where they were met by their little son Edward, who had travelled from Middleham to be with them. On the 30th they entered the city of York.

The people of York vied with each other in the loyalty and cordiality of their welcome. Richard III. was a most popular sovereign, and with good reason. Bishop Langton,[6] who accompanied him on this progress, thus wrote: 'He contents the people where he goes best that ever did Prince, for many a poor man that hath suffered wrong many days has been relieved and helped by him and his commands in his progress. And in many great cities and towns were great sums of money given him which he hath refused.[7] On my truth I never liked the conditions of any Prince so well as his. God hath sent him to us for the weal of us all.'[8] On September 8 King Richard and Queen Anne walked in solemn procession with the crowns on their heads, on the occasion of the creation of their son Edward as Prince of Wales.[9] The young Prince, his cousin the Earl of Warwick, and Galfridus de Sasiola, the Spanish Ambassador, were knighted. The royal party left York on the 20th, and proceeded by Gainsborough towards Lincoln, which city was entered on October 12.

Suddenly the news reached the King that the Duke of Buckingham had broken out in rebellion. Never was there an act so unprovoked and treacherous. The Duke seems to have been a weak unprincipled man, full of vanity and self-importance, and his worst qualities were worked upon by the insidious old intriguer Morton, who had been entrusted to his custody. Buckingham's ambition was to seize the crown. In accordance with the 'Titulus Regius,' only two persons stood in his way. These were King Richard III. and his delicate little son. The traitor's scheme was to strike them down and seize the coveted prize. The rebellion was carefully planned. All the Lancastrian and Woodville malcontents were invited to join, and there were to have been several simultaneous risings in the south of England, on October 18. On that day Buckingham unfurled his standard at Brecknock, while Dorset and Sir Thomas St. Leger rose in the west; and even the cautious Henry Tudor sailed across from Brittany, but feared to land. His mother, the wife of Stanley, intrigued actively with the Queen Dowager and the Woodville faction.

The energy and decision with which the King met the danger baffled the policy of the rebels. As Buckingham was Constable of England, it became necessary to appoint a Vice-Constable to try rebels in conjunction with the Earl Marshal, and Sir Ralph Ashton was selected for the post.[10] Owing to a great flood in the Severn the forces of Buckingham were unable to cross the river, their provisions failed, and they disbanded. The wretched traitor put on a disguise and fled; but he was betrayed and apprehended by the Sheriff of Shropshire. Meanwhile, the King had organised a sufficient force, and advanced rapidly to Salisbury, whither Buckingham was brought a prisoner. The traitor sought an interview with his injured sovereign, with the intention of assassinating him.[11] Fortunately the request was refused. He had been caught red-handed, and the Earl Marshal's court condemned him to death.[12] He was beheaded at Salisbury on November 2. Richard treated the Duke's widow, who was a Woodville, with his habitual generosity; granting her a pension out of the lordship of Tunbridge.

The other rebels fled. Dorset and old Morton escaped abroad. Sir Thomas St. Leger was caught and beheaded at Exeter, with Thomas Ramme and one other delinquent. Seven rebels suffered in London. There are a hundred names in the bill of attainder against the rebels; but most of them were subsequently pardoned, including Stanley's intriguing wife, who was merely given into the custody of her perfidious husband, an act of unwise leniency which amounted to recklessness.[13]

Richard had destroyed all opposition, and he now entered upon the serious business of government. Although his administration was profusely liberal, he checked corruption, reformed the public offices, and promoted economy in the service of the state. Parliament met on

January 23, 1484, and Master William Catesby was chosen Speaker. Its first business was to give full validity to the 'Titulus Regius' by embodying it in an Act of Parliament. The public acts of Richard's parliament are noted for their wisdom and beneficial effects. One of them gave security to purchasers of land against secret feoffments, another conferred power on magistrates to accept bail from persons accused of felony, another was intended to prevent the intimidation of juries. The abolition of benevolences was a most beneficent measure, designed to put an end to an oppressive system of extorting money. An elaborate statute was also passed to check malpractices in the manufacture of woollen goods. The statutes of Richard III. were the first that were published in English. The distinction between public and private acts was also first made in this parliament. The latter included the reversal of the attainder of the Percys, several other restitutions, and grants for endowments, including a grant for the endowment of Bishop Stillington's college at Acaster.

Lord Bacon, no friendly critic, said of Richard III. that he was 'a prince in military virtue approved, jealous of the honour of the English nation, and likewise a good law maker for the ease and solace of the common people.'[14] In speaking of the parliament of Richard III. Lord Campbell says: 'We have no difficulty in pronouncing Richard's parliament the most meritorious national assembly for protecting the liberty of the subject, and putting down abuses in the administration of justice that had sat in England since the reign of Henry III.'[15]

King Richard III. introduced reforms in the revenue departments, which were prepared under his own eye. He ordered the Auditor of the Exchequer to submit an annual return of all revenues, issues, and profits; while the Lord Treasurer was to make a return of all money received and disbursed in his office. Formerly the Pell Issue and Receipt Rolls only showed net sums paid into the Exchequer, 'reprises' and direct payments being ignored.

The principal source of revenue was from the customs. The 'antiqua costuma' consisted of 6s. 8d. on the sack of wool, and 13s. 4d. on the last of leather. The 'parva costuma' included 3s. 4d. on a sack of wool, a small tax on cloth and other imports and exports, and an ad valorem duty of 2d. in the pound, and 3d. from foreigners, on general merchandise. Tonnage and poundage was 1s. in the pound on the value of most goods, except wool and leather, and 3d. on each tun of wine. The 'antiqua costuma' and 'parva costuma' were hereditary, but tonnage and poundage had to be voted by parliament at the beginning of each reign. Customs duties brought in 18,629l. in the first, and 20,743l. in the second year of King Richard's reign. The old crown revenues yielded 17,900l., Hanaper 2,930l., and other receipts 5,297l. The total annual revenue was 50,356l. in the first, and 57,122l. in the second year.

The navy in those days was small, indeed it had ceased to exist during the wretched misrule of Henry VI. Richard had, as Lord Admiral during his brother's reign, been gradually restoring the navy to efficiency, and in 1480 his brother appointed a 'Keeper of the Ships,' the officer who had control of naval organisation. Thomas Rogers, a merchant and fishmonger of London, was continued as 'Keeper of the Ships' during King Richard's reign, the navy consisting of seven ships, the 'Nicholas,' 'Governor,' 'Grace Dieu,' 'Mary of the Tower,' 'Martin Garcia,' 'Falcon,' and 'Trinity.'

While parliament was sitting the Convocation also assembled. The bishops and clergy presented an adulatory address to the King, praying that he would redress their grievances, 'seeing your most noble and blessed disposition in all things.' In reply Richard granted a charter to the clergy, confirming their liberties and immunities; and he took the opportunity of enjoining a closer attention to their spiritual duties. With this object he issued a Royal Letter calling upon Churchmen to enforce discipline and promote morality among the people. The Convocation voted the King three-tenths, which yielded 5,600l.

Before the prorogation the King took measures to induce the Queen Dowager to come out of sanctuary with her daughters. He promised that, if they would be guided and ruled by him, he would treat them kindly and honourably as his kinswomen, marry them to gentlemen born, and give them suitable allowances. Elizabeth agreed to these terms, which were faithfully observed; and the King also undertook to grant a pension of 700 marks a year for her own maintenance. She not only came out of sanctuary with her daughters, but showed so much confidence in Richard's good faith that she sent to her son, the Marquis of Dorset, to return to England and submit himself to the King.

In March, 1484, the King and Queen left London, and proceeded northwards by way of Cambridge, reaching Nottingham on April 20. Here they received intelligence of the death of the young Prince of Wales, which took place at Middleham on the 9th of the same month. The unhappy parents were distracted with the most violent grief. 'You might have seen his father and mother in a state almost bordering on madness by reason of their sudden grief.'[16] The child was interred in the chapel built by Richard himself, on the north side of Sheriff Hutton church. The King had placed 'the sun in splendour,' the favourite device of his brother Edward, in one of the windows. An alabaster effigy of the young Prince of Wales, habited in a loose gown with a coronet on his head, was fixed on an altar tomb. The south side of the tomb is divided into compartments. In the centre one the heart-broken father is represented in armour, offering up prayer to the Almighty, who is supporting a crucifix. On each side, in other compartments, there are shields now quite plain, probably once painted, supported by angels; and on the window jamb there is a shield charged with a cross of St. George in bold relief, the badge of the garter. The charges on the other shields have probably been wilfully defaced, as well as any crowns or ensigns of royalty, to conceal the identity of the monument. This was perhaps done to avoid complete desecration at Tudor hands. Some months after the child's death, when Richard had to sign a warrant for the last expenses connected with the funeral of his 'most dear son,' he touchingly added, in his own handwriting, 'whom God pardon.'[17] This prayer may have suggested the subject of the sculptured panel on the tomb, where the petition is made to pass, in form of a scroll, from the suppliant's lips to the ear of God.

King Richard, after the death of his own son, declared his nephew Edward, Earl of Warwick, son of his brother Clarence, to be heir to the throne. It was no doubt intended to reverse the attainder in due time. Meanwhile young Warwick was given precedence before all other peers. He resided sometimes at Sheriff Hutton, sometimes with his aunt, as a member of the King's household.[18]

It is asserted by Rous that the King changed his mind soon afterwards, and declared his nephew the Earl of Lincoln to be his heir, closely imprisoning young Warwick.[19] Rous was a dishonest and unscrupulous writer, and this particular statement is disproved by documentary evidence. For on May 13, 1485, the Mayor and Corporation of York determined to address a letter to the Lords of Warwick and Lincoln and other of the Council at Sheriff Hutton.[20] The precedence here given to young Warwick above Lincoln, and the fact of his being addressed as one of the Council, prove the statement of Rous to be false. It shows also that Warwick had not been superseded, and that he was still heir to the throne, just before the battle of Bosworth.[21] He was probably a member of the King's household, and one of the children mentioned in the Royal Ordinance of July 23, 1484.

Richard III. made a progress in the north of England during the summer of 1484, superintending the coast defences, and in August he was again at Nottingham receiving an embassy from Scotland. The King gave audience to the Scottish envoys in the great hall of Nottingham Castle on September 16, seated under a royal canopy and surrounded by the chief officers of state. A truce was established for three years, and a marriage was agreed upon between the eldest son of James III. and the Lady Anne de la Pole,[22] niece of the King of England. At about the same time a friendly treaty was ratified between Richard and the Duke of Brittany.

In the autumn of 1484 the body of Henry VI. was, by the King's order, removed from Chertsey and interred in St. George's Chapel at Windsor, on the south side of the high altar, the tomb of Edward IV. being on the north side. The chapel was then nearly finished.

Richard III. returned to London on November 9. He was met by the Lord Mayor and Aldermen with upwards of four hundred citizens, who escorted him to his residence at the Wardrobe in Blackfriars. Christmas was kept at Westminster with all gaiety and splendour, the young niece Elizabeth being richly attired in a dress similar to that of the Queen, according to the gossiping old monk of Croyland. But the beloved consort of so many years, the playfellow of Richard's early days, who had shared all his joys and sorrows, the mother of his lost child, was passing away. Like her sister Isabella, Queen Anne was delicate, and she was now in a rapid decline. She died on March 16, 1485,[23] and was buried in Westminster Abbey; her sorrowing husband shedding tears over her grave.[24] As an aggravation of the King's grief, an odious report, probably originating in the wishes of the Queen Dowager and her daughter, was spread abroad that he meditated a marriage with his illegitimate niece. As soon as it came to Richard's ears, he gave it formal and public contradiction.[25]

As the spring of 1485 advanced it became known that encouraged and aided by the French court, the Lancastrian malcontents intended to attempt an invasion of England, and that, probably at the suggestion of Bishop Morton, they had put forward a pretender as a claimant of the crown. This was Henry Tudor, who was born at Pembroke Castle on January 28, 1457. His father, Edmund Tudor, was the son of a Welsh esquire with whom the widow of Henry V. had formed a clandestine connection. Thus Edmund was a half-brother of Henry VI., who created him Earl of Richmond, and his brother Jasper Earl of Pembroke. Henry Tudor was born two months after his father's death, when the widow was only in her fifteenth year. She was daughter of John Beaufort, Duke of Somerset, and at this time was the wife of Lord Stanley, her third husband. In 1471 Jasper Tudor fled into Brittany with his nephew Henry. Both Edmund and Jasper Tudor had been attainted and deprived of their earldoms. Edward IV. had created his brother Richard Earl of Richmond,[26] and the title had since merged in the crown. The earldom of Pembroke had been conferred on King Edward's son Edward. Henry Tudor, who was never Earl of Richmond, had lived in Brittany for many years, but in 1484 he had gone to France, where the desire to injure her English neighbours induced the Lady of Beaujeu, daughter of Louis XI. and Regent for her young brother Charles VIII., to encourage the conspirators. Henry's claim to relationship with the Kings of the House of Lancaster was derived from his mother's descent from an illegitimate son of John of Gaunt.[27] It was afterwards considered unadvisable to put this untenable claim forward, except in vague terms, and Henry's title was based on conquest.

The King, in anticipation of the threatened invasion, took up a central position at Nottingham Castle in the spring of 1485, and issued commissions of array. In the early part of the year he had found the treasury nearly exhausted, and had been obliged to resort to a loan, in order to raise funds for the defence of the country. His parliament had abolished the system of 'benevolences,' or forced contributions, which had often been resorted to by former kings and were very oppressive. Richard, in his difficulties, would not sanction this illegal practice, but he appealed to the people for a loan, delivering 'good and sufficient pledges' for its repayment.[28] Full payment was to be made in eighteen months, in two instalments. By Good Friday, April 1, about 20,000l. had been received, out of 30,000l. that had been asked for.

On June 23 a royal proclamation was issued declaring Henry Tydder alias Tudor and his followers to be traitors and outlaws, and announcing that this Henry, son of Edmund, son of Owen Tydder, actually pretended to have a title to the crown. The Earl of Warwick and the King's niece Elizabeth were sent to Sheriff Hutton for safety. Edward and Richard, the young sons of Edward IV., must have been sent to the Tower with the same object.

Meanwhile the French Regent, although there was no war and no pretext for hostilities with England, furnished the necessary funds to enable an expedition to be fitted out at Harfleur, and allowed French troops to be embarked under the command of a French officer named Philibert de Shaundé. Thus supported and accompanied, Henry Tudor landed at Milford Haven on August 8, 1485. He had with him a few Lancastrian exiles.

PEERAGE OF RICHARD III.

(Those printed in italic type were present at the Coronation.)

DUKES

  1. Duke of Buckingham, K.G. (Stafford),[1] held the train.
  2. Duke of Suffolk, K.G. (Pole), bore the sceptre.
  3. Duke of Norfolk, K.G (Howard), bore the crown.

ROYAL MINORS

  4. Earl of Salisbury (Plantagenet),[2] son of the King.
  5. Earl of Warwick   "   son of Clarence.
  6. Earl of March and Pembroke, K.G. (Plantagenet), illegitimate
    son of Edward IV.

EARLS

  7. Earl of Lincoln (Pole),[2] bore the orb.
  8. Earl of Surrey, K.G. (Howard),[2] bore the sword of state.
  9. Earl of Arundel, K.G. (FitzAlan).[1]
  10. Earl of Northumberland, K.G. (Percy),[1] bore the sword of mercy.
  11. Earl of Westmoreland (Nevill), sick.
  12. Earl of Wiltshire (Herbert), bore the queen's crown.
  13. Earl of Kent (Grey), bore the ecclesiastical sword of justice.
  14. Earl of Nottingham (Berkeley).
  15. Earl of Huntingdon, bore the queen's sceptre.
  16. Earl of Shrewsbury (Talbot) } minors
  17. Earl of Essex (Bourchier)   }

VISCOUNTS

18. Viscount Lovell, K.G., bore the civil sword of justice.
19. Viscount Lisle (Grey),[1] bore the rod with dove.

BARONS

20. Lord Abergavenny (Nevill).
21. Lord Maltravers, K.G. (Fitz-Alan).[2]
22. Lord Grey of Codnor.
23. Lord Grey of Wilton.
24. Lord Grey of Powys.
25. Lord Morley.
26. Lord Scrope of Bolton, K.G.
27. Lord Scrope of Masham.
28. Lord Beauchamp.
29. Lord Lumley.
30. Lord Audley.
31. Lord Stourton.
32. Lord FitzHugh.
33. Lord Zouch.
34. Lord Dacre.
35. Lord Ferrers, K.G.
36. Lord Cobham.
37. Lord Stanley, K.G.,[1] bore the mace of constable.

[1] Turned traitors.
[2] Eldest sons raised to the Upper House.

BARONS--Continued

38. Lord Strange.[2]
39. Lord Welles.[1]
40. Lord Greystoke, in the marches.
41. Lord Mountjoy, at Calais.
42. Lord Dudley, K.G., very old.
43. Lord Hungerford,[2] a minor.
44. Lord Ogle, in the marches.
45. Lord de la Warre, abroad.

PRELATES

1. Archbishop of Canterbury (Bourchier).
2. Bishop of Durham (Dudley).
3. "   " Rochester (Audley).
4. "   " Exeter (Courtenay).
5. "   " Norwich (Goldwell).
6. "   " Wells (Stillington).
7. "   " Salisbury (Woodville).
8. "   " Lincoln (Russell).

UNDER ATTAINDER

1. Earl of Oxford, Lancastrian.
2. Earl of Devonshire, "
3. Lord Rivers,   "
4. Lord Dynham,   "
5. Lord Beaumont,   "
6. Lord Clifford (minor) "
7. Marquis of Dorset, Woodville faction.
8. Jasper Tudor, late Earl of Pembroke.[3]
9. Henry Tudor, calling himself Earl of Richmond.[4]

MINISTERS OF RICHARD III.

Earl Marshal--The Duke of Norfolk.
Lord Chancellor--Dr. John Russell, Bishop of Lincoln.
Lord Chamberlain--Viscount Lovell, K.G. (at Bosworth). Slain at Stoke.
Lord Steward--Lord Stanley (traitor).
Lord Constable--Duke of Buckingham (traitor), then Sir Ralph Ashton.
Lord Admiral--Duke of Norfolk, K.G. (at Bosworth). Slain in battle.
'Keeper of the Ships'--Thomas Rogers.
Lord Privy Seal--John Gunthorpe, Dean of Wells.
Lord Treasurer--Lord Audley (died 1491).
Chancellor of the Exchequer--William Catesby (at Bosworth). Killed
 by Henry VII.

[1] Turned traitors.
[2] Eldest sons raised to the Upper House.
[3] The earldom of Pembroke belonged to young Edward, eldest illegitimate son of Edward IV.
[4] The earldom of Richmond had merged in the crown, having been granted to the Duke of Gloucester.

Chancellor of the Duchy--Thomas Metcalfe.
Secretary of State--John Kendall (at Bosworth). Slain in battle.
Lord Deputy of Ireland--Earl of Kildare (ob. 1513).
Clerk of the Council--James Harington (at Bosworth). Slain in battle.
Treasurer of the Household--Walter Hopton (at Bosworth). Slain
 in battle.
Comptrollers of the Household--Sir Robert Percy (of Scotton, near
 Knaresborough), (at Bosworth). Slain in battle. And Sir John

Buck (at Bosworth). Killed by Henry VII.
Keeper of the Great Wardrobe--Pierce Courteys.

COMMISSIONERS FOR PEACE WITH SCOTLAND, 1484.

John Bishop of Lincoln
Richard of St. Asaph
Duke of Norfolk
Earl of Northumberland
Lord Privy Seal
Sir W. Stanley
Lord Stanley
Lord Strange
Lord Powys
Lord FitzHugh
Lord Dacre
Master of the Rolls
Sir Richard Ratcliffe
William Catesby
Richard Salkeld.

JUDGES AND LAW OFFICERS OF RICHARD III.

Lord Chief Justice of the King's Bench . . William Hussey.
Lord Chief Justice of Common Pleas . . . . Thomas Brian.
Chief Baron of the Exchequer . . . . Sir Humphrey Starbury.
Master of the Rolls . . . . Thomas Barrow.
Judges--King's Bench . . . . Roger Townshend.
    " . . . . Guy Fairfax.
    Common Pleas . . . . William Jenney.
    " . . . . Richard Neele.
    Exchequer . . . . Brian Roucliffe.
    " . . . . Ralph Wolseley.

Attorney-General . . . . Morgan Kidwelly.[1]
Solicitor-General . . . . Thomas Lymon.[2]

[1] Morgan Kidwelly, King Richard's Attorney-General, was supposed, even by Miss Halsted, to have turned traitor and joined Henry Tudor. But Mr. Gairdner has cleared his character, and shown that the idea was due to a resemblance of names. The Attorney-General was true and loyal to the end.

[2] The Solicitor-General married Jane Shore, with the consent of King Richard.

King's Serjeants . . . . Thomas Tremayne.
   "   . . . . Roger Townshend.
   "   . . . . John Vavasour.
Recorder of London . . . . Nicholas Fitzwilliam.

KING RICHARD'S BISHOPS

1454-86.   Thomas Bourchier,[1][4] Cardinal Archbishop of Canterbury.
1480-1501. Thomas Rotherham,[4] Archbishop of York.
1448-89.   Thomas Kempe[4] (then aged 79), Bishop of London.
1447-87.   William de Waynflete,[2] Bishop of Winchester.
1476-85.   William Dudley,[1][2][3] Bishop of Durham.
1465-92.   Robert Stillington,[1] Bishop of Bath and Wells.
1478-1504. Edward Story,[4] Bishop of Chichester.
1478-86.   John Morton (traitor),[4] Bishop of Ely.
1478-86.   Peter Courtenay (traitor),[1][4] Bishop of Exeter.

1474-92. Thomas Milling (Abbot of Westminster), Bishop of Hereford.
1459-92. William Smith,[3] Bishop of Lichfield.
1480-95. John Russell,[1] Bishop of Lincoln.
1472-99. James Goldwell,[1][4] Bishop of Norwich.
1480-92. Edmund Audley,[1][4] Bishop of Rochester.
1482-85. Lionel Woodville (traitor),[1] Bishop of Salisbury.
1476-86. John Alcock,[2][3] Bishop of Worcester.
1478-95. Richard Bell,[4] Bishop of Carlisle.
1464-96. Thomas Ednam,[4] Bishop of Bangor.
1478-96. John Marshall,[4] Bishop of Llandaff.
1472-95. Richard Redman,[2][3] Bishop of St. Asaph.
1483. Thomas Langton,[2] Bishop of St. David's.
1480-87. Richard Oldham, Bishop of Sodor and Man.
1474-98. John Esteney,[1] Abbot of Westminster.

KNIGHTS OF THE GARTER, CREATED BY RICHARD III.

1. Sir John Conyers (at Bosworth). Escaped.
2. The Earl of Surrey (at Bosworth). Taken prisoner.
3. Viscount Lovell (at Bosworth). Escaped. Slain at Stoke. The
   King's dearest friend.

[1] At the coronation.
[2] Received the King at Oxford.
[3] With the King at Warwick
[4] At Henry Tudor's first Parliament.

4. Sir Richard Ratcliffe (at Bosworth). Slain in the battle.
5. Sir Thomas Burgh.

6. Lord Stanley (traitor).
7. Sir Richard Tunstall.

KNIGHTS

Sir Robert Dymoke (the champion)   was knighted on July 5, 1483.
Sir Robert Percy . . . .   "   "   "
Sir Walter Hopton . . . .   "   "   "
Sir William Jenney (Judge) . . . .   "   "   "
Sir Robert Brackenbury . . . . . .   "   "   " 1485.

KNIGHTS OF THE BATH, CREATED AT THE CORONATION OF RICHARD III.[1]

1. Sir Edmund de la Pole (son of the Duke of Suffolk).
2. Sir John Grey (son of the Earl of Kent).
3. Sir William Zouch (brother of Lord Zouch).
4. Sir George Neville (son of Lord Abergavenny).
5. Sir Christopher Willoughby.
6. Sir William Berkeley, of Beverston (traitor).
7. Sir Henry Babington. (Buck has Bainton.)
8. Sir Thomas Arundell.
9. Sir Thomas Boleyn. (Buck has Bullen.)
10. Sir Edmund Bedingfield.
11. Sir Gervase Clifton. Wounded at Bosworth.
12. Sir William Saye (son of Lord Saye, who fell at Barnet).
13. Sir William Enderby.
14. Sir Thomas Lewknor (traitor).
15. Sir Thomas Ormonde.
16. Sir John Browne.
17. Sir William Berkeley, of Wyldy.
18. Sir Edmund Cornwall, Baron of Burford.

[1] From Grafton, p. 799, and Holinshed, p. 733; Harl. MS. 293, fol. 208b, and 2115, fol. 152; Buck, p. 26.

[1] Morton in Grafton, p. 127.

[2] Harl MSS. 433, fol. 269. Their high rank is shown by the order that no livery is to exceed the allowance, 'but only to my Lord (Lincoln?) and the children.' See Davies, York Records, p. 212 n., who also makes the suggestion that these children were the offspring of Edward IV. and the young Earl of Warwick.

[3] King Richard's progress:

```
Windsor      22 July, 1483  | Gloucester   1 Aug. 1483
Reading      23  "     "    | Tewkesbury   4  "    "
Oxford       24  "     "    | Worcester    6  "    "
Warwick*      8 Aug.   "    | Doncaster   25  "    "
Coventry     15  "     "    | Pontefract  27  "    "
Leicester    17  "     "    | York        30  "    "
Nottingham+  22  "     "
```

* A week.
\+ Letter of Secretary Kendal to Mayor of York, Aug. 23; Drake, p. 116.

[4] Rous.

[5] Worcester, Lichfield, Durham, St. Asaph, and Bangor (Rous, 217).

[6] Of St. David's.

[7] See also Rous, p. 216.

[8] Sheppard's Christ Church Letters, 46, quoted by Gairdner, p. 115.

[9] Rymer, xii. 200, quoted by Gairdner, p.

[10] Buck, p. 31, who gives the Letters Patent.

[11] Confession of his son.

[12] It is generally alleged that there was no trial. The appointment of Sir Ralph Ashton proves that there was.

[13] King Richard's Traitors, Oct. 1483

In the bill of attainder (Rot. Part. v. p. 294) there are 100 persons. Of these were executed

The Duke of Buckingham at Salisbury.
Sir Thomas St. Leger at Exeter.
A person named Ramme at Exeter.
Some executed after trial at Torrington by Lord Scrope.

Wm. Collingbourne had offered another man 8l. to go to Hy. Tudor in Brittany and urge him to invade England. If they would land at Poole, he would get people to rise. Executed in London, and 6 others, 2 taken in Kent, 4 in Southwark.

  Courtenay, Bishop of Exeter }
  Woodville, Bishop of Salisbury }
  Morton, Bishop of Ely }
  Marquis of Dorset } escaped abroad.
    (son of the Queen Dowager) }
  Lord Welles }
    (uncle of Henry Tudor) }

Proclaimed Traitors—

  Henry Tudor, calling himself Earl of Richmond.*

Jasper Tudor, late Earl of Pembroke.*
Sir E. Courtenay.
Margaret, wife of Lord Stanley.
Sir William Cheney, to induce the Duke of Brittany to help.
John Cheney at Salisbury, and others.

Wm. Noreys, of Yachendon }
Sir Wm. Berkeley, of Beverton }
Sir Roger Tocotes, of Bromham, pardoned } 44 at Newbury and in
Sir Wm. Stonor, in Berks. } Berks.
Sir John Fogge, with 26 others }
Richard Beauchamp, of St. Amand }
William Knyvett, of Bodenham } with Buckingham at
John Hush, merchant of London } Bechurch
Thomas Nandike, necromancer of Cambridge }

Sir George Brown, of Bletchworth, and others executed at
    Maidstone (Oct. 18), Rochester (Oct. 20), Gravesend (Oct. 22).
Sir John Gifford.
Sir Thomas Lewknor.
Sir Richard Gilford.
Reynald Pympe.
Sir Edward Poynings.
Sir William Brandon.
Sir John Wingfield.
Arthur Keane.
Sir William Hunter, pardoned.
Sir Thomas Ferveys, "
Nicholas Gaynsford, "

One hundred named in the Bill, a considerable number afterwards pardoned.

Harl. MSS. No. 433, p. 128; Halsted, ii. 276 n.; Sharon Turner.

* Henry Tudor had never been Earl of Richmond. His father was attainted, and the title was given to Richard Duke of Gloucester, with whom it merged in the crown. Jasper Tudor had been Earl of Pembroke before his attainder. Hence Henry Tudor is named as 'calling himself Earl of Richmond,' while Jasper is 'late Earl of Pembroke.' After the attainder the Earldom of Pembroke was conferred by Edward IV. on his son Edward.

[14] Life of Henry VII.

[15] Lives of the Lord Chancellors, i. p. 407.

[16] 'Vidisses tantisper patrem et matrem, iis novis apud Nothinghaniam ubi tunc residebant, auditis præ subitis doloribus pene insanire'—Croyland, p. 571.

[17] Harl. MS. No. 433, fol. 183.

[18] Rous, pp. 217-218. 'Non multo post principe, ut dicitur, mortuo, juvenis comes Warwici Edwardus, filius primogenitus Georgii ducis Clarenciæ, proclamatus est apparens Angliæ in curia regali, et in serviciis ad mensam et cameram post regem et reginam primo ei serviebatur.'

[19] 'Postea sub arta custodia positus, conies Lincolniensis ei præferrebatur nomine Johannes Pole, filius et heres Johannis Pole ducis Suffolchiæ.'—Rous, p. 218.

[20] Davies, York Records, p. 210.

[21] Moreover, Lincoln fell at Stoke, fighting for the Earl of Warwick as rightful king, not for himself.

[22] This marriage never took place, and the Lady Anne became a nun at Sion.

[23] It is said by the Croyland monk (572) that there was an eclipse of the sun on the day of her death. This would make it March 16. Some authorities have the 11th.

[24] Buck, p. 129. 'Non cum minore honore quam sicut reginam decuit sepeliri.'—Croyland, i. 572.

[25] Croyland, York Records, pp. 208, 210.

[26] Rot. Parl. vi. 227.

[27] John of Gaunt, Duke of Lancaster, the third son of Edward III., who lived to marry, had for his first wife Blanche, heiress of Henry Duke of Lancaster, through whom he acquired the title. By her he had Henry IV., who usurped the crown, Edward and John, who died young, Philippa, married to Joam I., King of Portugal, and Elizabeth Duchess of Exeter. He married secondly Constanza, heiress of Pedro King of Castille and Leon, and had a daughter Catalina, wife of Enrique III., King of Castille and Leon. A governess was engaged for the daughters of the Duke of Lancaster. This was Catharine, daughter of a herald of Hainault, named Payn Roet, who had married Sir Hugh Swynford in 1367. The Duke had four children by this woman, named John, Henry, Thomas, and Joan, surnamed Beaufort from the castle in France where they were born. All were born during the lifetime not only of the Duke's wife, but also of the governess's husband. The Duchess died in 1394, and the realm was scandalised by the marriage of the Duke of Lancaster with this woman on January 13, 1396. The Duke died in February 1399, Catharine Swynford on May 10, 1403. Their children were granted letters of legitimation by

Richard II. in February 1397, confirmed by Henry IV. on February 10, 1407, 'excepta dignitate regali.' Henry Tudor's mother was granddaughter of John, the eldest of the Beauforts.

[28] Every act of Richard III. has been persistently misrepresented. This loan is usually alleged to have been a return to the illegal system of 'benevolences,' which Richard had himself abolished a year before, by Act of Parliament. Even Miss Halsted is led into this error. But Mr. Gairdner has completely disposed of the accusation. See Croyland, p. 572, and Lingard's remarks, iv. 255. Gairdner, p. 198.

CHAPTER XI THE BATTLE OF BOSWORTH

Richard's headquarters were at Nottingham Castle, the 'Castle of Care' as he had called it, since he received the news of his son's death there. With the aid of the loan a force had been raised and armed; while reinforcements were on their way from several directions. Here the news arrived that Henry Tudor[1] had landed at Milford Haven with 2,000 mercenaries. He would never have run this risk unless he had previously received distinct promises of adherence from the Talbots and Stanleys. His mother, the wife of Stanley, was an inveterate intriguer. She had already been detected in treasonable practices and contemptuously forgiven by the King. Now she had persuaded her treacherous husband that it would be more for his interests to be step-father to a new King owing everything to his treason, than to continue loyal to his generous and forgiving master. This explains the conduct of the Stanleys, which emboldened the invader to venture upon such an enterprise. The insurgents advanced by Cardigan and Welshpool to Shrewsbury. They were joined by several Welsh chiefs, and by Sir Gilbert Talbot with 2,000 men. Henry Tudor was accompanied by his uncle Jasper, and by John Vere, son of the attainted Earl of Oxford. Reginald Bray,[2] his mother's steward, was in attendance on him, and Dr. Richard Fox[3] acted as his secretary. Most of the leaders of his troops were exiles who had been concerned in Buckingham's abortive treason. William Brandon,[4] Sir John Cheney, Sir Giles Daubeny, Sir Robert Willoughby, Sir John Byron, Richard Edgcombe,[5] and Sir Thomas Bourchier, all come under this category. Sir John Savage and Simon Digby[6] joined the invaders after they had landed, and Walter Hungerford[7] deserted just before the battle. No peer, except Stanley, joined the rebels.

Lord Stanley and his brother Sir William had raised forces in Lancashire and Cheshire, with the base intention of turning traitors to their King if a good opportunity offered, but of being on the winning side in any circumstances. With this object their design was to hold aloof until the last moment. Sir William Stanley had a secret interview with Henry at Stafford. On August 20 the insurgents, about 8,000 strong, arrived at Atherstone, nine miles beyond Tamworth. Here the Stanleys again met Henry secretly. They pretended to the King that they were retreating before the invaders.

Richard was undoubtedly a man endowed with great military talent. He had shown remarkable generalship, when quite a boy, at Barnet and Tewkesbury. He had conducted the Scottish campaign with signal success. He had promptly stamped out the Buckingham revolt. He was now to encounter the rebels. There can be no doubt that if he had waited for the reinforcements which were on their way, especially from the north, the result would never have been doubtful. But alas! he despised his enemy, and his open and generous nature prevented him from harbouring a suspicion of the foul treachery of the Stanleys until it was too late.

English pluck has been a motive power which has helped to place the English-speaking race in the forefront of the world's history. That dogged courage facing overwhelming odds rather than wait for help or give ground is the secret of England's success. Often leading to decisive victory it has sometimes resulted in disaster. Never more conspicuous than in the audacious campaigns of Crecy and Agincourt, when fortune was on the side of reckless valour, it was equally present on the fatal field of Beaugé, when Thomas Duke of Clarence lost his life. We find it again at Wakefield, a battle which resembles Bosworth in several respects. The brave and chivalrous father lost his life on the former, the gallant son on the latter field. Both Richards were full of English pluck. Both scorned to wait for succour; and preferred, like the men of Zutphen and of Balaclava, to charge into the midst of countless odds. Both were betrayed—the Duke of York by Nevill, the King by the Stanleys. These Plantagenets were fitting leaders of the people of England. While their dogged English pluck led some of them to destruction, the very same quality has secured decisive victory for England on a hundred fields.

On August 14 King Richard was hunting in Beskwood Park. He was an ardent sportsman, and this was fated to be his last day's sport. Monday the 15th was the Feast of the Assumption of the Virgin, and he devoutly kept it, as we learn from the Duke of Norfolk.[8] He commenced his march from Nottingham on Wednesday morning. He was surrounded by loyal and devoted friends. Viscount Lovell and Sir Robert Percy, the companions of his childhood, rode by his side. The veteran Duke of Norfolk, who had fought with the great Talbot at Châtillon, was hurrying up with a contingent from the eastern counties. His son, the gallant Earl of Surrey, was with him. Lords Ferrers and Zouch had arrived from the Midlands. The loyal old Constable, Sir Robert Brackenbury, had come by forced marches from London. The Earl of Northumberland, who owed much to his royal cousin,[9] was bringing a first instalment of troops from the north. The faithful city of York was represented by eighty of her citizens, stout-hearted and well equipped.[10] Other troops were on their way, and if the King had waited for them his victory was certain. All the loyal gentry of the north were in arms, but Richard did not give them time to reach his camp. Among them were the two Lords Scrope, Lords Dacre and Ogle, Lord Greystoke of Hinderskelf, the King's cousin,[11] who 'brought a mighty many,' and among the Yorkshire names of those loyal to King Richard were Gascoigne and Conyers, Strickland and Constable, Mauleverer and Plumpton, Tempest and Pudsey, Pilkington and Musgrave.

The King formed his army in two divisions, marching five abreast, with the cavalry on the flanks. Richard himself was on a white horse richly caparisoned, and he wore a golden circlet on his helmet. He entered Leicester in the evening of August 19, and lodged at the 'White Boar'[12] in North Gate Street. In the morning of Sunday the 21st the army marched out of Leicester, reaching the little village of Stapleton, a distance of eight miles, in the afternoon. A camp had already been prepared in a field near Stapleton, called 'the Bradshaws,' which is on a slight eminence.

This part of Leicestershire consists of a succession of hills and dales, with streams flowing westward, and uniting to form the Anker, a tributary of the Trent. The 'Bradshaws' is on the brow of a gentle slope, at the base of which flows a rivulet called the Tweed. The Duke of Norfolk's camp was at Cadeby, about two miles to the north, but he only arrived at Stapleton the day before the battle. Stanley, still pretending to retreat, marched with 2,000 men, by Stoke Golding, to a field now called 'Gamble's Close,' facing the 'Bradshaws,' with the Tweed flowing between the two positions. Sir William Stanley had a similar force encamped on the northern side of the field, in front of the town of Market Bosworth, and near the Duke of Norfolk. Between, but to the west of Stapleton and Cadeby, there is a ridge known as Sutton Fields, in front of the village of Sutton Cheney. A gentle slope sinks thence to Redmore Plain[13] and Ambien Leys, between which is the hill called Ambien. Further west, across the stream, there are some fields called the White Moors, with the village of Shenton to the north, and those of Dadlington and Stoke Golding to the south-east.

Henry had arrived at Atherstone on August 20, and lodged at the 'Three Tuns,' while the rebel troops and their French allies under Philibert de Shaundé encamped in the meadows north of the church. Tudor was here joined by another traitor, Robert Hardwicke of Lindley. Next day the insurgents advanced nearly due east, crossed the bridge over the river Anker at Witherley, and then turned up the Fenn Lanes, encamping on White Moors. Hardwicke of Lindley acted as their guide. They were a mile from Ambien Hill, with Lord Stanley in advance of their right flank, and Sir William Stanley between their camp and Bosworth, on their left flank.

The King had thrown up a breastwork to protect his camp, 300 yards long, with flanks of fifty yards, facing Lord Stanley. At length the suspicious conduct of Stanley forced him to entertain the idea of treachery. But it was too late. He had about 8,000 men, while Norfolk's contingent numbered 4,000. The Stanleys had about 8,000 men, and the insurgent army was composed of 2,000 French mercenaries, 2,000 retainers of Sir Gilbert Talbot, and 4,000 Welsh and English traitors, in all 8,000 men. Including the Stanley contingents, the enemy largely outnumbered the royal army.

During the night Sir Simon Digby got into the royal camp as a spy, and returned with the report that the troops were in motion. The rebel leaders, therefore, sounded to arms. This must have been at dawn of Monday, August 22, 1485. The sun rose that day at a quarter after five.[14] King Richard marched north-eastward for two miles to effect a junction with the Duke of Norfolk. The royal army was then formed in two lines, along the ridge of Sutton Fields. The archers were in the front line, with a few small pieces of artillery, under the Duke of Norfolk. The bill-men formed the rear line, and the horse were on the flanks.

Stanley marched at the same time as the King, and halted to the rear of his left flank. The Earl of Northumberland arrived the same morning, but he seems to have thought that his men needed rest. He took no part in the battle. This slackness and want of zeal were punished in after years by the loyal people of Yorkshire.[15]

King Richard was dressed in the same suit of polished steel that he had worn at Tewkesbury, with a golden circlet round his helmet. He rode to a knoll, since called 'Dickon's Nook,' and addressed the army in a spirit-stirring speech, calling on all true Englishmen to resist the foreign invaders, and appealing to their loyalty and patriotism. He then led them down the slope, placing his right towards Ambien Leys. In front of his centre there was a well, since known as King Richard's Well.

Philibert de Shaundé had formed the insurgents across Redmore Plain, with a morass on their right flank. In their first line was John Vere in the centre, Sir Gilbert Talbot on the right, and Sir John Savage on the left wing. Jasper Tudor commanded the second line, and his nephew Henry kept well in the rear. John Vere ordered his men not to advance more than ten paces in front of their standard; for he knew of the contemplated treachery, and that the royal troops would be attacked in the rear.

As soon as the King saw that the insurgents had left their camp and advanced round the morass, he gave the order for the attack at about 10 A.M. A volley of arrows was discharged on either side: probably a few shots from some small pieces of ordnance were fired by the rebels.[16] Then the traitor Stanley threw off the mask and fell upon the left rear of the royal army, throwing it into confusion. The Duke of Norfolk fought gallantly and fell in the thickest of the battle.

The young King beheld this treason, and at once made up his mind. He saw that a desperate charge of cavalry was the only remaining chance. He received a report that Henry Tudor was skulking in the rear, and resolved to attack him. It was a well-concerted plan, though made on the spur of the moment. Richard was surrounded by loyal and devoted knights. It is said that he stopped to quench his thirst at the well. Then, putting spurs to his horse, he galloped forward, followed by the Chancellor of the Exchequer, the Secretary of State, the Clerk of the Council, the Constable of the Tower, Lords Lovell, K.G., Ferrers, and Zouch; Sir Bryan Stapleton, Sir Thomas and Humphrey Stafford, Sir Richard Clarendon, Sir Gervase Clifton, Sir Robert Percy,[17] Sir Richard Ratcliffe, K.G.,[18] the flower of England's loyal chivalry. Sir William Parker was the standard-bearer. Never was the valour of the kingly race of Plantagenet more gloriously displayed. Sir Robert Brackenbury was encountered by the traitor Hungerford, who slew the grey-headed old warrior, loyal to the last. Sir Gervase Clifton was overthrown and badly wounded, but he was shielded from further harm by Sir John Byron, his old friend and neighbour in Nottinghamshire, who eventually obtained his pardon from the usurper.[19] The King himself felled William Brandon to the ground. He was the adventurer's standard-bearer, and the red dragon worked on white and green sarcenet was hurled into the mud. The lions of England still waved over their defenders. The King then unhorsed Sir John Cheney, a French pensioner, and was on the point of reaching Henry Tudor himself, when the last and foulest act of treachery was perpetrated. Sir William Stanley suddenly attacked the right flank of the royal army with 3,000 men. King Richard was surrounded. He was urged to fly by the loyal knights who stood by him to the last. 'Never,' exclaimed the young hero, 'I will not budge a foot; I will die King of England,' and he dashed into the thickest of the fight. Like a sturdy oak sinking under a thousand blows, at length King Richard fell, fighting an army and covered with wounds. 'Fighting manfully in the thickest press of his enemies,' confessed one of the most unscrupulous among them.[20] He fell at the foot of the hill in Ambien Leys. Lord Ferrers, Lord Zouch, Sir Richard Ratcliffe, the Secretary of State, and the Clerk of the Council fell fighting by his side. Sir William Conyers and Sir Richard Clarendon were also among the slain, with many other loyal knights and gentlemen. Sir William Parker (or Thurleball?), the King's standard-bearer, is said to have kept the lions of England on high until both his legs were cut from under him, nor, when on the ground, would he let go while breath was left in his body.[21]

The royal charge commenced at 11 A.M. and lasted about half an hour. Each side lost a hundred men in battle, but the treason of the Stanleys was followed by the flight of the royal army towards Stoke Golding, and during the pursuit, which continued for fifty minutes, there was considerable slaughter.

Henry then came to the front, and was at Stoke Golding when Sir William Stanley brought him the golden circlet off the late King's helmet, saluting him as King. The place is called 'Crown Hill.' Stanley was made Lord Chamberlain by the usurper; but such a traitor could not be trusted. Henry was conscious that 'though Stanley came in time to save his life, he delayed long enough to endanger it.' The astute and patient King, brought up in the school of Louis XI., bided his time. Before many years his saviour was beheaded.

Shameful indignities are said to have been perpetrated on the lifeless body of King Richard. They could have been prevented by a word from Henry, but that word was not spoken. 'Insults offered by the victor to the corpse of a soldier slain in battle evince a great degree of meanness or cowardice on the part of the former.'[22]

Richard III. was buried in the church of St. Mary, belonging to the Grey Friars, at Leicester, and a tomb was erected over his grave. Not only has the tomb long since disappeared, but the church also. In 1808 a stone pyramid was built over the well on the battlefield, with a suitable inscription by the learned Dr. Parr, to commemorate the gallant death of the King:

> AQUA EX HOC PUTEO HAUSTA
> SITIM SEDAVIT
> RICABDUS TERTIUS REX ANGLIAE
> CUM HENRICO COMITE DE RICHMONDIA
> ACERRIME ATQUE INFENSISSIME PRAELIANS
> ET VITA PARITEB AC SCEPTRO
> ANTE NOCTEM CARITURUS
> II KAL. SEPT. A.D. MCCCCLXXXV

In 1871 the arms of King Richard III., impaling those of Queen Anne, were placed on an abutment of the new bridge at Nottingham, as a memorial. Richard III., the last of our Plantagenet kings, is the only one since the Norman Conquest who has fallen on the field of battle. He was also the youngest of our actual reigning sovereigns when he died.[23]

Richard passed through the first thirty years of his life, before his accession, with honour and repute. He displayed brilliant courage as a knight, and remarkable ability as a general. In France he upheld the honour of England against the corrupt faction which surrounded his sovereign. In Scotland he did admirable service by the capture of Berwick. He was an efficient and energetic administrator of the Northern Marches, and was the first to establish postal communication by means of relays of horses. He was justly popular throughout the country, and was beloved in Yorkshire, where he was best known. When the news of his death reached York, the people were plunged in grief. The following entry was made in the City Register: 'He was piteously slain and murdered to the great heaviness of this city.'[24]

On his accession to the throne his character did not alter. He loved his country, and was a King of great administrative ability. He was prompt and vigorous in suppressing insurrections, and baffling the schemes of conspirators; but he was lenient, often unwisely so, when the immediate danger was over. No other King would have spared such mischievous traitors as Stanley and Morton. His generosity to the families of attainted rebels will not find any parallel in our history. Not only did he show liberal clemency to the wives of Rivers, Hastings, Buckingham and others: but he actually pensioned the wives of men who were plotting against him in foreign countries, like John Vere, Lord Dynham, and Alexander Cheney. His uprightness and good faith were relied upon by enemies and friends alike. Lord Rivers appointed him supervisor of his last will, well knowing him to be an honourable and magnanimous foe. Lady Latimer sought the same service from him, as a kind and trusty friend. As an arbitrator in family disputes, like that between Sir Robert Plumpton and his relations, Richard, by his impartial justice, established peace and concord where there had been ill-will and litigation.[25] There was nothing mean or sordid in his nature; he was liberal, open-handed, and generous.

Richard's Parliament was the best that had met since the time of Edward I. His administration was patriotic. He checked corruption in the public service, refused large sums of money that were offered to him as gifts by several towns,[26] and anxiously sought the welfare of his people. He took great interest in the administration of justice, and it is recorded that in Michaelmas term of 1484 he personally attended in the Star Chamber and propounded questions of law to the judges. He encouraged trade, and especially voyages to Iceland and the northern fisheries. In Ireland he was very popular and his government was successful. His foreign policy was wise and judicious. He made peace with Scotland, established friendly relations with Brittany and Spain, observed strict neutrality between Maximilian and the Flemish towns, while promoting commercial intercourse, and watched the treacherous regency of France with well-founded suspicion.

King Richard was a great builder.[27] He founded collegiate churches at Middleham, Barnard Castle, and All Hallows Barking, built a memorial chapel at Towton, another at Sheriff Hutton, endowed Queens' College, Cambridge,[28] and erected a handsome tower at Westminster. He pushed forward the works at St. George's Chapel, Windsor, begun by his brother, and repaired the castles of Skipton, Carlisle, Nottingham, and Warwick. His cognizance of the white boar is still to be seen on the stonework of an oriel window at Barnard Castle. Richard was a prince of literary tastes, and among his books a manuscript copy of the romance of Tristan de Leonnais and a Wickliffe Bible have been preserved. He was the friend and patron of Caxton, who dedicated a book 'Of the Ordre of Chyvalry and Knyghthode' to 'his redoubted Lord King Richard.' By letters patent, dated March 21, 1484, he gave the Heralds a charter of incorporation, and was thus the founder of the College of Arms. He also granted them 'a right fayre and stately house,'[29] called Pulteney's Inn. He was devout and religious, striving to promote greater activity among the clergy in improving the morals of the people. Richard was a keen sportsman, devoted to the chase both with hawk and hound. He kept large hunting establishments at Westminster and in Yorkshire.

King Richard was probably conscious of the political change that was impending in the world, for he was a vigilant observer of the signs of the times, and was well versed in the political questions which were engaging the attention of European statesmen. He had witnessed the fall of his brother-in-law, Charles the Bold, and the collapse of the system he upheld. He must have seen that feudalism was giving way to a new era, in the age of the Renaissance. The young Plantagenet was well fitted by nature to rule the destinies of England during this period of change. He had received an excellent training. For years he had been accustomed to confer with the authorities at York on their local affairs, he had often been in consultation with clerical advisers when framing statutes for his collegiate churches, and from early youth he had had unusual opportunities of acquiring a knowledge of the needs and wishes of the people. He desired to reign in the hearts of his countrymen. His proclamations and letters show that he wished to take his people into his counsels, to consult public opinion, and to be guided by it. He was an administrator of no mean ability, and although he was bold even to recklessness in facing the consequences of his acts, he always showed anxiety to have the public feeling with him. He would, in all probability, have respected the rights and liberties of his subjects while leading them into new ways.

In all respects Richard was better fitted to reign over England in the days of change that were inevitable than the two tyrants who succeeded him. Henry Tudor caused a beautiful chapel to be built at Westminster for his own tomb, but his son robbed and destroyed scores of far more beautiful tombs and churches in all parts of England. There might have been an age of English Renaissance under Richard. There actually was an age of Vandalic destruction under the Tudors. The father was a miserly foreigner, the son a rapacious and remorseless tyrant,[30] both despots by nature, and haters of constitutional freedom. The battle of Bosworth was a calamity from which England did not soon recover. But after seventy-three years of tyranny the Great Queen began to reign. Though a Tudor by name her high qualities were derived from her mother's English ancestors. She was a true Englishwoman at heart. Descendant of the brave and loyal Norfolk who fell fighting for King Richard at Bosworth, the grand-niece of Richard III. was by blood even more truly English than were her Yorkist great-uncles.

Richard was most agreeable and ingratiating in his manners, and where he was best known he was most liked.[31] He formed friendships which endured the test of time. Those who knew and loved him in boyhood fought by his side on the fatal field at Bosworth.[32] Richard III. was the only one of our kings who made a true love match. His cousin Anne, the playmate of his childhood, was his first love. United before they were twenty, they passed ten years of happy married life together at Middleham. Their love is proved by their constant companionship. When the Protector was surrounded by perils and difficulties, his wife hurried up to London to share them with him. Together they were crowned, together they sat at public banquets, made progresses and walked in royal processions. Together they mourned over the death of their beloved child, and sought comfort in mutual sympathy. Richard only survived his wife's death for five short months; having shared with her their joys and sorrows for fourteen years.

The true picture of our last Plantagenet King is not unpleasant to look upon, when the accumulated garbage and filth of centuries of calumny have been cleared off its surface.

CONTEMPORARY SOVEREIGNS

Scotland	James III.	1460-1488
France	Anne of Beaujeu (Regent for Charles VIII.)	1483
Brittany	Francis II.	1458-1488
Low Countries	Mary and Maximilian	1477-1493
Germany	Emperor Frederick III.	1440-1493
Denmark, Sweden, and Norway	Hans	1481-1513
Bohemia	Vladislaus	1471-1510
Hungary	Matthias Corvinus	1458-1490
Poland	Casimir IV.	1445-1492
Castille	Isabella	1474-1504
Aragon	Ferdinand	1479-1516
Portugal	Joam II.	1481-1495
Naples	Ferdinand of Aragon	1458-1494
Pope	Sixtus IV. (delle Rovere)	1471-1484
"	Innocent VIII. (Cibo)	1484-1492
Tuscany	Lorenzo de' Medici	1469-1492
Milan	Gian Galeazzo Sforza	1476-1494
Grand Seigneur	Bayazid II.	1481-1512

[1] Henry Tudor was not, and never had been, Earl of Richmond. His father had been deprived by attainder and outlawry. Richard Duke of Gloucester was created Earl of Richmond by King Edward IV., and when Richard succeeded, the title merged in the crown.

[2] Sir Reginald Bray was made a K.B. at Henry's coronation, and afterwards a Knight of the Garter. He was an architect, and has the credit of having finished St. George's Chapel at Windsor and built Henry VII.'s Chapel at Westminster.

[3] Fox was a priestly conspirator who had been acting as one of Morton's agents. He was rewarded with the Bishopric of Winchester.

[4] Henry's standard-bearer.

[5] Knighted after the battle.

[6] Made Lieutenant of the forests of Sherwood, Beskwood, and Clipston, on Sept. 22, 1485.

[7] Knighted after the battle.

[8] Paston Letters, ii. p. 334.

[9] Their mothers were sisters. Richard III. had passed an Act restoring all their rights and possessions to the Percys.

[10] Davies, York Records, p. 216.

[11] Their mothers were sisters.

[12] Afterwards the 'Blue Boar.'

[13] The battle was sometimes called Redmore, 'apud Rodemore juxta Leicestre' (York Records, p. 217). See also Drayton's Polyolbion, xxii.

'O Redmore then it seemed thy name was not in vain,
When with a thousand's blood the earth was coloured red.'

[14] Thirty-first of Gregorian era. Sun rises at 5.15 A.M.

[15] They killed him near Thirsk, on April 28, 1488, when he was engaged in enforcing the payment of extortionate taxes levied by his new master (Dugdale's Baronage, p. 282).

[16] Four cannon balls were found on Ambien Hill in the last century. They are now in possession of Mrs. Park Yates, of Sandiway, near Northwich, who allowed Mr. Gairdner to examine them. One is of lead, weighing 14-¾ lbs., another 8-½ lbs., another 4 lbs., and the fourth is of stone and larger. Mr. Gairdner suggests that the guns may have been brought by the rebels from Tamworth Castle, which was on their line of march.

[17] Son of Robert Percy of Scotton, near Knaresborough.

[18] Eldest son of Sir Thomas Ratcliffe of Derwentwater. Sir Richard married Agnes, daughter of Lord Scrope of Bolton.

[19] Sir Gervase Clifton of Clifton lived until 1493. His tomb is in Clifton Church.

[20] Polydore Virgil, p. 224. 'Attamen si ad ejus honorem veritatem dicam ut nobilis miles licet corpore parvus et viribus debilis ad ultimum anhelitum suum modo defensorio clarissime se habuit, sæpius se proditum

clamans et dicans "Treason! Treason! Treason!" et sic gustans quod aliis sæpius propinaverat miserrime vitam finivit.'—Rous, p. 218. 'Nam inter pugnandum et non in fuga, dictus Rex Richardus, multis vulneribus ictus, quasi princeps animosus et audentissimus in campo occubuit.'— Croyland Chron., Gale, i. p. 574.

[21] Hutton's Bosworth. The only detailed account of the battle is in the history of the Italian Polydore Virgil, who came to England in about 1503. Hall, Grafton, and Holinshed copied from Polydore, or from each other. Hutton visited the ground in 1788, and again in 1807, and wrote a history of the battle. Mr. Gairdner also went over the ground and wrote an account of the battle in the Archæologia, lv. pt. vii. p. 159 (1896), read Jan. 24, 1895. The present writer has twice been over every part of the ground, and examined it carefully with Polydore Virgil and Hutton as his guides, the first time accompanied by an accomplished antiquary, the present Earl of Liverpool.

[22] Brooke, Visits to Battle Fields in England, p. 170.

[23] Mary II. was two months younger, but she was only a joint sovereign. Edward VI. never actually reigned.

[24] Davies, York Records, p. 218.

[25] The history of this Plumpton arbitration illustrates the difference between Richard III. and Henry VII. The former appears as a just and upright king, studying the good of his subjects; the latter, as a pettifogging tyrant, seeking pretexts and excuses for robbery and spoliation.

The dispute was between Sir Robert Plumpton and his heirs general as to rights of succession. At last there was an agreement to abide the award of the King's Majesty.

Richard III. gave the matter his careful attention, and decided on the merits, solely actuated by the desire of doing substantial justice. His judgment was given on September 16, 1483. Impartial justice was actually done by Richard's award, and its conditions were peacefully acquiesced in by both parties, for several years.

'But,' as the Editor remarks, 'it was the misfortune of Sir Robert Plumpton to have lived on into the days of Henry VII., who, under the pretence of a rigid enforcement of the law, sought only the means to gratify his avarice.' Every defect of title, which might furnish the pretext for a suit or fine, was eagerly caught at in order to swell the revenue. In this manner the claim of the Plumpton heirs general was re-opened by the infamous Empson, the tool of Henry; and after years of persecution, Sir Robert was reduced to beggary and a debtors' prison.' Plumpton Correspondence, pp. xc. to cxviii. (Camden Society, 1839).

[26] London, Gloucester, and Worcester.

[27] 'Erat iste Rex Ricardus in edificiis laudandus, ut Westmonasteriensi, Notinghamiæ, Warwici, Eboraci et apud Midlam, multisque aliis locis, ut ad oculum manifesta evidet.'—Rous, p. 215.

[28] Rous, p. 216.

[29] Stow. Henry Tudor, when he usurped the crown, seized upon this property, and turned out the Heralds. They remained houseless until 1555, when the Earl Marshal purchased a house on St. Benet's Hill for them, the site of the present Heralds' College.

[30] Henry VIII. was never known to exercise the prerogative of mercy. Even poor young Lord Dacre was among his victims, for a trivial offence.

[31] 'Richard was bold in conceiving and reckless in facing the consequences of his acts, of high and brilliant courage, and seductive manners.'—W. Campbell, Introduction to Materials for the History of the Reign of Henry VII., p. xiv.

[32] Lord Lovell and Sir Robert Percy.

PART II

CHAPTER I THE AUTHORITIES

The dynasty of the Plantagenets had reigned over England for more than three centuries, when the last King of that royal race fell at the battle of Bosworth. Under the Plantagenets, Normans and Saxons were welded into one nation. The House of Commons became a firmly established institution. The cherished liberties of England took form and shape. The victories of the Plantagenet kings are the most glorious traditions of the English people. No other dynasty became so thoroughly national, and the Yorkist kings were almost pure Englishmen in blood.[1] A halo of romance would naturally have gathered round our last Plantagenet, our youngest reigning sovereign,[2] and the only English monarch since the Conquest who fell in battle, fighting valiantly for his crown and country.

Instead of this being the case, the accusations of his enemies have received full credence. He was charged with the committal of a series of atrocious crimes, his name has been execrated by posterity, and historians have vied with each other in heaping opprobrium on his memory.

Yet there are obvious reasons for closely criticising the accusations against King Richard, and for examining them with more than ordinary care before accepting them as proved. For his successor had no valid title to the crown. It was not only the new King's interest, but a necessity of his position, that he should cause grave charges to be brought against his predecessor, and that they should be accepted as true. Henry VII. had the power and the will to silence all comment, and to prevent any defence from being published. Evidence in favour of Richard was destroyed.

Authors employed by Henry, and others who were anxious to please him and his successors, were alone permitted to write histories. Not a syllable was allowed to be uttered on the other side for one hundred and sixty years. The story thus put forward was dramatised by Shakespeare, and became so familiar to posterity that even writers of our own day approach the subject with unconscious prejudice which they cannot resist. If Richard performs kindly acts, and many such are recorded, he is trying 'to get unsteadfast friends.' If he punishes treason he is 'a venomous hunchback.' If a rebellion is put down during his reign he is an inhuman tyrant. His ability is cunning, his justice is cruelty, his bravery is fury, his generosity is artfulness, his devotion is hypocrisy.

In giving some account of the original authorities upon whose testimony the charges against King Richard rest, I only propose to state general conclusions with regard to them in the present chapter; because proofs and arguments will be embodied in the detailed discussions which follow.

Bernard André, Archbishop Morton, and Polydore Virgil were actually in the pay or under the direct influence of the first Tudor King. In this trio only one was an Englishman. John Rous and Robert Fabyan wrote during Henry's reign, accepted his version of events, and sought his favour. The continuator of the Chronicle of Croyland Abbey is the sole independent source of information.

By far the most important of the original authorities, and the one on which all subsequent history has been based, is Archbishop Morton. His narrative is contained in the 'History of Richard III.,' erroneously attributed to Sir Thomas More, who was in Morton's household when a boy. This work first appeared in Hardyng's Chronicle, printed by Grafton in 1543. It was embodied in Hall's Chronicle, and copied by Holinshed. Fourteen years after its publication, another and somewhat different version was brought out by Rastell in 1557. Rastell was related to Sir Thomas More, and he alleged that his version was taken from a manuscript in More's handwriting written about 1513. A Latin version, written long before its publication, was printed at Louvain in 1566, with various additions to the imaginary speeches, and an address to Henry VIII. and the Earl of Surrey. Sir George Buck[3] and Sir John Harington[4] had heard that the work was written by Morton. The Latin version could not have been, for it is addressed to Henry VIII., and Morton died in 1500.

The history, as we have it, contains long speeches and dialogues which must have been fabricated by the writer. The narrative from the death of Edward IV. to the accession of Richard was certainly written or dictated by Morton, for no one else could have been cognizant of some of the facts. The title given by the publisher is misleading. It is not a 'history of Richard III.,' but a very detailed narrative of the events from his brother's death to his own accession, covering a period of less than three months. It ends abruptly at a point just before the date of Morton's flight from England. His personal knowledge ceased with his departure, and here the story suddenly comes to an end. He was evidently acquainted personally with every detail, and he possessed an exceptionally accurate memory.[5] The errors and alterations of dates in the narrative must consequently have been made intentionally and with an object. Morton's character and the value of his testimony will be discussed more fully in a future chapter. The story of the murder of the young princes at the end of the book cannot have been written by Morton, for it alludes to events which happened after October 12, 1500, the date of that prelate's death. The outline of the story of the murder was no doubt inspired, as Lord Bacon shrewdly suspected, by Henry VII. himself.

Rastell assumed that the English version of this 'History of Richard III.' was composed by Sir Thomas More because a copy in his handwriting was found among his papers. The previous publication by Grafton proves that there were other copies abroad, differing slightly from each other, and there is no reason for assuming that the copy in More's handwriting was the original. Indeed there is evidence that it was not. Grafton's version contains a good deal at the end which is not in the narrative attributed to More by Rastell. The latter ends abruptly, as if the whole had not been copied. More merely made an unfinished copy. The respect with which this production has been treated is due to Sir Thomas More's reputed authorship, and to this is to be attributed its comparative freedom from criticism. It is in reality an unscrupulous party pamphlet, and its authorship ought not to affect its character. Yet the reply to any objection to statements contained in it has hitherto been that it was written by the good and virtuous Sir Thomas More, and therefore must be true.[6]

Internal evidence makes it certain that More did not write it. The author speaks of the death-bed of Edward IV. as an eye-witness.[7] More was then only five years of age. He was born in February 1478. This seems conclusive. Sir Thomas made an incomplete copy, when a young man, of a work which was attracting a good deal of attention, and of which there were other copies in circulation. The date of the copy is said by Rastell to be 1513, when More's age was about thirty-five. The actual compiler of the book, as we have it, is unknown. But the information and the inspiration of the whole work, with the exception of the story of the murder of the young princes at the end, is undoubtedly from Archbishop Morton. I have, therefore, referred to the work as by Morton, and to the story of the murders, which is clearly not by Morton, as by Rastell's anonymous historian.

Henry VII. began the business of vilifying his predecessor very early in his reign. It was indeed a matter of the utmost moment to him, for he appears to have considered that a belief in the alleged crimes of Richard was essential to the security of his own position. He brought over a blind Gascon from France, named Bernard André, whom he appointed his poet laureate and historiographer. André began to write a life of Henry VII. in 1500. It is very brief, with several gaps, and he left it incomplete when he died in about 1522.

But the Italian who arrived some years later in Henry's reign was far more serviceable. Polydore Virgil was the paid historian of the Tudors. He was a native of Urbino, and was sent to England by his patron, the infamous Pope Alexander VI., in 1501 as the assistant collector of the tax called Peter's pence. Henry requested him to undertake the history, placing all official materials at his disposal, and doubtless indicating the line he was to take. He proved an apt pupil and was well rewarded. He was made absentee Rector of Church Langton, received a prebend at Lincoln, another at Hereford, and was appointed Archdeacon of Wells. In 1513 he was made a Canon of St. Paul's with a house, and he had other preferment. His history was completed in 1534. Polydore Virgil was a man of learning, and his work is based on original research. But he did not hesitate to misrepresent facts not only to please his patrons, but in order to gratify his own spite and malignity.[8] In his account of events in the life of Richard III. he merely recorded the version that would be pleasing to his employer. His imperfect knowledge of the English language impairs the value of his evidence when obtained from oral sources. The tale of the assassination of young Edward of Lancaster by a King of England and his chief nobles is peculiarly Italian, and may be claimed by Polydore as his original conception. It is worthy of this protégé of the Borgias. His statements respecting King Richard deserve little credit, unless they are corroborated by independent evidence. Polydore had access to the written statements of Morton, of which he made considerable use. He also had the run of all official documents, and he is said to have made away with numerous original papers, which may be presumed to have disproved his assertions.[9] One most important document, which Henry ordered to be destroyed, has been preserved through a fortunate accident.[10]

These three writers, André, Morton, and Virgil, were employed by the Tudors, and considering the sources from whence their statements come, little weight ought to be attached to them. They are the paid, and very well paid, counsel and witnesses of King Richard's cunning enemy. 'The sagacious, patient, unchivalrous man,' says Mr. Campbell, 'although he rewarded his panegyrists with, for him, prodigal liberality, estimated with mercantile keenness the worth which their eulogies would bear in his own age.'[11]

The authors who wrote during the reign of Henry VII., but not in his pay or directly under his influence, next come under review. John Rous, the so-called hermit of Guy's Cliff, was an antiquary and an heraldic draughtsman. He knew Richard personally. He was the author of 'Historia Regum Angliæ,' which he dedicated to Henry VII., and in which he heaped virulent abuse on King Richard, crowding his venom into a page or two at the end—an after-thought to please his new patron. He also prepared two pictorial heraldic rolls, representing the pedigree of the Earls of

Warwick. Both were executed during the lifetime of King Richard. One is at Kimbolton, the other at the Heralds' College. To the latter Rous had access after the accession of Henry. To the former he had not. In the former Richard is described as 'a mighty Prince and special good Lord,' and as 'the most victorious Prince Richard III. In his realm full commendably punishing offenders of the laws, especially oppressors of his commons, and cherishing those that were virtuous, by the which discreet guiding he got great thanks and love of all his subjects rich and poor, and great laud of the people of all other lands about him.' The latter roll was still in the hands of Rous when Richard fell. The above passage is expunged. The portraits of the two Yorkist Kings are taken out. Queen Anne Nevill is despoiled of her crown, her son is deprived of crown and sceptre, and Richard is merely alluded to as Anne's 'infelix maritus.' The testimony of such an unblushing time-server as Rous must be rejected as worthless. Yet, in one or two instances, he has inadvertently revealed the truth, where the official writers have intended to conceal it.[12]

Robert Fabyan was a clothier and alderman of London, who recorded the events of earlier times and of his own day in a chronicle which was written during the reign of Henry VII.[13] He was a fulsome Tudor partisan, anxious to please the reigning powers, and ready to record any story against the fallen King, even to wholesale falsification of dates. It will be shown further on that, in concocting part of his chronicle, he must have been in dishonest collusion with Morton. Fabyan died in 1513, and his chronicle was first published in 1516. It was used by Polydore Virgil.

Dr. Warkworth, Master of Jesus College, Cambridge, wrote a diary which has chiefly been relied upon as evidence of the date of the death of Henry VI.,[14] but that question will be fully discussed in a future chapter.

Morton, Polydore Virgil, Rous, and Fabyan will be found to be dishonest and untrustworthy narrators, who can be shown to use deception deliberately, with a full knowledge of the truth. The second continuation of the Chronicle of Croyland Abbey occupies an entirely different position. There is every reason for believing that the monks who wrote it, though the first was prejudiced, and the second was credulous and easily deceived, intended to relate what they believed to be true. This continuation long remained in manuscript, in which state it was seen by Sir George Buck. It was not printed until 1684. It occupies twenty-eight folio pages.[15]

The first part of the continuation bears internal evidence of having been written by one monk who concludes with some local notices respecting the abbey and its inmates. Then another monk took up the chronicling pen, and ends his part in the same way. It is capable of absolute proof that this continuation of the Croyland Chronicle was written by at least two monks. In referring to the death of Henry VI., the first monk prays that the tyrant who caused it may be given time for repentance. This part must, therefore, have been written while the tyrant in question was alive, whether Edward IV., Richard, or Lord Rivers the Constable (who was really the responsible person) is intended. The second monk says at the end, that the work was finished on April 30, 1486, and that it was written in ten days. Edward, Richard and Rivers were all dead in April 1486. Consequently these two passages must have been written by different hands.

The first of these monks was the more judicious of the two, and he had probably once mixed in the world. He mentions a councillor of Edward IV. who was doctor of canon law, and who was sent to Abbeville on an embassy to the Duke of Burgundy in 1471. In the margin there is a note to the effect that the same man compiled that part of the chronicle. If this note is to be relied on, the first monk had once been in the service of Edward IV., but he had Lancastrian sympathies like Morton. He refers to the executions after Tewkesbury as vindictive, and he hints at a rumour that Henry VI. met his death by order of his successor. His part of the chronicle includes ten pages, and covers the period from 1471 to the death of Edward IV.

The second monk seems to have known nothing of the outer world, and was very credulous. It is with him that we have to do in this inquiry. He relates the events leading to the accession of Richard III. with general accuracy, and correctly as regards dates, the same dates being falsified by Morton and Fabyan. He even gives the true grounds on which Richard's claim to the crown rested, which are falsified by Morton and by Polydore Virgil, and which were forbidden by Henry VII. to be mentioned on pain of imprisonment. The chronicle remained in manuscript, and the truth-telling monk was not found out. The contribution of the second monk to the continuation of the Chronicle of Croyland Abbey was written out in ten days, and finished in the time of Henry VII., on April 30, 1486. Though generally trustworthy it contains several errors. It follows Morton, Polydore Virgil, and Fabyan in stating that Hastings was beheaded on the day of his arrest. It will be seen in Chapter III. that this is disproved by an investigation of dates given by those writers, and by Stallworthe. It follows Morton in the statement that Lord Rivers and his companions were beheaded without trial. This is disproved by Rous. It asserts that, after King Richard's coronation, there was a rumour that his nephews had been put to death. There is no other contemporaneous mention of this rumour, and reasons will presently be given for believing that there was no such rumour. It also states that Richard was crowned a second time at York. Mr.

Davies, in his 'York Records,' has shown that no such coronation ever took place.

The interesting question arises how the monk was misled on these four points, when his information was so accurate, and so directly contradicts Morton, Polydore Virgil, and Fabyan, as regards the dates of events immediately preceding Richard's accession, and as regards the nature of his claim to the throne. Could Morton have been at his elbow? If he was, these errors would be explained, for they are the most telling points in Morton's case. We know that Morton was sent to Brecknock Castle, in the custody of the Duke of Buckingham, in August 1483. Later in the autumn he escaped, crossed England in disguise, and was concealed for some time in the fen country near Ely, before taking ship for Flanders. He even mentions his object in going there. 'If he were in the Isle of Ely,' he told Buckingham, 'he could make many friends to further the enterprise.'[16] He went there to plot and intrigue. The secluded Abbey of Croyland is a likely asylum for Morton to have selected as a place of concealment. A political bishop who had been a principal actor in the recent events would be a Godsend to the chronicling monk; while the intriguer would be in his element, sowing the first seeds of his future crop of calumny. The second Croyland monk would be as clay in the potter's hand. He gives us a striking instance of his gossiping credulity. He had been told that the King's niece, Elizabeth, once appeared at Court in a dress similar to that of the Queen. Instead of the obvious deduction that Queen Anne had kindly provided the girl with a dress like her own, we are treated to dark hints about a rival who was to supplant the Queen, and modern historians have taken the old monk's nonsense in all seriousness. Morton would have found such a man quite ready to accept without further inquiry any statement he might make, and to be the channel of any rumour he chose to spread.

Such are the witnesses arrayed against the last Plantagenet King by his Tudor successors. It will be our business to test the value of their testimony. They had it all their own way. No one was allowed to answer them. For those who knew the truth it was a choice between silence and ruin. The accused had no counsel. Whether the Tudor writers are trustworthy or not, there can be no question that, aided by these advantages, they served their employers well. They have completely succeeded in their object. They have blackened the memory of King Richard III. for all time.

The chief evidence in Richard's favour can only now be found in the contradictions, admissions, inadvertent lapses into truth, and suppressions of his traducers. Official documents and private letters also tell their tale. Falsifications of dates, and the objects of such falsifications by the Tudor writers, are often detected by means of these unimpeachable sources of information. Among the Harleian manuscripts there is a book kept by Dr. Russell, the Bishop of Lincoln and Richard's Chancellor, containing all the documents that passed the Great or Privy Seal during his reign, as well as correspondence with foreign sovereigns and ambassadors.[17] This manuscript has been a mine of rebutting evidence. There is also valuable testimony derivable from the Rolls of Parliament, Patent Rolls, and from Rymer's 'Foedera.' It is worthy of special note that the undesigned evidence of official documents often exposes the true character of Tudor testimony.

Enough has been said to show that the statements of the Tudor writers call for more than ordinary caution in their use; and that the nearest approach to the truth, which is all we can hope for, will not be reached if any fact or insinuation alleged or hinted by them is accepted without being first subjected to very rigorous scrutiny.

The later chroniclers, such as Hall, Grafton, Holinshed, Stow and Buck, copied from the earlier writers. They cannot be considered as original authorities. Hall is little more than a translation of Polydore Virgil, served up with embellishments invented by himself. Stow is much more trustworthy.

These later writers must not be relied upon for facts. It was their habit to add numerous minor details to the stories they received from their predecessors, and it cannot reasonably be doubted that these additions were inventions intended to add force or interest to their narratives. When they quote from or insert documents the case is different. Thus Hall and Grafton give the conversation between Morton and the Duke of Buckingham at Brecknock, being a copy of some original document. Buck gives the substance of a letter from Elizabeth of York to the Duke of Norfolk, the original of which he had actually seen. He also quotes some older narrative for the imprisonment and death of King Richard's illegitimate son. Hall gives the proceedings of the Council when the imprisonment of the Queen Dowager, at Bermondsey, was ordered. In such cases only ought the evidence of the later writers to be accepted.

There was a reaction against the acceptance of all the statements put forth by Tudor writers, which began from the moment that it became safe to discuss the subject. The caricature was too gross, and too coarsely drawn for general acceptance. As soon as the last of the Tudors had passed away, Sir George Buck[18] wrote a defence of Richard III. He was followed by Carte in his History of England.[19] Rapin, although he felt obliged to repeat the stories of the Tudor writers, evidently had no confidence in their accuracy, and warned his readers against them more than once. Stronger views on the subject were adopted by

Horace Walpole in his 'Historic Doubts'[20] (1768), by Bayley in his 'History and Antiquities of the Tower of London,'[21] by Laing in his continuation of 'Henry's History of England,'[22] by Mr. Courtenay in his 'Commentaries on Shakespeare,'[23] by Miss Halsted in her 'Life of Richard III.'[24] and by Mr. Legge in his 'Unpopular King.'[25] Mr. Thorold Rogers rejects the story of the assassination of Henry VI.; Sharon Turner[26] and Jesse[27] acquit the accused King on all the counts except the murder of his nephews; while Dr. Hook,[28] Dr. Stubbs and Sir Harris Nicolas[29] are unable to believe all the accusations. The arguments put forward by some of these authors are not always tenable. But they show that there has been, from the time when discussion was first allowed, a revulsion of feeling among well-informed students against the acceptance of these accusations without close scrutiny. It was felt that the statements of Tudor writers must at least be considered as those of prejudiced and ex parte witnesses. Miss Halsted's 'Life of Richard III.' is by far the most complete and the most valuable. Her interest in the slandered young King led her to pay frequent visits to the ruins of Middleham Castle, the scene of Richard's boyhood and of his happy married life. Miss Halsted eventually married the dean of the college founded by Richard and lies buried in Middleham Church.

Tudor fables discredited
On the other hand, there have been a few historians who have approached the questions at issue either without considering the other side at all or with a strong though possibly unconscious bias. Hume only had a superficial knowledge of the subject. The most authoritative and important upholder of the Tudor accusations is Dr. Lingard.[30] He defends them in their entirety, and in this he stands alone among those who have really studied the subject. Mr. Gairdner[31] rejects some of the accusations

and supports other Tudor stories with hesitation, and in an apologetic and more or less doubtful tone. But Mr. Gairdner's knowledge of the subject is so exhaustive, and his position as a historian is so justly high, that I have devoted a separate chapter to the consideration of his views on the chief accusations against King Richard III.

The Tudor fables are now discredited and are dying, but they are dying hard.

[1] Richard II. was the first of our Kings, after the Norman Conquest, who was partly an Englishman. Henry V., Edward IV., and Richard III. were almost pure Englishmen. So was Edward VI., and Elizabeth was a thorough Englishwoman. Mary II. and Anne were half English.

[2] See p. 159, note 1.

[3] 'Dr. Morton had taken his revenge and written a book in Latin against King Richard, which came afterwards to the hands of Mr. More. The book was lately in the hands of Mr. Roper of Eltham, as Sir Edward Hoby, who saw it, told me.'—Buck, p. 75.

[4] 'Written as I have heard by Morton.'—Harington's Metamorphosis of Ajax, p. 46. Mr. Gairdner has suggested that the book attributed to More is a translation of one written in Latin by Morton. See Letters and Papers illustrative of the Reign of Richard III., &c. Preface xviii. (n). It is really the English version that was dictated or inspired by Morton.

[5] More's Utopia, p. 20.

[6] See for instance Sharon Turner (iii. 462), who claims unquestioning belief in this scurrilous production, because 'all confess More's ability and integrity.' See also Jesse (p. 156 n. and p. 500).

In the same spirit Sir John Harington defended his own filthy treatise because 'the worthy and incorrupt Master More' was dirty in his History of Richard III. These writers seem to think that falsehood becomes truth, and obscenity becomes decency in this book, merely because its authorship is attributed to More. See Metamorphosis of Ajax, p. 46.

[7] 'As I myself, who wrote this pamphlet, truly know.' This is not in Rastell's version; but in the continuation of Hardyng's Chronicle.

[8] Speaking of Polydore Virgil in his Life of Henry VIII. (p. 9), Lord Herbert of Cherbury adds: 'in whom I have observed not a little malignity.' The story of Cardinal Wolsey's ingratitude to Fox owes its parentage to the spite of Polydore Virgil; whom Wolsey imprisoned. It was quite untrue.—Brewer.

[9] 'Polydore Virgil committed as many of our ancient manuscript volumes to the flames as would have filled a waggon, that the faults of his own work might pass undiscovered.'—Caius, De Antiquitate Cantabrigiæ (1574), p. 52.

'Polydore caused all the histories to be burnt which by the King's authority and the assistance of his friends he could possibly come at.'—La Poplinière, Histoire des Histoires, ix. 485.

[10] The Act of Parliament explaining the title of Richard III. to the crown.

[11] Mr. Campbell's Introduction to the Materials for the History of the Reign of Henry VII.

[12] Rous was one of the Chantry Priests at Guy's Cliff. He died in 1491, and was buried at St. Mary's, Warwick.

[13] One proof of this is that he calls Lord Stanley the Earl of Derby. He was created Earl of Derby by Henry VII.

[14] Rerum Anglicarum scriptorum veterum. Tom. i. (Oxoniæ, 1684.)

[15] Alia Hist. Croylandensis continuatio, pp. 549-578.

[16] Grafton, p. 130.

[17] Harl. MS. 433.

[18] Sir George Buck was descended from John Buck, comptroller of King Richard's household, who was put to death after the battle of Bosworth. Sir George served with the Earl of Essex in the Cadiz expedition of 1596. He was knighted by James I. in July 1603, and became Master of the Bevels in 1610, a post which he held until 1622. He died on September 22, 1623. His History of the Life and Reign of King Richard III., composed in five books, was published in 1646, with 'George Buck, Esq.,' as author. But the existence of the manuscript in the British Museum, with Sir George as the author, and in his handwriting, proves the substitution of 'Esquire' for 'Sir' to be a mistake. Camden speaks of Buck as a man of distinguished learning.

[19] Thomas Carte, History of England to 1654 inclusive. 4 vols. folio. 1753.

[20] Horace Walpole, Historic Doubts on the Life and Reign of Richard III., 4to. 1768.

[21] John Bayley, History and Antiquities of the Tower of London, 2 vols. 4to. 1821.

[22] Laing, Continuation of the History of Great Britain by Dr. Henry. 1795.

[23] J. P. Courtenay, Commentaries on the Plays of Shakespeare, 2 vols. 8vo. 1840.

[24] Miss Halsted, Life of Richard III. 2 vols. 8vo. 1844.

[25] Alfred O. Legge, The Unpopular King. Life and Times of Richard III. 2 vols. 8vo. 1883.

[26] Sharon Turner, History of England during the Middle Ages. 5 vols. 8vo. 1830.

[27] John H. Jesse, Memoirs of King Richard III. 8vo. 1862.

[28] Dr. W. F. Hook, D.D., Lives of the Archbishops of Canterbury. 9 vols. 8vo. 1860-72. He considers the slander of the Duchess of York incredible.

[29] Sir N. H. Nicolas, Privy Purse Expenses of Elizabeth of York. 1830. He utterly rejects the story of Richard having poisoned his wife, and having wanted to marry Elizabeth of York (p. liii.) Dr. W. Stubbs, Constitutional History of England, vol. ii. Thorold Rogers, Work and Wages, ii. 212.

[30] Dr. Lingard, History of England to the Revolution. 4th ed. 1837; 6th ed. 1854.

[31] James Gairdner, Letters and Papers Illustrative of the Reigns of Richard III. and Henry VII. 1861-63. Memorials of Henry VII. 1858. History of the Life and Reign of Richard III. 1878. Life of Henry VII. 1889. Article in the English Historical Review. 1891.

CHAPTER II EXAMINATION OF THE CHARGES AGAINST RICHARD III

1. The Deformity.
2. Murder of Edward of Lancaster.
3. Murder of Henry VI.
4. Marriage with Anne Nevill.
5. Treatment of the Countess of Warwick.
6. Death of Clarence.

An indictment, in many counts, was brought against Richard III. after his death, by the authors who wrote during the reign of his successor, and in the interests of that successor's dynasty. It will be seen, in the course of the discussion, with what object these accusations were made, and why a belief in them was considered to be so important to the success of the Tudor usurpation. The reckless profusion of abuse was due to the complete license of the traducers. No one could appear for the accused. The brave young King was dead, his body subjected to cowardly insults, his friends proscribed, his people silenced. Calumny was triumphant and unchecked. Yet there was method and system in the scheme of the Tudor writers. Their accusations were all intended to lead up to a belief in the dead King's guilt with regard to one central crime. If he was to be deformed, if he was to be an assassin at the age of eighteen, the murderer of his brother and his wife, a ruthless usurper and tyrant, it was because such a monster would be more likely to commit a crime of which he must be thought to be guilty in the interests of his wily successor. It will now be our business to examine these charges one by one. The first concerns Richard's personal appearance.

It is stated that he was two years in his mother's womb,[1] that he was born feet foremost,[2] with a complete set of teeth,[3] and with hair down to the shoulders,[4] that he was hump-backed, that his right shoulder was higher than his left,[5] that his left shoulder was much higher than his right,[6] and that one of his arms was withered.[7]

Passing over the obvious fables with the remark that they throw just suspicion on other statements from the same sources, we come to the hump-back. We do not find this deformity mentioned by any contemporary except Morton. If it had existed it is certain that so conspicuous a blemish would have been dwelt upon by all contemporary detractors. Stow, the most honest of the later chroniclers, told Sir George Buck that he had talked to old men who had seen and known Richard, and who said that he was in bodily shape comely enough.[8] In the two portraits drawn by Rous no inequality is visible. Richard here has a handsome youthful face, slight build and good figure. The portrait at Windsor shows a face full of energy and decision, yet gentle and melancholy. The shoulders are quite even.

Rous, Polydore Virgil, and Morton are the authorities for the unequal shoulders. Rous says that the right shoulder was higher. Morton makes the left shoulder much higher. Their contradictory testimony shows the worthless character of both these authorities. Polydore Virgil merely mentions an inequality. Fabyan and the Croyland monk do not say a word against Richard's personal appearance. A curious piece of evidence was discovered by Mr. Davies of York, which bears on the question.[9] From the 'York Records' it appears that, six years after King Richard's death, a man named Burton was brought before the Lord Mayor accused of calling that prince, whose memory was so beloved in the north, 'a crouchback.' One John Poynter, who heard this remark, told Burton that he lied, and struck at him with a little rod he had in his hand. It would seem, therefore, that if there was any defect in Richard's figure, it was so slight that its very existence was matter of dispute among those who could well remember the King, while it was imperceptible to Stow's informants. On the whole, we may accept the conclusion of Miss Halsted that Richard was of slight and delicate build, and that the severe martial exercises in which his youth had been spent had caused the shoulder of his sword-arm to be very slightly higher than the other.

The story of the withered arm comes from Morton. That astute prelate always had an object in making his statements. This particular tale was invented to draw off attention from the real charge made by the Protector against the Woodvilles. It served its turn, and may be dismissed as false without any hesitation. For it is not mentioned by a single other authority. The victor of Barnet and Tewkesbury, the leader of the brilliant charge at Bosworth, who unhorsed Sir John Cheney[10] and William Brandon, must have had serviceable arms.

The object of the Tudor historians in commencing their grotesque caricature of an imaginary monster with these stories of his personal deformity is transparent. They intended to make him detestable from the outset. They calculated that improbable crimes would be more readily believed if the alleged perpetrator was a deformed hunchback born with teeth. They were right. Nothing has more conduced to an unreasoning prejudice against Richard, and to a firm belief in his alleged crimes, than the impression of his personal repulsiveness.

Modern writers have also understood this method of treatment. Lord Macaulay was careful to prepare the minds of his readers for the alleged judicial crimes of Sir Elijah by telling them that little Impey was in the habit of stealing cakes at school.[11] The great essayist, as well as the Tudor historians, knew their public. The one invented the pilfering story and the others the deformity with the same motive. If a judge had been a juvenile thief, or if a king had been a deformed little monster, the charges against them in after life would be more readily accepted as true. It is illogical, but it is human nature.

Richard was described as a venomous hunchback[12] and made to commit several atrocious crimes in order to prepare men's minds to receive, without incredulity, the story of the murder of his nephews. It was evidently anticipated that this final draft on their powers of belief would be dishonoured unless the alleged murderer had been steeped in crime from his infancy.

At the early age of eighteen Richard is accordingly accused of having committed a cowardly and inhuman murder in cold blood after the battle of Tewkesbury, on evidence which would be insufficient to hang a dog.[13]

The battle took place on May 4, 1471. The young Duke of Gloucester had displayed valour and generalship, and had won for himself a name in chivalry. On the other side, Prince Edward of Lancaster, who was exactly one year younger than Richard, led the main battle of his army, and bore himself manfully. Carried away in the rout and closely followed by his victorious enemies, he was slain on the field of battle. There was one eye-witness who wrote an account of the battle of Tewkesbury. He said that young Edward of Lancaster 'was taken fleeing to the townwards and slain in the field.'[14] A drawing accompanies this writer's report, in which we see a horse on its knees, the rider receiving his deathblow, the helmet struck off, and the bright golden locks sinking on the horse's mane.[15] This was the plain truth. He fell, fighting bravely, on the battlefield. All contemporaries, without an exception, corroborate this evidence. The next writer was Warkworth, but he was not present. He wrote 'There was slain on the field Prince Edward, which cried for succour to the Duke of Clarence.'[16] Bernard André, the paid historian of Henry VII., says the same, 'Is enim ante Bernardi campum Theoxberye proelio belligerens ceciderat.' The Croyland monk says that some of the Lancastrian leaders fell in the battle, others 'by the revengeful hands of certain persons afterwards,'[17] referring to the fact that some were executed after trial before the Earl Marshal and Constable. There is no hint here of the alleged assassination of Edward. Comines tells the same story, 'et fut le Prince de Galles tué sur le champ et plusieurs autres grans seigneurs.' Such is the unanimous testimony of contemporaries.

We now come to the other Tudor writers and their versions of young Edward's death. Fabyan, writing to please Henry VII., is the first who said that the Prince was captured and brought before Edward IV., and he added the following tale: 'The King strake him with his gauntlet in the face, on which the Prince was by the King's servants incontinently slain.'[18] Fabyan's baseless gossip came before Polydore Virgil, and the protégé of Pope Alexander VI. conceived the idea of giving it a lurid Borgian colouring, better suited to the latitude of Urbino than to that of Tewkesbury and calculated to make our flesh creep. It was thus that his ideas found words: 'King Edward gave no answer, only thrusting the young man from him with his hand, whom forthwith those that were present, who were George Duke of Clarence, Richard Duke of Gloucester, and William Lord Hastings, crewelly murderyd.'[19] This story was improved upon by Grafton, Hall, Holinshed and other Tudor chroniclers. Dorset was added to the list of alleged assassins by Habington, Grafton, and Hall. Gloucester is made to strike the first blow by Holinshed. Here we have a striking example of the gradual growth of a legend which has eventually become embedded in history.[20] Its original conception was due to an Italian, not to an English brain. It is thus that the fable has become a part of the history of England. Honest John Stow is alone in rejecting the Italian's embellishment. He discredits the version of Polydore Virgil as a palpable fraud, and merely repeats Fabyan's statement.

It is very remarkable that three authorities patronised by Henry VII. give no countenance to the fable of Polydore Virgil. Bernard André is in perfect agreement with the contemporaries, simply because Virgil's story had not been invented when he wrote. Rous is silent for the same reason. He was the originator of the birth with teeth and with hair to the shoulders. He heaped calumny on calumny, and would have eagerly repeated the Tewkesbury story if it had existed in his time. Morton's silence is still more singular except on the hypothesis that the slander was not then in existence.

Dr. Morton was actually present at Tewkesbury. If young Edward was murdered he must have known it. Yet in a work prepared for the express purpose of enumerating the alleged crimes of Richard he said nothing. He had no scruples. He repeats all he can think of, with the object of heaping opprobrium on Richard's memory. But there is not a hint about assassinating Edward of Lancaster. Morton's silence, under these circumstances, amounts to a proof that the story was a fabrication of later times. André, Rous, and Morton wrote before Polydore Virgil, and when the Italian's calumny had not yet been invented. It cannot be that Virgil found out what the less vigilant André, Rous, and Morton overlooked. If anyone knew all the details of the battle of Tewkesbury at first hand, it was Morton. He was there. His silence explodes the fable. It also convicts

Polydore Virgil of having fabricated an exceptionally foul slander, with a rank scent of its Borgian origin:—

'Virgilii duo sunt: alter Maro: tu Polydore
   Alter: Tu Mendax: ille Poeta fuit.'[21]

Unless the testimony of those who were absent, and for the most part unborn, is to be preferred to that of eye-witnesses, and that of future generations to contemporaries, the fable of young Edward's murder ought never again to find a place in serious history.

The charge against the Duke of Gloucester that he murdered Henry VI. is an insinuation rather than an accusation. None of his traducers state it as a fact. One says 'as men constantly say,' another, 'it was the continual report,' another, 'as many believe.' We must, therefore, first treat this alleged 'continual report' as a rumour only, and judge of it from probabilities.

We are asked to believe that young Richard, a boy of eighteen, who had just won great military renown, arrived at the Tower in the evening of one day with orders to proceed on active service very early the next morning; that, although fully occupied with preparations for his departure, he found time to induce Lord Rivers, the Constable of the Tower, and his political enemy, to deliver up charge to him in order that he might assassinate a defenceless and feeble invalid with his own hand, a deed which might just as well have been perpetrated by any hired jailer; that it was done without his brother Edward's knowledge, and that, although the deed must have been done with the knowledge of Lord Rivers and his officials, of Henry's ten servants and three readers, yet there was never any certainty about the matter. Rivers, be it remembered, was not Richard's friend.

This grossly improbable rumour bears the evidence of its origin clearly marked. It was put forward in the reign and in the interests of Henry VII. It was a rumour manufactured by his paid writers and their followers. We can examine the process.

Morton says: 'He slew with his own hand King Henry VI. as men constantly say, and that without knowledge or commandment of the King.'

Polydore Virgil has the following version: 'King Edward, to the intent that there should be no new insurrections, travelled not long after through Kent, which business being despatched, to the intent that every man might conceive a perfect peace to be attained, Henry VI. being not long before deprived of his diadem, was put to death in the Tower of London. The continual report is that Richard Duke of Gloucester killed him with a sword, whereby his brother might be delivered from all hostility.'

Dr. Warkworth tells us that 'the same night that King Edward came to London, King Harry being in ward in prison in the Tower of London, was put to death on the 21st of May on a Tuesday night between eleven and twelve of the clock, being then at the Tower the Duke of Gloucester, brother to King Edward, and many others. On the morrow he was chested, and brought to Paul's and his face was open that every man might see him. And in his lying he bled on the pavement there, and afterwards at the Blackfriars was brought, and there bled afresh.' This Dr. Warkworth was Master of St. Peter's College, Cambridge, from 1473 to 1500. He kept a private diary, receiving his facts from informants he saw at Cambridge. His account of Henry's death shows that he was superstitious and credulous. His second-hand report of the time and manner of the death cannot be received as of any authority. His mention of

Gloucester's presence has been assumed to be intended, by the writer, to imply that the Duke was concerned in the crime. This does not follow and, in a mere private diary, such innuendo would be out of place and improbable. The date of the 21st, given by Warkworth and Fabyan, would be approved by Henry VII. as throwing suspicion on his predecessor, and would be fixed as the obit of Henry VI. Any subsequent repetition of that date gives it no additional authority. Such repetition has as much or as little authority as is given to it by the assertions of Warkworth and Fabyan.[22]

Fabyan gives the same date as Warkworth, and adds, 'of the death of Henry divers tales were told, but the most common fame went that he was stikked with a dagger, by the hands of Richard of Gloucester.'[23]

Rous says, 'He killed by others or, as many believe, with his own hand, that most sacred man Henry VI.'[24]

The continuator of the Croyland Chronicle insinuates nothing against Richard. His words are: 'The body of King Henry was found lifeless in the Tower; may God pardon and give time for repentance to that man, whoever he was, that dared to lay his sacrilegious hand upon the Lord's anointed. The doer may obtain the name of a tyrant, the sufferer of a glorious martyr.'[25] The antithesis of tyrant and martyr shows that the monk alluded to King Edward and King Henry. The prayer that 'the doer' may have time for repentance is a proof that the passage was written during Edward's lifetime, and that there was then a rumour that Henry had met with foul play. But it also furnishes a proof that rumour had not then imputed the supposed act to Richard.

Of these authorities, Warkworth's informant and the City Chronicler are the only two who perceived that in order to give any plausibility to the alleged 'continual report,' Henry's death must be made to tally with young Richard's presence in the Tower. They, therefore, fixed upon May 21, the single day when Richard was there. Their fabrication is exposed by the evidence of the accounts for Henry's maintenance, as will be seen directly; and also by the contradiction of Polydore Virgil. That author, who had access to all official sources of information, places Henry's death in the end of May, after King Edward's progress through Kent. Thus these authorities do not agree, and are quite unworthy of credit.

We are not altogether without the means of ascertaining the truth. Henry VI. was not an old man. His age was 47. But he was feeble and half-witted. His health was very precarious, his constitution having been weakened by long illnesses. He inherited the mental and physical imbecility of his grandfather Charles VI. of France. Shortly before his liberation by the Earl of Warwick in 1470, some ruffian had stabbed him[26] and then fled. Henry was said to have been convalescent, but, with his feeble hold on life, it is not likely that his recovery was permanent. He gradually sank, and died on May 24, or perhaps in the night of the 23rd. Queen Margaret of Anjou arrived at the Tower as a prisoner on the 21st, just in time to soothe her husband's last moments, and to be with him when he died. The Lancastrian leanings of the family of Lord Rivers, who was Constable of the Tower, make it likely that the unhappy queen was granted access to her dying husband. We know that Margaret was treated with consideration, and allowed to reside with her most intimate English friend, the old Duchess of Suffolk, at Wallingford, until her ransom was paid.

The date of Henry's death is fixed by the evidence of his household accounts, which are given by Rymer.

'Accounts of the costs and expenses for the custody of King Henry, The Wednesday after the feast of Holy Trinity, June 12.'

'To the same William Sayer for money to his own hand delivered for the expenses and diet of the said Henry and of ten persons his attendants within the tower, for the custody of the said Henry, namely, for fourteen days the first beginning on the 11th of May last, as per account delivered 14l. 5s.'

'To William Sayer for money delivered at times, namely at one time, 7s. for the hire of three hired readers for the said William and other attendants within the tower in charge of the King for xiv days and for the board of the same for the same time, and on another time 3s. 10d. for the board of said Henry within the said tower as per account delivered 10s. 10d.'[27]

It is clear from these entries that Henry's accounts were made up on May 11, and that they were again made up when he died, fourteen days after May 11, that is, on May 24.[28] We also gather that he was maintained in becoming state, at a cost of 400l. a year, equivalent to upwards of 2,000l. of our money, and that he had ten servants, and three readers to read aloud to him. Mr. Thorold Rogers says: 'I make no doubt that Henry was used well during the nine years of his residence in the Tower: nor do I believe that he was done to death after Tewkesbury. The story of his assassination in the Tower is, I am persuaded, a Tudor calumny.'[29] 'I conclude that nature which had hid his misfortunes from him more than once by a lethargy which seemed almost like death, at last released him in the same merciful fashion from the recurrent sorrows of his life.'[30]

The only contemporary writer was the author of a letter to the citizens of Bruges, giving an account of the events which led to the restoration of Edward IV. Speaking from personal knowledge he reported that Henry VI. died on May 23, and his accuracy is established by the evidence of the accounts.

These are the plain facts connected with Henry's death. They are fatal to the story of the murder. Warkworth and Fabyan give the 21st for the date of Henry's death, because Gloucester was in the Tower on that day only. Their assertions are disproved by Polydore Virgil, by the writer of the letter at Bruges, and by the accounts which show the date of Henry's death to have been May 23 or 24. On those days Gloucester was at Sandwich, upwards of seventy miles from the Tower. The tale of Henry's assassination by the Duke of Gloucester is a Tudor calumny, and was invented many years afterwards to please Henry VII. It is possible that a false rumour of foul play may have been spread by the enemies of Edward IV., and this seems likely from the words of the Croyland Chronicle. But the absurd accusation against the King's young brother was concocted after Richard III. had fallen at Bosworth, and when any calumny against the dead was welcomed and rewarded by a successor, who believed that his security depended upon a belief in his predecessor's infamy. Habington, in his life of Edward IV., has pointed out the absurdity of charging Richard with the alleged murder.[31]

The next charge against the Duke of Gloucester is that he forced the Lady Anne Nevill to marry him, immediately after he had murdered young Edward of Lancaster, who was her husband.[32] The answers to this are that Edward was not her husband,[33] that Richard did not murder him, and that Richard did not force Anne's inclinations. No marriage between Edward and Anne ever took place. The Croyland monk always speaks of Anne, at this time, as the 'maiden' and the 'damsel.'

But there is more to be said. The two young cousins, Richard and Anne, were brought up together, and their union was most natural. Miss Halsted has well remarked that Richard showed peculiar delicacy towards Anne, in placing her in sanctuary at St. Martin's before the marriage, where her inclinations could in no way be forced. Anne was her husband's constant companion at every important crisis of his life, and there is good reason to believe that the marriage was a happy one.

A very bitter enemy of Richard's memory, in later times, has attempted to draw conclusions to his disadvantage from the marriage settlements. There had been no time to obtain the usual dispensations, and it therefore became advisable that the trustees, for the sake of the offspring, should guard against any possible informality in the marriage. A protecting clause was inserted, in case the property could not be held without a renewal of the marriage ceremony; arising from any alleged informality in the nuptials. This clause, framed by the lawyers, was to the effect that if the Duke of Gloucester and the Lady Anne Nevill should be divorced, and afterwards marry again, the Act for the partition of property should nevertheless be valid, and that in case of a divorce, and if the Duke shall do his continual diligence and effectual devoir by all lawful means to be lawfully married to the said Anne, he shall have as much of the premises as pertained to her during her lifetime. It was merely a formal clause inserted by the lawyers, and probably never even read by Richard or Anne.

Miss Strickland calls this 'an ominous clause relating to a wedlock of a few months; proving Anne meditated availing herself of some informality in her abhorred marriage; but if she had done so her husband would have remained in possession of her property. The absence of the dispensation is a negative proof that Anne never consented to her second marriage, and that it was never legalised may be guessed by the rumours of a subsequent period when the venomous hunchback meditated in his turn divorcing her.'

This is a good example of the sort of stuff which rooted and unreasoning prejudice allows to pass for argument.

The next charge is made by only one of the Tudor writers. Rous alleged that 'Richard imprisoned for life the Countess of Warwick who had fled to him for refuge.'[34] This is untrue. The Countess of Warwick heard of the defeat and death of her husband at Barnet, when she landed in England. She took sanctuary at Beaulieu in Hampshire, was attainted, and all her property passed to her daughters Isabella and Anne, who married the Dukes of Clarence and Gloucester. The Countess remained at Beaulieu for two years, from 1471 to 1473. We next hear of her in a letter from Sir John Paston dated June 3, 1473. 'The Countess of Warwick is now out of Beaulieu, and Sir James Tyrrel conveyeth her northward, men say by the King's assent, whereto some men say that the Duke of Clarence is not agreed.'[35] Evidently the King had given his assent to a request of Gloucester that his wife's mother might be allowed to come and live with her daughter at Middleham. There was no prison but a home with her child. Tyrrel, who was then an officer of Edward's Court, was sent to escort her from Beaulieu to Middleham.[36]

There is evidence of Richard's kindly feeling towards his wife's family. He interceded for the heirs of the Marquis

Montagu, Warwick's brother, and it was at the request of Gloucester that the King allowed them to inherit part of their father's property.[37] Another indication of the Duke's friendliness, as regards his mother-in-law and her relations, is afforded by their confidence in him. Lady Latimer, a sister of the Countess of Warwick, appointed Richard the supervisor of her will, which was a position of great trust in those days. Such kindly offices performed for those who were near and dear to the Countess of Warwick are cogent, though indirect, proofs that the statement of Rous is a calumny.

Shakespeare and others have further accused Richard of having abetted and aided in the death of his brother George Duke of Clarence. No serious historian, except Sandford, has ventured to bring forward the charge directly. The Croyland monk, Polydore Virgil, André, Rous, Fabyan are all silent on the subject.[38] But Morton is equal to the occasion. The passage in which he insinuates suspicion is a good specimen of the style of this unscrupulous slanderer:

'Some wise men also ween that his drift, covertly conveyed, lacked not in helping forth his brother of Clarence to his death; which he resisted openly, howbeit somewhat, as men deemed, more faintly than he that were heartily minded to his wealth. And they who thus deem think that he, long time in King Edward's life, forethought to be King in case that the King his brother (whose life he looked that evil diet should shorten) should happen to decease (as indeed he did) while his children were young. And they deem that for this intent he was glad of his brother's death, the Duke of Clarence, whose life must needs have hindered him so intending whether the same Clarence had kept him true to his nephew the young King, or enterprised to be King himself. But of all this point there is no certainty, and whoso divineth upon conjectures may as well shoot too far as too short.'

The object of this involved passage is to leave a sort of general impression that Richard had something or other to do with the death of Clarence.[39] By throwing up a dust cloud of verbiage the central fact that Richard intervened in his brother's favour is obscured and thrown into the background.

The guilt of the death of Clarence rests with Rivers and the Woodville faction. He was a great danger to them, as will be seen in the next chapter, while they benefited by his attainder and got the wardship of his son. All Richard did was to protest against the execution of his brother.

[1] Rous, 214. 'Biennio matris utero tentus, exiens cum dentibus et capillis ad humeros.' This is false, for Richard was born three years after his brother George, and there was another child, named Thomas, between them.

[2] Morton.

[3] Rous.

[4] Rous.

[5] Rous.

[6] Morton.

[7] Morton.

[8] Buck, p. 79.

[9] Davies, York Records, May 14, 1190, p. 220.

[10] 'A man of much fortitude, and exceeding the common sort.'—Polydore Virgil, p. 224.

[11] In Macaulay's review of Gleig's Life of Warren Hastings.

[12] Miss Strickland.

[13] Mr. Gairdner gives the evidence. 'Each crime rests on slender testimony enough, though any one of them being admitted, lends greater credit to the others. From this point of view it is not at all improbable that Richard was a murderer at nineteen' (p. 13). Richard killed his nephews, consequently he assassinated a prisoner when he was nineteen. It thus having been shown that he was a murderer

when he was nineteen, what more probable than that he killed his nephews? This method of arguing has been perfectly satisfactory to generations of historical students, and appears to be so still.

[14] Fleetwood Chron. p. 30. This is the narrative of the recovery of his kingdom by Edward IV., in Harl. MS. no. 543, printed by the Camden Society.

[15] The drawing is in the abridgment sent to Bruges, reproduced in the Archæologia, xxi. p. ii.

[16] Warkworth Chronicle, Camden Society, p. 18.

[17] The Croyland monk wrote: 'As well in the field as afterwards by the revengeful hands of certain persons, Prince Edward, Devon, Somerset,' &c.: that is Prince Edward and Devon on the field, Somerset by 'the revengeful hands': by which phrase he is pleased to refer to the Earl Marshal's Court which was a constitutional tribunal (Chron. Croyland, p. 555). 'Tum in campo tum postea ultricibus quorundam manibus, ipso Principe Edwardo unigenito Regis Henrici, victo Duce Somersetiæ, Comiteque Devoniæ ac aliis dominis omnibus et singulis memoratis' (p. 555).

[18] Fabyan, p. 662.

[19] Polydore Virgil, p. 336.

[20] Hall is notorious for the embellishment of fables that were passed on to him by Polydore Virgil, by adding names and incidents of his own invention. In the case of the death of the young Earl of Rutland, he first took several years off his age and made a little child of him, then gave him a tutor and supplied the tutor's name. With these properties he got

up a very effective scene on Wakefield Bridge. When Rutland's real age is known, Hall's story becomes absurd, and he is convicted of intentional inaccuracy. Again when he described the burial of Henry VI., he said that the corpse was conveyed to Chertsey 'without priest or clerk, torch or taper, singing or saying.' This is something worse than embellishment, it is absolutely false. The payments are recorded (and the records are still preserved), for obsequies and masses said by four orders of brethren, for linen cloth, spices, and for wages of men carrying torches. The statements of Hall are certainly unreliable. In retailing Polydore Virgil's calumny about the assassination of Prince Edward at Tewkesbury, Hall cannot refrain from similar inventions and embellishments. He adds that Edward was taken prisoner by Sir Richard Croft and delivered up to the King in consequence of a proclamation offering a reward of 100l. a year to whosoever should yield up the Prince dead or alive: accompanied by an assurance that his life should be spared (Hall, p. 301). Habington repeats this and adds, as his own contribution, that 'the good knight repented what he had done, and openly professed his service abused and his faith deluded' (Life of Edward IV. p. 96). This statement is confuted by the fact that it was on the battle-field of Tewkesbury that Richard Croft received his knighthood from King Edward. This would not have been so if he had 'openly declared his service abused.' He afterwards received benefits from King Richard (Paston Letters). The fable of Fabyan was embellished and added to by various hands, until it became a very elaborate and highly finished lie circumstantial.

[21] The name of Virgil borne by two,
    One Maro and one Polydore.
    The first a Poet wise and true,
    The last a lying slanderer.

[22] Mr. Gairdner mentions that there is a MS. City Chronicle among the Cottonian MSS. (Vitell. A. xvi. f. 133), which states that Henry's body was brought to St. Paul's on Ascension Eve (May 22), 'who was slain, as it was said, by the Duke of Gloucester.' In MS. Arundel, 28, in the British Museum, there is an old Chronicle, on a fly-leaf of which, at the end, there are some jottings relating to Edward IV.'s time in a contemporary hand, and among others—'eodem die decessit Henricus sextus,' meaning the day of Edward's arrival in London. A MS. in Heralds' College (printed by Mr. Gairdner) dates the death 'in vigilia Ascencionis Dominicæ'; a MS. at Oxford (Laud, 674) gives the same date; a MS. in the Royal Library at the British Museum says: 'Obitus Regis Henriei Sexti, gui obiit inter vicesimum primum diem Maii et xxiim diem Maii.' Henry's obit is set down May 22. None of these documents have any date. Their statements about May 21 are the same as those of Warkworth or Fabyan, from whom they must have been derived. But Warkworth and Fabyan are proved to be wrong by the evidence of the accounts for Henry's maintenance: and by the evidence of Polydore Virgil, as well as by the letter at Bruges.

[23] Fabyan, p. 662.

[24] Rous, p. 215. 'Ipsum sanctissimum virum Henricum Sextum per alios vel multis credentibus manu pocius propria interfecit.'

[25] Croyland Chron. p. 557.

[26] 'Collectarum et mansuetudinum et bonorum morum regis Henrici VI., et ex collectione magistri Joannis Blakman bacchalaurii theologiæ et post Cartusiæ monachi Londini.'—Hearne, p. 202.

[27] Rymer's Foedera, xi. pp. 712, 713.

[28] Laing, in his continuation of Henry's History of Great Britain, in referring to the accounts for the maintenance of Henry VI. in Rymer's Foedera, mistook the day on which they were audited and passed, namely June 12, for the day on which the expenses were incurred; and concluded that Henry was alive on June 12. This is triumphantly pointed out by Dr. Lingard. But the triumph is imaginary. Dr. Lingard ought to have seen that the date of auditing does not affect the question. The fact remains that Henry's board was paid, and that he was consequently alive, for fourteen days after May 11, that is until May 24, which is fatal to the story of the murder.

This is shown by Bayley, who quotes the accounts in his History of the Tower of London, and points out that they furnish satisfactory evidence of Henry having been alive at least until May 24 (second ed. p. 323). Mr. Gairdner has suggested that the payments up to the 24th were to Henry's servants who were not discharged until then, and do not prove that Henry was alive. But this is untenable, for they are for Henry's keep as well.

[29] Work and Wages, ii. 312.

[30] Ibid. ii. 313.

[31] 'I cannot believe a man so cunning in declining envy and winning honour to his name, would have undertaken such a business and executed it with his own hand. Nor did this concern the Duke of Gloucester so particularly as to engage him alone in the cruelty.'—Habington, in Kennet, p. 455.

[32] Gairdner, p. 22.

[33] Sharon Turner, iii. p. 323. Anne had been contracted to Edward of Lancaster in July 1470, she being only fourteen, and he sixteen; but she was never married to him. The marriage was not to take place unless certain conditions were complied with by Anne's father, the Earl of Warwick. The conditions were not fulfilled, and the contract, ipso facto, was null and void.

[34] Rous, p. 215. 'Durante vita sua incarceravit.' The Countess out-lived Richard III.

[35] Paston Letters, iii. p. 92.

[36] Mr. Gairdner quotes a letter from William Dengayn to William Calthorp (Third Report of Hist. MSS. Commission, p. 272), from which it appears that the Countess of Warwick was actually with the Duke of Gloucester in June 1473.—Gairdner's Richard III. p. 27 (n).

[37] Rot. Parl. vi. 124.

[38] Gloucester was in London at the opening of Parliament on January 16, 1478; but there is no evidence where he was in February, the month of Clarence's death. He was certainly at Middleham in March. Mr. Gairdner pronounces Gloucester 'guiltless of his brother's death' (p. 40).

[39] Morton did this so successfully that his imitators soon began to make a direct accusation. The slander grew and prospered until at last we find the following passage in Sandford: 'He was drowned in a butt of malmsey, his brother the Duke of Gloucester assisting thereat with his own proper hands!' He refers to Hall, p. 246.—Genealogical History (London, 1707), p. 438.

CHAPTER III FURTHER CHARGES AGAINST RICHARD III

7. Execution of Hastings.
8. Execution of Rivers, Vaughan, Grey, and Haute.
9. The 'Usurpation.'
10. Refusal of Buckingham's petition.
11. Second coronation at York.
12. Poisoning of his wife.
13. Intended marriage with Elizabeth of York.
14. Intended execution of Lord Strange.

The most elaborate and detailed part of the indictment against Richard III. refers to the so-called 'usurpation,' including the period from his arrival in London to his coronation. The events of the interregnum had to be represented in such a way as that it should appear that Henry Tudor was righteously superseding an unscrupulous usurper. This was a matter of vital importance to the intruding dynasty. Accordingly much art was devoted to the preparation of a plausible story, while careful but not always effectual efforts were made to destroy all documents that would contradict it.

The portion of the history published by Grafton and Rastell was undoubtedly written or dictated by John Morton himself. It is on Morton's story that all subsequent historians have relied for their facts; and as it is on this period that the whole career of Richard as a sovereign hinges, it is necessary that we should bear in mind what manner of man this Morton really was. He was born at Beer Regis in Dorsetshire, but the year is very uncertain, and he received his first instruction at Cerne Abbey. Thence he proceeded to Oxford, and began life as a lawyer, practising in the Court of Arches. He became a Master in Chancery, increasing his income by taking orders, and was Parson of Bloxworth in Dorsetshire. He took the Lancastrian side, and was at York when the battle of Towton was fought. In 1462 he fled to the Continent with Queen Margaret. His fortunes were then at a low ebb, but they brightened when the Earl of Warwick came to France to betray the cause of Edward IV. Morton attached himself to Warwick at Angers, went with him to England in August 1470, escaped from Barnet to join Queen Margaret at Weymouth, and was with her at Tewkesbury. Nothing but ill luck had attended his fortunes since he had joined the Lancastrian party. So he changed sides, obtained a pardon from Edward IV. and wormed himself into that good-natured monarch's confidence. He became one of the greatest pluralists on record. 'He was avaricious and grasping.'[1] He received a bribe from Louis XI. for inducing his own sovereign to accept dishonourable terms of peace, and was further bribed with a pension of 2,000 crowns a year.[2] The contrast between the upright conduct of the Duke of Gloucester and his own corrupt practices on that occasion explains the wily priest's malignant hostility to Richard. Morton was made Bishop of Ely in 1479. On the death of Edward he saw a wide opening for his ambition in the chances of a long minority. The facts revealed to the Council by Bishop Stillington were, consequently, distasteful to him. He was the heart and soul of the conspiracy of Hastings and the Woodville faction against the Protector. He brought Hastings to his death, but escaped himself. The incorrigible plotter was entrusted to the custody of the Duke of Buckingham. By his cunning artifices he induced that weak nobleman to become a traitor, and claim the crown for himself. He led Buckingham to his death; but secured his own safety. He then joined Henry Tudor's conspiracy, and it was doubtless through Morton's advice that the Welsh adventurer put forward a claim to the crown. Success at length attended the intriguer's schemes. Henry VII. made him Chancellor in 1486, Archbishop of Canterbury in 1487, and, after much importunity, a cardinal's hat was obtained for him, from the Borgian Pope.[3] He became enormously rich. He revealed to Henry VII. 'the confessions of as many lords as his grace listed.'[4] He was one of the most odious instruments of Henry's extortions. The argument that those who spent little must have saved much, and that those who spent much must have much, was called 'Morton's fork.'[5] He died in 1500, hated and execrated by all ranks of the people.

This is the man from whom history derives the narrative of Richard's accession. We must remember the circumstances in which he wrote or dictated his version. He was then Archbishop of Canterbury under Henry VII. He had to traduce Richard in the interests of his master, and at the same time he had to conceal from Henry himself certain parts of his own proceedings, especially as regards his intrigue with Buckingham.

Morton was most unscrupulous in fabricating his story, throwing out misleading insinuations, garbling and suppressing facts, making false statements, and altering dates. He was a leading actor in, and an eyewitness of what he described, he was an able and clever man, and he was intimately acquainted with the facts as they really happened. Moreover, we are informed by Sir Thomas More, who knew him, that he had an extraordinary memory.[6] Consequently every mistake that is detected in his narrative, every date that is altered, must have been inserted with a special object. It is fortunate for the cause of truth that he was more careless, and wrote in greater detail, than he certainly would have done, if there had been any chance of an answer being put forward by one equally conversant with the facts. But he knew that he was safe— power unscrupulously enforced was on his side.

Morton opens his case with the assumption that the Duke of Gloucester had always intended to supplant his nephew. He asserts that the Duke concerted plans with Buckingham and Hastings against the Queen and her relations; that he then, secretly, and by divers means, caused the Queen to be persuaded to advise her son not to come with a large force to London; and that he and other lords wrote to the Queen's friends so lovingly that they, nothing mistrusting, brought the young prince up in good speed with sober company. Gloucester and Buckingham then went to Northampton and met Rivers there. For all that appears in this part of the narrative, Gloucester was in London, and came thence with Buckingham to Northampton. Gloucester was really in the marches of Scotland, and he could not possibly have carried on all these intrigues at that distance, between April 9 when King Edward died and the 23rd when Rivers left Ludlow. He could not even have heard of the King's death for several days. It is true that, towards the end of his lampoon, when telling his story about an alleged quarrel between Gloucester and Buckingham, Morton does mention the Duke being at York, and Buckingham having sent a messenger to him who met him at Nottingham.[7] But this messenger could not have been the channel of all the intrigues he describes. There was no time.

The Duke may have received some hasty notice from a messenger, but the first real news of what had been going on in London came from Buckingham at Northampton.

Morton's story about Gloucester's intrigues at this time is therefore a fabrication. The truth is exactly the reverse of Morton's version. Richard's conduct was straightforward and loyal. After attending solemn obsequies of his brother in York Minster, he called on the nobility and gentry of Yorkshire to swear allegiance to his young nephew. When he arrived in London, he ordered preparations to be made for his nephew's coronation, and he sent summonses to forty esquires to receive knighthood of the Bath on the occasion.[8] He also caused the dresses to be worn by his nephew at his coronation to be got ready.[9] These acts were well known to Morton, who passed them over in silence, because they would tend to give a true impression, where he wanted to leave a false one.

Having thus raised a prejudice against the Protector, Morton's next object was to instil a belief that Hastings worked against the Woodvilles throughout in concert with Richard. In order to create this impression he gives two false dates. He makes young Richard leave sanctuary on June 9. The true date was the 16th.[10] He asserts that Lord Rivers was beheaded on June 13, the very day of the arrest of Hastings, and he makes a great point of it, observing as a striking coincidence that Hastings suffered death on the self-same day and about the self-same hour as Rivers whose execution he had approved.[11] He knew this to be false. Rivers made his will on the 23rd, and was not beheaded until the 25th.[12] Morton had a motive for falsifying the dates, and it is obvious. He wanted it to appear that Hastings was an enemy of the Woodville faction to the end, that he was a party to the removal of young Richard from sanctuary and to the execution of Rivers. But why? Clearly because Hastings was not an enemy of the Woodvilles to the end, because he had, with Morton and others, formed a coalition with them, and entered into a conspiracy with them against the Protector. It was important to conceal this, because it justified the Protector's action against Hastings; and Morton did so by resorting to a falsification of dates. He then proceeds to enter into minute details, in describing the scene when Hastings was arrested on Friday, June 13.

Morton makes the Protector ask him for a mess of strawberries from his garden at Holborn. He then alleges that Gloucester suddenly altered his tone, accused the Queen-Dowager of witchcraft, displayed a withered arm as having been injured by sorcery, upbraided Hastings for having Jane Shore as a mistress, and ordered Hastings to be beheaded on a log of wood before dinner. We are also informed that Master William Catesby made the mischief between the Protector and the Lord Chamberlain, and that a proclamation was issued setting forth the cause of the execution of Hastings.

These details enable us to obtain some glimmering of the truth. We have the reminiscences of an eyewitness, who was also a schemer so dealing with the facts as to leave false impressions clothed in the similitude of veracious recollections. The tale of the strawberries is doubtless true, and is a masterly touch designed to give an air of reality to the scene. The withered arm is a fabrication intended to conceal the real charge made by the Protector. That charge was contained in the proclamation which Morton mentions as having been well indited and written on parchment. He professes to give the substance of it. The seeker after truth would very much prefer the original text. But it was destroyed. Its destruction is a strong presumption in favour of the Protector, and justifies the conclusion that the real charge was a serious one. It is incredible that Catesby merely revealed the nonsense about Jane Shore's sorcery. Morton has inserted this rubbish in order to conceal the real charge made by the Protector. Morton further tells us that 'Shore's wife was of all women the one the Queen most hated,' and that she was the mistress of Hastings. She was really the mistress of Dorset,[13] the Queen's son, and the motive for bringing in the Queen's alleged hatred, in this place, is to conceal the real position of Jane Shore, which was that of a secret agent between the party of the Woodvilles and Hastings.

The fullness of Morton's details defeats his object. He draws attention to the truth which he elaborately endeavours to hide. We are thus enabled to deduce from the garrulity of the designing priest the facts that, probably through his prompting, Hastings had formed a coalition with the Queen-Dowager and her party against the Protector, and that the negotiation had been conducted through Jane Shore as intermediary. We learn that Catesby revealed the plot to the Protector, who promptly arrested Hastings, and brought a charge of treason against him.

Morton would have us believe that Hastings was beheaded on the spot without trial. This version of the story is also told by Fabyan, and adopted by Polydore Virgil. It was told to the second Croyland monk, who wrote that Hastings was beheaded on June 13.[14] It was a version industriously spread by Morton, as a charge of lawless cruelty and indecent haste against the Protector. It can be proved to be false.

Morton's story is that Hastings was hurried out of the council room and beheaded on a log of wood in the court of the Tower, that the Protector and Buckingham appeared to the citizens in rusty armour, pretending that they had been in mortal danger from Hastings, and that the Protector swore he would have the head of Hastings before he dined.

This is a grossly improbable story on the face of it; but Bishop Morton, on the accession of Henry VII., was evidently very anxious that it should be accepted, for he must have given it publicity at a very early date. It was supplied to the credulous old Croyland monk, and was accepted by Fabyan, who must have known it to be false, with such zeal that he added a few extra touches to the story. Fabyan was a citizen of London and knew the truth. Yet he clearly implies that the delivery of young Richard and the execution of Rivers took place before the arrest of Hastings, adopting the falsifications of Morton. He also falsified dates in order to reconcile the alleged date of the execution of Hastings with other events, following Morton in this also. This justifies the conclusion that Fabyan and Morton were in collusion; for they both were aware of the truth from personal knowledge, and they both perverted it in the same way.[15]

There is other testimony on this point which is quite above suspicion. Simon Stallworthe, a prebendary of Lincoln, wrote a letter from London to Sir William Stonor, a gentleman of Oxfordshire, on Saturday June 21, 1483,[16] in which he said that 'on Friday last was the Lord Chambleyn [Hastings] hedded sone after noon.' As Saturday was the 21st, Friday last was the 20th. We here have evidence that Lord Hastings was not beheaded until a week after his arrest and, as there was no indecent haste, we may assume that there was a trial and sentence by a proper tribunal. The story of Morton about the hurried execution on the 13th, and the log of wood, is therefore false. It has been suggested that when Stallworthe wrote 'Friday last,' he did not mean Friday last, but the Friday before Friday last. This theory is exploded by the very next line in Stallworthe's letter. He there says that 'on Monday last' young Richard came out of sanctuary. This is certainly the correct date. But it contradicts both Morton and Fabyan, though it is corroborated by the Croyland Chronicle. If 'Monday last' meant 'Monday last,' 'Friday last' must be taken to mean 'Friday last' in Stallworthe's letter, and not any other date that the exigencies of calumniators may require.

The evidence that the story of the hasty execution of Hastings is false does not rest solely on Stallworthe's letter. Morton and Fabyan are convicted out of their own mouths.

This is a point which should be clearly understood. It must be borne in mind that we have certain fixed dates. Hastings was certainly arrested on June 13. It is also certain that Thursday, June 26, was the date of Richard's accession: it is fixed by the year book. Dr. Shaw's sermon was preached on the previous Sunday, that is June 22. Fabyan, as well as Stallworthe, tells us that the execution of Hastings took place on the previous Friday. These are fixed beacons, and will lead us to the truth. They will also enable us to detect the false lights thrown out by Morton and Fabyan. They both knew the truth well, but they had to manipulate the dates so as to make it appear that Hastings was executed on the 13th. It must be borne in mind that, on Fabyan's own showing, the execution took place on the Friday before Shaw's sermon was preached.

In order to give a plausible appearance to the assertion that Hastings was beheaded on the 13th, Fabyan tried to get rid of the week between the 13th and the 20th. He thought he was bound to recognise the fact that the execution was on the Friday before Shaw's sermon, so he brought the sermon back a week too. But Shaw's sermon was well known to have been preached on the Sunday before the accession. So he had to move back the accession also, and he placed it on June 20. Here Fabyan's dishonesty is detected, for the 20th was not a Thursday, and that the 26th was the date of the accession is beyond dispute.

Morton was, of course, in the same difficulty as regards his dates. But he was far better practised in the manipulation of evidence. Such an old hand would commit himself to dates as little as possible. He would fear them as a thief fears a detective. He gives only one, and he selects the right day of the week, which Fabyan did not. But this is quite enough to convict him. He chose the 19th for the day of Richard's accession with the very same object as Fabyan, to get rid of the gap between the 13th and the 20th; well knowing that the right date for the accession was the 26th.

We can now perceive the truth, both through the direct testimony of Stallworthe and through the detection of the dishonesty of Morton and Fabyan. Lord Hastings was arrested on June 13 on a charge of treason, tried and sentenced. He was executed, after a decent interval, on Friday, June 20. The admission of Morton that a proclamation was issued, announcing the details of the Hastings-Woodville conspiracy, is important. This document, and all others relating to the business, were destroyed in the same way as the Act of Parliament recording Richard's title was destroyed. The object of making away with the Act was to conceal the truth. The disappearance of all documents relating to the execution of Hastings can only be explained in the same way.

But what must we think of Morton and Fabyan, who are thus proved to have been guilty of such a fraud? Their evidence against Richard, on all other points, must be held to be utterly worthless.

The trial of Lord Rivers, with Grey, Vaughan and Haute, followed on that of Hastings. They had been charged with treasonable designs, immediately after the death of King Edward, on the very clearest evidence. But the long delay in bringing them to trial justifies the belief that their capital punishment was not intended, if fresh charges had not been brought against them, arising out of the Hastings conspiracy. Morton brings forward the same accusation in their case, and he gives a false date for their execution. He would have us believe that Rivers and his companions were also put to death 'without so much as the formality of a trial.' So he appears to have told the second Croyland monk. But his untruthfulness is exposed by the evidence of another Tudor witness. Rous inadvertently let out the truth, not knowing there was any reason for concealing it. He certainly did not do so out of any good will for King Richard. There was a trial and the Earl of Northumberland presided at it. He was not the sole judge, but the President acting with other judges.[17] He probably sat as a Commissioner to execute the office of Lord Steward, with a jury of northern Peers, to try Rivers. Morton falsified the date of the executions, making them earlier by twelve days. One object of this falsification has already been pointed out. It also served to indicate such haste in the executions as would make the absence of any trial appear probable.

The overt acts of Rivers and his associates show that their condemnation was just; and their punishment was necessary for the safety and tranquillity of the country. It was a righteous retribution for the death of Clarence, by whose fall the Woodvilles had so largely profited.

Morton next proceeds to falsify the title of King Richard III. to the crown. This point is of great importance and merits close attention. The statement of Richard's title to the crown was drawn up, and adopted by the Lords Spiritual and Temporal and Commons, after considering all the evidence between June 8 and 25. The document was afterwards embodied in an Act of Parliament entitled the 'Titulus Regius,' with which the writers employed by Henry VII. must have been well acquainted. When Henry came to the throne, he ordered this Act to be repealed without quoting the preamble, with a view to its purport being concealed. He caused it to be destroyed, and threatened any one who kept a copy with fine and imprisonment during his pleasure. The reason he gave for this was that 'all things in the said Act may be forgot.' In spite of this threat the truth was told by the Croyland monk, but his chronicle remained in manuscript, and he was not found out. Henry's conduct affords a strong presumption that the title was valid. But he did more. He granted an illusory pardon to Bishop Stillington, who was the principal witness to the truth of the main statement in the 'Titulus Regius.' This was done with the object of keeping silence on the subject of his real offence, which was telling the truth. Henry then arrested him on another trumped up charge, and kept him in close and solitary imprisonment in Windsor Castle until his death in June 1491.

These proceedings show the immense importance attached by Henry VII. to a suppression of the truth relating to Richard's title to the crown. It is certain that if the alleged previous contract with Lady Eleanor Butler was false, the falsehood would have been eagerly exposed, and there would have been no occasion to invent any other story. On the other hand, if the alleged previous contract was true, the evidence would have been suppressed and another story would have been invented and promulgated. The evidence was suppressed, and a different tale was put forward. The conclusion is inevitable that the previous contract of Edward IV. with Lady Eleanor Butler was a fact.

By a mere accident the original draft of the 'Titulus Regius' was not destroyed. It was discovered long afterwards among the Tower records. Its tenor was given in the continuation of the Croyland Chronicle.[18] Richard's title rested on the statement that Edward IV. was already married to Lady Eleanor Butler, a daughter of the first Earl of Shrewsbury,[19] when he went through the ceremony with Lady Grey. It is certain, therefore, that this and this only was the statement made in inspired sermons and speeches at the time; for it was the official case of those who advocated Richard's accession. It is impossible that one ground for the claim should have been put forward officially, and another which was not only different but contradictory, in the sermons and speeches directed to be made at the same time.

Now all this was well known to Morton, and to Polydore Virgil, when they concocted their stories. They had free access to all official sources of information. But they clearly believed that the evidence had been so effectually placed out of reach, that it was safe for them to adopt what tale they chose. They, therefore, stated that Dr. Shaw preached a sermon at Paul's Cross on June 22, in which he calumniated the Duchess of York by maintaining that Edward IV. and Clarence were her children by some other man, and that Gloucester was the only legitimate son of the Duke her husband. The object was to throw the reader off the scent respecting Edward's own connubial proceedings, by bringing an infamous and very absurd charge against his mother. This is clearly the line that Polydore Virgil was instructed to take, for he alludes to the common report that Edward's children were called bastards, and declares it to be 'void of all truth,' that there was such a report. He goes further, alleging that the Duchess of York complained of the injury done her, and that Dr. Shaw died of sorrow for having uttered the slander.[20] With the 'Titulus Regius' before us, it will be allowed that this witness did not stick at trifles.

But Morton was not to be outdone by the Italian. He puts the slander about the Duchess of York into Dr. Shaw's mouth, and he also makes the preacher tell another tale which would make bastards of Edward's children. According to Polydore Virgil the report that the preacher made bastards of Edward's children was 'voyd of all truthe.'

According to Morton the preacher said that Edward was previously married to a woman named Lucy. It will be seen that these authorities contradict each other. Morton proceeds to knock down his own ninepin, by telling us that Lucy confessed she was never married to the King. No one but Morton ever said she was.

Morton farther alleged that when Edward IV. proposed to marry the widow of Sir J. Grey he was opposed by his mother, who represented that he was already contracted before God to Elizabeth Lucy. Morton knew perfectly well that this never happened, and that Edward went through a marriage ceremony with Lady Grey without the knowledge of his mother or any one else. He has only introduced the name of Elizabeth Lucy as a herring drawn across the scent. His great object was to conceal the name of Lady Eleanor Butler.

The absurdity of Morton's fabrications respecting the woman Lucy will be appreciated when we remember that she actually had two children by Edward IV.[21] We are asked to believe that Dr. Shaw, in preaching a sermon in support of Richard's right to the throne, put forward a statement which, if true, would make two children legitimate, whose legitimacy would at once bar any claim on the part of Richard.

These misrepresentations discredit the authority of Polydore Virgil and Morton. Of course there can be no doubt that Dr. Shaw in his sermon, if indeed he ever preached it, and the Duke of Buckingham if he ever made a speech at the Guildhall, simply explained to the people the contents of the petition stating Richard's title, which was about to be presented to him: namely that Edward IV. was previously contracted to the Lady Eleanor Butler, and that the children by Lady Grey were consequently illegitimate.

The invention of the infamous slander against the Duchess of York by Morton and Polydore Virgil, the careful exclusion of Lady Eleanor's name and of any allusion to her, and the elaborate efforts of Henry VII. to destroy all traces of the evidence are very significant. They amount to a proof that the Butler contract was a reality, and that (if the children of Clarence were incapacitated by their father's attainder) King Richard's title was sound and just.

The Croyland monk and Rous do not mention Dr. Shaw's sermon. Fabyan tells us that the preacher stated that King Edward's children were not legitimate, thus contradicting Polydore Virgil, who declares that the preacher never made any such allegation. But Fabyan does not mention the slander against the Duchess of York. This is a further proof that it was invented by Morton. Virgil, in adopting it, had, however, been instructed to avoid all allusion to Edward's own matrimonial affairs.

Having misrepresented Dr. Shaw's sermon on Sunday the 22nd, Morton goes on to say that on the following Tuesday the Duke of Buckingham went to the Guildhall and made a speech to the people. On Wednesday, according to Morton, the Lord Mayor and aldermen came to Baynard's Castle, with Buckingham and divers noblemen, besides many knights and gentlemen.

This is another falsification of dates made as usual with a purpose. Nothing really happened on Wednesday. On Thursday the 26th, Morton says that Richard III. went to Westminster Hall in royal state. What Morton has done is to transfer the events of Thursday to Wednesday, and to make as little as possible of them, in order to draw off attention from a very momentous event. No one would gather from Morton's narrative that on Thursday, June 26, the Convention Parliament, as it would have been called in later days, consisting of the Lords Spiritual and Temporal and the Commons, which had been summoned for the 25th and actually met, proceeded to Crosby Place with the petition embodying Richard's title, and urged him to accept the crown.[22] Morton ignores all this, in order that his readers may be kept in ignorance of the solemn and deliberate proceedings which accompanied Richard's acceptance of the crown. Polydore Virgil does the same.

We next come to the treason of the Duke of Buckingham. Its motive was misrepresented by Morton, with the object of creating a belief that the Duke advocated the cause of Henry Tudor. A long conversation between Buckingham and Morton at Brecknock is recorded by Grafton. It is very characteristic, and is no doubt authentic, so far as that it was written or communicated by Morton. But whether it ever took place as narrated is quite another matter. This conversation sets forth the arguments by which the mischievous old intriguer alleged that he induced Buckingham to rebel, and the pretended object of the insurrection.

It is asserted by Morton and Polydore Virgil that the cause of Buckingham's discontent was the refusal of Richard III. to grant him the moiety of the Bohun lands. It is added that Buckingham's suit was rejected by the King, with many spiteful words, and that there was ever afterwards hatred and distrust between them. This can be proved to be false. Richard granted Buckingham's petition, and made him a grant[23] of the lands under the royal sign manual, giving him the profits from the date of signature, until the formality was completed by authority of Parliament.

This story must have been fabricated to conceal the true motive of Buckingham's treason. He probably aspired to the throne as the next heir of the Plantagenets after Richard and his son, in accordance with the 'Titulus Regius.' He had himself concurred in declaring the children of Edward IV. to be illegitimate, and those of Clarence to be incapacitated. Next came Richard III. and his delicate son, of whom he would dispose if the rebellion was successful. He ignored the sisters of the King and their children.[24] This completed the descendants of the second son of Edward III. The legitimate descendants of the third son came to an end with Henry VI. Buckingham himself represented the fifth son of Edward III.

Assailed by the insidious flattery of Morton, he was prematurely hurried into a rash attempt which cost him his life. When Morton recorded the conversation with his victim many years afterwards, he was Archbishop of Canterbury, Henry VII. was King, and it was advisable, in order to gratify the new sovereign, that Richard should be accused of murdering his nephews, and that Buckingham should be made to give up the scheme for his own aggrandisement, in order to risk his life for the sake of an unknown adventurer in Brittany. It will be admitted that this is a grossly improbable story.

It is certainly astounding that the childish nonsense which Morton puts into Buckingham's mouth should have been gravely accepted as true by subsequent historians. We are first told that when Buckingham heard of the murder of the two innocents, to which he never agreed, he abhorred the sight of the King and could no longer abide with the Court. So he took his leave at Gloucester with a merry countenance but a despiteful heart. According to this, the murders took place in July, for Buckingham left Gloucester on August 1. The more detailed story directly contradicts Morton, and places the murders in the end of August. Both are false, but this is one out of many instances of the utter recklessness of these slanderers. Buckingham is then made to say that he stopped at Tewkesbury for two days to think. The result was that he came to the conclusion that he ought to be King, not on the ground of his descent from the fifth son of Edward III., but because his mother was a daughter of Edmund, Duke of Somerset. His mother was the fourth daughter of that Duke, who had not the remotest right to the throne, and never put forward a claim. If there had been such a claim, Buckingham would not have first found it out, by thinking for two days at Tewkesbury. After this mental effort he continued his journey towards Shrewsbury, and met Margaret Lady Stanley, the mother of Henry Tudor, on the road. She told him that she was the daughter of John Beaufort, Duke of Somerset, Edmund's elder brother. This, we are asked to believe, was quite a new idea to Buckingham. We are to suppose that he knew nothing about his relations before his cogitations at Tewkesbury and his chat with Lady Stanley, and that the receipt of the information made him give up his own ambitious plans altogether. He is made to propose to his fellow-traveller that her son should be king and that he should marry the eldest daughter of Edward IV. Buckingham, after examining the evidence, had just concurred in a solemn declaration that this daughter was illegitimate. But he now evolved from his inner consciousness the discovery that the evidence was derived from suborned witnesses. The Duke then took his leave of Margaret, and proceeded with Morton to Brecknock Castle. Margaret's steward, Reginald Bray, conveyed messages between the conspirators, and an insurrection was arranged. Morton acknowledges that he originally advised Buckingham himself to claim the crown at Brecknock, on which the Duke related the above wonderful story. To complete the absurdity of this childish romance, it must be remembered that Morton was travelling with Buckingham, all the way from Gloucester to Brecknock.

A man who could be guilty of fabricating such a fable is wholly unworthy of credit in his reckless accusations against King Richard, though his minute knowledge of the real facts renders any inadvertent admissions most important. Such are the statements that witnesses and other evidence were produced to establish the illegitimacy of King Edward's children,[25] and that Richard intended to treat his nephews with kindness and consideration.[26] But it is incredible that Buckingham should have contemplated the idea of setting his own claim aside for the sake of an obscure adventurer in Brittany who had no claim at all; while the pretence that Buckingham was horrified at the murder of the young princes contradicts Henry's own clumsy fable. The whole pretended conversation must have been an afterthought to please the Tudor usurper.

The next accusation against Richard refers to his conduct at York, and is derived from the second Croyland monk, who too readily accepted the gossip that was current when he wrote, and which was pleasing to the Tudor Government. It is alleged that Richard appropriated to his own use the treasure which his brother had amassed, and had committed to the care of his executors after his death. This statement, as Mr. Gairdner has shown,[27] is contrary to the fact. The whole property had been placed under ecclesiastical sequestration by the Archbishop of Canterbury, because the executors had declined to act, and no further steps had been taken. It was also stated, on the authority of the same Croyland monk, that Richard went through the ceremony of a second coronation at York.[28] The deduction intended to be drawn, and which often has been drawn, was that his title was so doubtful that he hoped a double coronation might strengthen it. But there was no second coronation at York. Nothing of the kind ever took place.

One is loth to refer to the malignant slander involved in the insinuation that King Richard poisoned his wife. Polydore Virgil says: 'But the Queen, whether she was despatched with sorrowfulness or poison, died within a few days after.' The wretched wasp of Guy's Cliff adds his sting: 'Dominam Annam reginam suam intoxicavit.'[29]

Richard and Anne were cousins, and companions from childhood. Their union had been a happy one in their hospitable Yorkshire home. In all the important events of his life Richard had always had the companionship of his wife. They had been together in sorrow and in joy. Anne's illness was a lingering decline, during which she was assiduously watched and cared for by her physicians, and by her sorrowing husband, who deeply mourned her loss. She was buried, as a Queen, in Westminster Abbey. It is true that no writer has done more than insinuate this calumny. But most of the Tudor slanders take the form of insinuations. 'It is a charge,' wrote Sir Harris Nicolas, 'which is deserving of attention for no other reason than as it affords a remarkable example of the manner in which ignorance and prejudice sometimes render what is called history more contemptible than a romance.' The same may be said of most of the Tudor stories about Richard III.

The rumour that King Richard had an intention of marrying his illegitimate niece Elizabeth is unsustained by any evidence,[30] and is contrary to all probability. Such a project would have stultified the Act of Parliament on which his title to the crown was based. The King was a politician and was not entirely deprived of his senses. He could not have entertained an idea so absurd. But there is evidence that the scheme was favoured by the girl herself and her mother, and this fully accounts for the existence of the rumour. Their ages were suitable, the King being thirty-two and his niece in her twenty-first year; and in a letter to the Duke of Norfolk Elizabeth expressed a strong wish to become the wife of her uncle.[31] The Church of Rome granted, and still grants, dispensations for such marriages. But, be this how it may, Richard himself can never have contemplated a marriage with his niece. 'The whole tale,' says Sir Harris Nicolas, 'was invented with the view of blackening Richard's character, to gratify the monarch in whose reign all the contemporary writers who relate it flourished.' As soon as the rumour came to Richard's ears he publicly and emphatically denied its truth.

The Tudor writers tell various stories about Henry, while in Brittany, having promised to marry Elizabeth; and this is used as an argument that he must have believed her brothers to be dead, for if they were alive, there would be less object in the marriage. Looking at the source whence these stories come, there is no reason whatever for accepting them as true. They are derived from the apocryphal conversation between the Duke of Buckingham and the Bishop of Ely at Brecknock. In order to conceal the real object of Buckingham and his own duplicity, Morton, as has been seen, fabricated a story about his dupe having conspired with Henry Tudor's mother to set him up as a claimant to the crown, and a suitor for the hand of Elizabeth of York. It is likely enough that the intriguing wife of Stanley did conspire with Buckingham in the hope of advancing her son's interests, and that she opened negotiations with the Queen Dowager. Her design in the latter intrigue would be to secure the Woodville interest for supporting the contemplated rising. She despatched her steward Reginald Bray to Brecknock, her confessor Urswick to Brittany, and her doctor Lewis to Westminster Sanctuary. Her treacherous husband was feigning loyalty all the time, and was in zealous attendance on the King. She was found out and contemptuously forgiven by Richard. But the story of a contemplated marriage at that time between Henry Tudor and Elizabeth was an afterthought of Morton, at a time when Henry and Elizabeth were actually married. The story was repeated by Polydore Virgil, and retailed, with the customary embellishments, by Hall and Grafton.

It is scarcely necessary to notice the imputed intention of King Richard to avenge the treachery of Lord Stanley on his son Lord Strange, who was in the royal camp at the time of the battle of Bosworth. He remained unharmed. This is the fact. We are asked to believe that the King intended to behead him, but could not spare the time before the battle began. There was plenty of time, but no intention of using it for such a purpose. The proof of this is that Lord Strange was not injured. The evidence for the alleged intention to behead him rests solely on the assertions of men who wrote long afterwards, and the value of whose testimony we are now pretty well able to estimate.

[1] Hook, v. p. 409.

[2] He was then Master of the Rolls.

[3] Alexander VI., 1492-1503.

[4] Tyndale, The Practice of Prelates, p. 305. Parker Society.

[5] Lord Bacon, Henry VII.

[6] Utopia, p. 20.

[7] Morton was intimately acquainted with the real facts. He makes no mistakes. His mis-statements are all prepared designedly and with an object. He even knew the name of Buckingham's messenger, and that of Gloucester's servant to whom he applied for a secret interview with his master.—P. 134, ed. 1821.

[8] Ellis's Original Letters, second series, i. p. 147.

[9] Wardrobe Accounts.

[10] Stallworthe's letter of June 21 (Exc. Hist. pp. 14-10). The Croyland monk also gives the surrender of young Richard after the arrest of Hastings (p. 566).

[11] He misled Horace Walpole (p. 49), and Dr. Lingard (iv. p. 227) on this point. But Dr. Lingard was quite ready to continue in his error. His account is as follows:—'On the same day that Hastings suffered (and the time should be noticed) Ratcliffe entered Pomfret Castle at the head of a numerous body of armed men, seized Rivers, Grey and Vaughan, observed no judicial forms, and struck off the heads of the victims.' He calls the Yorkshire troops that

came to London 'the ruffians who had murdered the prisoners at Pontefract.' This is not very temperate language. Dr. Lingard afterwards found that this was all wrong. But he would not alter his erroneous text. He merely added a note in a later edition, showing that he knew Rivers to have been still alive on the 23rd, and that Rous named the Earl of Northumberland as presiding at the trial. Yet he retains the assertion in the text that there were no judicial forms!

[12] Croyland, p. 567. Polydore Virgil gives the correct date; and the Croyland monk also places the execution of Rivers after the arrest of Hastings.

[13] Rymer, xii. p. 204.

[14] 13 die mensis Junii veniens in Turrim ad consilium, jussu Protectoris capite truncatus est.—Croyland Chron. Gale, i. 566.

[15] The Croyland Chronicler is quite free from suspicion of intentional falsification. He was informed that Hastings had been beheaded on the 13th, the day of his arrest, and he stated what he believed to be the fact. He, therefore, made no attempt to make this fit in with other events by falsifying dates, as was the course taken by Morton and Fabyan. The monk places the delivery of young Richard and the execution of Rivers in proper order of time, and gives the correct date for Richard's accession.

[16] Excerpt. Hist. p. 16.

[17] 'Eorum principalis judex.'—Rous, p. 213.

[18] Sir George Buck ascertained the truth through having access to the manuscript of the Croyland Chronicle. The

writer simply mentions the pre-contract with Lady Eleanor Butler; but the Chronicle was not printed until 1084. Speed was the first to print the full text of the 'Titulus Regius' in his History of Great Britain, 1611.

[19] The first Earl of Shrewsbury had a large family by two wives, but the names of all his daughters have not been recorded. Dugdale mentions none. Collins gives Jane married to James Lord Berkeley. There were also Elizabeth wife of John Mowbray, Duke of Norfolk, and others, including Eleanor. Buck is mistaken in supposing that Eleanor's first husband was Sir Ralph Butler, Lord Sudeley. His wife was Alice Deincourt, and he was too old. Eleanor's husband may have been an unrecorded son of Ralph Butler, Lord Sudeley, who died when a young man before his father. She must have married Edward IV., when a widow, in or before 1464. She died at Norwich, and was buried in the church of the White Friars Carmelites.— Weever's Funeral Monuments, p. 805.

[20] Morton says that 'within few days after he withered and consumed away' (p. 103).

[21] I. Arthur was married to a daughter and heiress of Edward Grey, Viscount Lisle, the brother-in-law of Lady Grey. She was the widow of Edmund Dudley. In 1533 Arthur was created Viscount Lisle. He had three daughters, and from the second, Frances wife of John Basset of Umberleigh, co. Devon, General Monk was descended. Arthur Viscount Lisle died, without male heirs, in 1541.

II. Elizabeth wife of Thomas, eldest son of George Lord Lumley, who died before his father. From her descends the present Earl of Scarborough.

[22] Letter from King Richard to Lord Mountjoy.

[23] The text of the grant is given by Dugdale, with the King's signet and sign manual, given at his manor at Greenwich on July 13, 1483. A list of the manors follows.—Dugdale's Baronage, i. 168.

Mr. Gairdner argues that, in spite of this grant, the Duke had reason to doubt the fulfilment of the promise when Parliament met. I am unable to follow him. The King had done all that he possibly could do until Parliament met, and he had put his good faith and sincerity beyond doubt by giving Buckingham the profits beforehand, in anticipation of the approval of Parliament. What could he possibly do more? There was no shadow of a pretext for any such doubt on the part of Buckingham.—Gairdner's Richard III., p. 136.

[24] He also had to ignore the children of Henry Bourchier, Earl of Essex, by the Princess Isabel, a sister of Richard Duke of York.

[25] Morton, in Grafton, p. 126.

[26] Ibid. p. 127.

[27] Richard III. p. 146, quoting from Royal Wills, pp. 345-347.

[28] Rous, p. 217. Drake's Eborac. p. 117. The fable is fully exposed by Mr. Davies in his York Records.

[29] Rous.

[30] This rumour never reached Fabyan or Rous. It is mentioned by the Croyland monk.

[31] On the authority of Sir George Buck. His words are as follows:—'When February was past, the Lady Elizabeth, being more impatient and jealous of the success than every one knew or conceived, writes a letter to the Duke of Norfolk intimating first that he was the man in whom she most affied, in respect of that love her Father had ever borne him. Then she congratulates his many courtesies, in continuance of which she desires him to be a mediator for her to the King in the behalf of the marriage propounded between them, who, as she wrote, was her only joy and maker in the world, and that she was his in heart and thought, withal insinuating that the better part of February was past, and that she feared the Queen would never die. All these be her own words written with her own hand, and this is the sum of her letter, which remaineth in the autograph or original draft under her own hand, in the magnificent cabinet of Thomas Earl of Arundel and Surrey.' (Buck, p. 128.)

Sir Harris Nicolas (Privy Purse Expenses of Elizabeth of York, p. 1), as an admirer of Elizabeth of York, was much troubled by this letter. He attacked Sir George Buck as 'one whose violent prejudices do not sufficiently account for the mendacity for which his work is remarkable.' But this is unjust. Buck no doubt was prejudiced, but not more so than the Tudor chroniclers. He blunders and is uncritical, yet there is no reason to impugn his good faith. Nor did Sir Harris Nicolas himself think that the case was sufficiently disposed of by abusing Sir George Buck. He made various attempts to explain away the letter, but none satisfactory or even plausible. Dr. Lingard did not doubt the authenticity of the letter (v. pp. 355-359, ed. 1823, iv. p. 252, ed. 1849). It is not now known to exist, but that proves nothing if Buck wrote in good faith.

Mr. Gairdner approaches the subject more calmly. 'Positive testimony like this,' he says, 'is not to be lightly set aside as incredible. Yet Buck, if not altogether dishonest (and I see no reason to think him so), was certainly by no means an impartial historian. At the same time Buck's abstract of the letter is very minute, and such as would seem to follow pretty closely the turns of expression in a genuine original, and he expressly declares the manuscript to be an autograph or original draft. If it be not a forgery palmed off upon Buck himself, I am inclined to think it was written, not by Elizabeth, but by her mother who bore the same Christian name. Every word might just as well have come from her, except the mention of the father, which may be a mistake; and there is nothing inconceivable in her anxiety that Richard should marry her daughter.' He adds 'that Elizabeth could have been eager to obtain the hand of her brother's murderer is really too monstrous to be believed.' Why then is it not 'too monstrous to be believed' that the mother should have been eager to obtain the hand of her son's murderer for her daughter? It is clear that the grounds for accepting the letter are too strong for Mr. Gairdner to be able to reject them. Yet that Elizabeth should wish to marry her brother's murderer appears incredible to him. The conclusion is inevitable. Richard was not her brother's murderer, if the letter was authentic (see Gairdner's Life of Richard III. pp. 256-257, and note p. 257).

CHAPTER IV THE MAIN CHARGE AGAINST RICHARD III

15. Murder of the Princes in the Tower. Acquittal.

In attempting an impartial consideration of the question of the fate of King Edward's sons, it must always be remembered that the main argument against their uncle is made to rest upon the truth of his previous alleged crimes. This argument is destroyed if Richard was not a venomous hunchback born with teeth, if he was not a cold scheming and calculating villain who had already committed two atrocious murders, drowned his brother in a butt of malmsey, poisoned his wife, and waded through the blood of innocent men to an usurped throne. A careful study of the evidence establishes the fact that these accusations are false, and that they were put forward by the writers under a new dynasty in order to blacken the character of the last Plantagenet King, and to make the accusation that he murdered his nephews more plausible. For it was a matter of the most vital importance to Henry VII., not only that the boys should have been murdered, but that it should be believed that the crime was perpetrated before his accession.

We have to deal with a different man altogether. The real Richard, who is accused of the murder of his nephews, was not previously steeped in crime. The accusation must now be considered as being brought against an ordinary prince of the fifteenth century, if not better certainly not worse than his contemporaries. This at once destroys the chief points of the evidence against him. His accusers rightly felt that it was necessary to blacken Richard's character, and this they did coarsely enough, but very successfully. They knew that, without this poisoning of the wells, the case against him lost all its force. 'Nemo repente turpissimus.'

We must now approach the question relating to the fate of the two young sons of Edward IV., without having constantly before our minds the grotesque caricature portrayed by the Tudor writers. Although it is not possible, especially at this distance of time, to account for the workings of any man's mind, or for the motives which may control his actions, it is yet necessary to consider this phase of the question, with as much light as we can bring to bear upon it.

It is not disputed that Edward IV. always evinced unshaken love and affection for his young brother, and showed the most absolute confidence in him at the time of his death. Richard returned this affection with devoted loyalty. He had no love for the Woodville faction, but he must have felt some regard for his brother's children, being such a man as we believe he has been proved to have been. This feeling of regard would decrease the strength of any motive producing a desire to destroy them for his own ends. But there was no such motive. The boys had been declared to be illegitimate, after an examination of evidence, by the unanimous voice of Parliament. When the Cardinal Archbishop, surrounded by his suffragans, placed the crown of St. Edward on Richard's head, he proclaimed the belief of the Church, and released from their oaths all who under a misapprehension had sworn allegiance to Edward V. The boy, as a claimant to the throne, had ceased to be dangerous.

It should be borne in mind that Parliament was unanimous in recognising the title of Richard III. Excepting half a dozen Lancastrian exiles who were equally opposed to any member of the house of York,[1] the whole peerage was at

Richard's coronation except those whose absence is accounted for by extreme age or youth, or by the calls of duty.[2] Even the Woodville faction had submitted, and was represented at the coronation by Viscount Lisle and the Bishop of Salisbury. Henry Tudor's mother bore the train of Richard's Queen, and his uncle Lord Welles was also at the coronation. There was absolutely no party for the illegitimate sons of Edward IV. at the time of their alleged murders, and consequently no danger to be apprehended from them. If the story had put the murders after Buckingham's rising it would have been a little more plausible. But it placed them two months before the rising, when the King had not the shadow of a suspicion that any opposition was contemplated. Setting aside all natural or religious feeling, and even assuming Richard to have been the impossible monster depicted by Tudor writers, he certainly had no motive for the crime.

But it may be argued that the workings of men's minds are inexplicable, and that Richard may have committed the crime from a motive which would seem insufficient to any reasonable man. To decide upon this proposition we can only turn to a consideration of his conduct as regards other persons in the same relationship and position as the two boys, and who were likely to cause Richard as much or as little trouble. There were seven such persons, namely, the five daughters of Edward IV. and the two children of the Duke of Clarence. The King treated his nieces with kindness and consideration as near relations, when they came under his protection. The young Earl of Warwick, son of Richard's elder brother Clarence, was a far more formidable rival than the sons of Edward. The former was incontestably legitimate; while the latter had been declared to be illegitimate by both Houses of Parliament. Richard knighted the son of Clarence, placed him at the head of the nobility, and made him a member of council and of his own household. We, therefore, know that Richard did not look upon the children of his elder brothers as enemies to be destroyed, but as relations to be cherished.

We find, then, that the two young sons of Edward IV. went to reside in the royal lodgings of the Tower in June 1483. The statement put forth by Henry VII. is that they were murdered there in the following August. But there are two pieces of evidence, one of them positive evidence, that they were alive throughout the reign of Richard III.

In the orders for King Richard's household dated after the death of his own son, children are mentioned of such high rank that they were to be served before all other Lords. The only children who could occupy such a position were the sons of Edward IV. and the son of Clarence. The conclusion must be that all his nephews were members of his household, and that they were only sent to Sheriff Hutton and to the Tower when danger threatened the realm from the invasion of Henry Tudor.

The other piece of evidence is found in a warrant in Rymer's 'Foedera,' dated March 9, 1485, to the following effect: it directs Henry Davy 'to deliver unto John Goddestande, footman unto the Lord Bastard, two doblets of silk, one jacket of silk, one gown of cloth, two shirts, and two bonets.'[3] There are other warrants to pay for provisions. Dr. Lingard[4] tried to destroy the significance of these warrants by suggesting that they referred to John of Gloucester, an illegitimate son of the King. But this boy is mentioned in Rymer's 'Foedera,' and is designated as a bastard son of the King[5] simply and not as a lord, for no such title belonged to him. Edward, on the other hand, although he was officially called a bastard, was also a lord. In his case the designation of Lord was correct. In the 'Wardrobe Account' he was called the Lord Edward; after the accession of his uncle.[6] The royal titles of Wales and Cornwall were no longer consistent or proper, and had indeed been transferred, in due course, to the King's son. But the earldoms of March and Pembroke, conferred on him by his father, still belonged to Edward. He would properly be styled the Lord Bastard, while John of Gloucester could not be and was not. There was only one 'Lord' Bastard.[7] The warrants, therefore, show that Edward was alive and well treated in March 1485, four months before the death of Richard III.

These two pieces of evidence are in keeping with Morton's statement that King Richard had declared his intention of maintaining his nephews in honourable estate. But there is strong collateral evidence pointing to the same conclusion. If there had been foul play, it is scarcely credible that the mother could have been induced by any promises to throw her remaining children on the protection of one who had already violated the most sacred ties as regards her two sons. It is, however, just possible that a very unfeeling and selfish woman (though Elizabeth was neither), weary of confinement in sanctuary, might have been induced to make terms with the murderer of her sons, in order to obtain a comfortable provision for herself. But she did more than this. She sent for her other son, who was safe in France, advising him to return home and submit himself to the King. It is incredible that she could have done this unless she knew that the two boys were alive and well treated. She remained on friendly terms with Richard until his death, and her daughters attended the festivities at his Court. Still stronger evidence in the same direction is afforded by the letter to the Duke of Norfolk, whether it was written by the King's niece Elizabeth or by her mother, as Mr. Gairdner suggests. The writer could not have spoken of Richard as her 'joy and maker in the world,' or have said that she was 'his in heart and thought,' if he had just murdered the brothers of one and the sons of the other. The thing is quite impossible.

The conduct of their mother and sister is a strong corroboration of the positive evidence that the young princes were alive and well throughout King Richard's reign.

On the other hand, there is no evidence whatever that they were dead; beyond rumours of which we only hear long afterwards. We are told that there were rumours that they had been murdered, and rumours that they were alive, and had been taken abroad. Rumours but no evidence.

If they had been smothered the bodies would have been exposed to allay suspicion, and would have received Christian burial. To hide them would have been an act of incredible folly.

There remain then, for consideration, these rumours which are alleged to have prevailed during the reign of King Richard to the effect that his nephews had been murdered. It is maintained that if these rumours were generally believed, Richard must have been guilty, because if he had been innocent he would have taken some steps to disprove the rumours, and he took no such steps, or rather—no such steps are recorded by his enemies.

The points for investigation are whether such rumours actually existed, and if so, whether they were so general as to reach the King's ears and make it advisable that anything should be done to refute them.

It is alleged that these rumours took shape during the King's progress to York in the summer and autumn of 1483. There is no evidence that they prevailed at this or any other time during Richard's reign.[8] The authority for a rumour about the fate of the two boys in the summer of 1483 is the Croyland Chronicle; and there can be no doubt that the statement was made in good faith; although the writer may have been deceived.

The passage in the Croyland Chronicle is to the effect that the princes remaining in custody in the Tower, the people in the south and west of England became anxious for their liberation, that meetings were held on the subject, and that proposals were made to arrange the escape of the daughters of Edward IV. so that, if anything happened to his sons, there might still be heirs of his body. It was also reported that the sons of Edward were dead, though it was unknown by what violent means they met their end.[9] So far the Croyland monk.

No doubt there were partizans of the defeated factions of Hastings and the Woodvilles who were ready to spread any rumours injurious to the King. The question is whether the rumours which reached the ears of the Croyland monk were ever generally credited by the people, so as to call for action from the Government. Is it true that they led to loud murmurings from meetings and assemblages of the people in the south and west of England, such as would attract general notice? The only proof offered is that an officer named Nesfield was ordered to watch the approaches of the Sanctuary at Westminster, and see that no one left it secretly. But this was a precaution which would have been taken under any circumstances. Polydore Virgil alleges that Richard himself spread a report that his nephews were dead; and this is magnified and embellished by Grafton and Hall, according to their wont. The statement is grossly improbable in itself, is wholly unsupported, and is entirely unworthy of credit.

There is, then, no evidence that these rumours existed, beyond the passage in the Croyland Chronicle. But there is strong reason for rejecting the monk's story. If the rumours had really existed, and if in consequence there were mutinous assemblages of the people preliminary to an insurrectionary movement, the vigilant and energetic young King would have made all necessary preparations to meet the danger. Nothing is more certain in his history than that he was taken absolutely by surprise when he received tidings of an outbreak in Kent on October 11, 1483. It was a concerted rising, secretly arranged by Buckingham. This Duke had taken leave of the King at Gloucester on August 2 before the alleged action of Richard at Warwick with a view to the murders, which was on August 8. According to the story, Buckingham can have known nothing of the murders when he arranged his plot. Consequently it is not possible that the rising in Kent, arranged by Buckingham, can have had anything to do with the alleged murder of the young princes.

Yet the Croyland monk had certainly been told that there was a rumour that the boys were dead. If it had not reached him as general talk, it must have come direct to him from some malignant enemy of the King. Was there such a man lurking in the fen country round Croyland? We know that Morton had taken refuge in the fen country (Isle of Ely) at this very time. If that schemer was at the chronicler's elbow, the rumour is fully accounted for. It probably originated with Morton while he was lurking in the fens, and ceased to exist when he sailed for Flanders. His own narrative, as we have received it, comes to an abrupt termination while he is conversing with the Duke of Buckingham at Brecknock. If it had been continued, we should doubtless have had a highly coloured version of the rumour mentioned in the Croyland Chronicle. Morton and his slanders went abroad together. The rumour that the young princes had been put to death appeared no more in England during Richard's life. But as soon as Morton went to France, it appeared there. In the autumn of 1483 Morton left England. In January 1484, the murder of the princes was alleged as a fact by the Chancellor of France in a speech to the States-General at Tours. 'Regardez, je vous prie, les événements qui après la mort du Roi Édouard sont arrivés dans ce pays. Contemplez ses enfants, déjà grands et braves, massacreé impunément, et la couronne transportée a l'assassin par la faveur des peuples.'[10] The Chancellor may have received this statement from another Lancastrian exile, but it is most likely that it came from Morton. Louis XI. had hated Richard because he opposed the peace which the French King bought from Edward IV., and because he refused the French bribes with contempt.[11] This hatred was inherited by the Lady of Beaujeu who became Regent on the death of Louis XI. in August 1483. Any calumny was seized upon as an opportunity for reviling the King of England; and with Morton in France there would be no dearth of such wares.

The insult to the King of England uttered by the French Chancellor may not have reached Richard's government. If it did, it must have been apologised for or explained away, for some months afterwards, in September 1484, King Richard granted a safe-conduct for an embassy from the French Regency to treat of peace.[12] The calumny was clearly received by the French Chancellor from Morton, or some other unscrupulous outlaw, and not from any general rumour. For it is stated as a fact; the truth being that it was never known what became of the two boys, or pretended to be known until after the alleged confession of Tyrrel in 1502.

Fabyan, writing in the time of Henry VII., talks of a rumour, and of its having been the common fame that King

Richard put his nephews to secret death. This was merely what Henry VII. wanted to be the 'common fame'; and no one dared to gainsay it. In the year after his accession the usurping Tudor ordered it to be given out that the boys were murdered by their uncle, and his paid agents had to repeat the statement. André said they were killed with a sword.[13] Rous stated that they were put to death by some means unknown.[14] Polydore followed Rous. Comines, naturally enough, told the story officially promulgated in England. But Henry never dared to make the accusation publicly in his first so-called Parliament, and there can have been only one reason for this silence. The boys were then alive.

Henry's chroniclers, however, testify that nothing was known, and thus prove the falsehood of the French Chancellor's statement, while furnishing additional proof that no general rumour existed during Richard's reign that the boys were dead.

It is not to be supposed that Sir William Stanley would have entertained for a moment the belief that Perkin Warbeck was a son of Edward IV. unless he knew that the princes were alive throughout Richard's reign. No one had better means of knowing. The story put forward by Henry VII. tells us that it remained in doubt whether the boys were destroyed or not in Richard's day. Polydore Virgil mentions a rumour that they had escaped abroad. Perkin Warbeck's story was believed by a great number of people, which could not have been the case if the rumour of the death of the princes had been generally credited.

No question arose before King Richard's death. Many persons must have known that his nephews were alive and well treated. Their mother and brother knew, and they were silenced by imprisonment. Sir William Stanley and his fellow-sufferers knew, and they were beheaded. After Henry's accession, there were dozens, if not hundreds, of people who knew the truth. They had a choice between silence and ruin or death. The truth might have been, and probably was, mentioned in private correspondence; but even that would be very perilous, and scarcely any correspondence of that date has been preserved. In one letter in the 'Plumpton Correspondence,' the dislike of Henry's illegal attainders is referred to, but with bated breath. Among the mass of the people there was no certain knowledge of what had happened to the boys. Of course many baseless rumours then became current. The statements accusing Richard, and the assertions that these rumours received popular credit during his reign, merely indicate what his successor wanted to be believed on the subject.

[1] Earls of Oxford, Devonshire, and Pembroke, Lords Rivers, Dynham, and Beaumont. Lord Clifford was a minor, and in hiding in Yorkshire.

[2] Lord Dudley in extreme old age, Earls of Shrewsbury and Essex, and Lord Hungerford minors, Lords Greystoke and Ogle in the Marches, Lord Mountjoy at Calais, Lord de la Warre abroad. The Earl of Westmoreland was dangerously ill.

[3] Bayley, Antiquities of the Tower of London. (8vo. ed 1830, p. 343 n.)

[4] iv. p. 580 (5th ed. 1849).

[5] Rymer, xii. p. 265. 'Pro filio bastardo regis.' 'Cum summa dilecti filii nostri bastardi Johannis de Gloucestriæ ingenii vivacitas, membrorumque agilitas, et ad omnes bonos mores magnam et indubiam nobis de futuro ejus servitio bono spem, gratiâ divinâ promittant.' This warrant granted the wardship of Calais to John of Gloucester, so soon as he should have reached the age of twenty-one.

[6] Archæologia, i. p. 367.

[7] Sir Richard, K.G., the second son, was not then a lord. The title of York was a royal one, like that of Wales, and he could not hold it when proved to be illegitimate. Those of Norfolk and Nottingham came from his intended wife, Anne Mowbray, and when she died, they went to her heirs Howard and Berkeley, by creation of the King on June 8, 1483. Young Richard, as well as Edward, was a Knight of the Garter, but Edward was the only 'Lord Bastard.'

[8] A letter from the King to the Mayor of York, dated April 11, 1485, is on the subject of the suppression of false

reports and lies. But this refers to the false report that Richard intended to marry his niece. Davies, York Records. Drake incorrectly places this letter in 1484. Drake's Ebor. p. 119.

[9] 'Vulgatum est dictos Regis Edwardi pueros, quo genere violenti interitus ignoratur, decessisse in fata.'

[10] Journal des Etats-Généraux de France tenus en 1483-84 (Documents Inédits), quoted by Gairdner in his Richard III. p. 160.

[11] He accepted a present of horses from Louis as a matter of courtesy.

[12] Rymer's Foedera, xii. p. 234.

[13] 'Nepotes clam ferro feriri jussit.'—André.

[14] 'Ita quod ex post paucissimis notum fuit qua morte martirizati sunt.'—Rous.

CHAPTER V HENRY TUDOR IN THE DOCK

Murder of the Princes in the Tower. Conviction.

Henry Tydder, alias Tudor, must now take his place in the dock. Let us first see what manner of man this fortunate adventurer was. In 1485 he was twenty-eight years of age. He is described as a man of slender build, about five feet nine inches high, with a saturnine expression, grey restless eyes, yellow hair, and very little of it. Having passed his life as a fugitive and conspirator, cunning and dissimulation had become a second nature to him. The victory gained for him at Bosworth, by the foulest treachery, placed despotic power in his hands. His first acts were the illegal and unjust executions of William Catesby,[1] Chancellor of the Exchequer, of John Buck, the Comptroller of the late King's Household, of William Bracher, Yeoman of the Crown, and of his son. These executions were in violation of all law. They were simply murders; for Henry Tudor himself had no legal status, and was in fact an attainted outlaw. Catesby was the faithful and loyal minister of a King who studied the welfare of his subjects, and was the Speaker of the best Parliament that had sat since the time of Edward I. He was an able and diligent public servant. This was his only crime. Nothing tangible has ever been alleged against him, except that he did his duty by reporting the meditated treason of Hastings. If the fables of Morton and his colleagues are accepted, the executions of Rivers, Grey and Vaughan were doubtful acts. But the executions of Catesby, Buck, and the Brachers were heinous crimes. Richard was the Chief of the State, though it may be held that his measures were unjust. Henry was an outlaw without legal authority of any kind, and his executions were ruthless murders. Thus did this adventurer wade through the blood of innocent men to his usurped throne.[2] His next proceeding was to send Sir Robert Willoughby to

Sheriff Hutton, to get possession of young Edward Earl of Warwick, the heir to the throne, and of the late King's niece Elizabeth.

Henry Tudor then marched to London and seized the government. He became responsible for the surviving members of the royal family of England, legitimate or otherwise. What did he do with them? There were Edward and Richard, the illegitimate sons of Edward IV., there was Edward the legitimate son of the Duke of Clarence, and now the rightful King of England, and there was John, the illegitimate son of Richard III. They all fell into his power, and he alone became answerable for their lives. There is too much reason to suspect that they all met with foul play at his hands.

Henry Tudor, on usurping the crown of England, necessarily found himself in a very difficult position. His mother's claim, as heiress to an illegitimate son of the third son of Edward III., was worthless in itself, for even if the descent had been legitimate, she must come after all the descendants of the second son of Edward III. Moreover the claim, such as it was, had not yet descended to Henry Tudor and never did, for his mother survived him. He wisely refrained from stating such a claim as this, although he alleged a vague hereditary right of some sort, which he did not try to explain. There remained the right of conquest with the aid of French mercenaries, and he ventured to put it forward. But he soon saw that he would have to find some other prop to support his usurpation.

Henry must certainly have been a man of great ability, with an acute but narrow mind, marvellous powers of dissimulation and of self-deception, with considerable tact and skill in guiding and influencing those around him. He was essentially un-English. He was a near relation of Louis

XI., and he made that mean tyrant his model. He hated English freedom, and that intimate contact with the people which made the Plantagenets popular. He loved mystery. He surrounded himself with an armed guard which constantly went about with him, a thing never done before by former kings.[3] He originated a tribunal with despotic powers, consisting of a committee of his Council, the infamous Star Chamber. He established 'a close and secret, a tyrannical and often a most cruel government.'[4] He extorted money by means of those illegal 'benevolences' which had been abolished by the patriotic Parliament of Richard III. He was penurious, greedy, and mean. He was the first English King who increased his revenue by forfeitures enforced through legal chicanery. He began the practice of setting agents to ferret out any claim which the Crown could make, and a subservient judge would affirm. For he loved the forms of law, which apparently soothed his conscience. He was very superstitious. When his own interests were not concerned he was not devoid of natural affection and he recoiled from crime. Yet he became capable of any foul deed if he deemed it necessary for his own security. But he meditated a crime for months and years, and stood trembling on the brink for a long time before he summoned up courage to act. Even then he much preferred the forms of law, thinking that if he shared the deed with others, the guilt became a limited liability.

Henry had the wisdom to see that, although his claim of conquest and vague assertion of right by descent[5] might serve for a time, he must establish some better title to secure any stability for his throne. He had obtained his position by the favour of a treacherous faction, and was confirmed in it by a pretended Parliament of his adherents, many of them still under attainder. Unlike the grand ceremony of King Richard's coronation, when the whole peerage was present, that of Henry was very thinly attended. He felt that some step must promptly be taken, with a view to strengthening his position, and reconciling the nation to his usurpation.

There was Elizabeth, the late King's niece, whose person he had secured. If she was made queen it might propitiate the powerful Yorkist party. But she was illegitimate, and consequently young Warwick was the rightful King. There was another more fatal difficulty, a knowledge of which was shared with the girl's mother, if not with the girl herself. All evidence of the illegitimacy might be destroyed. Henry caused the Act of Parliament recording and legalising King Richard's title to be expunged. He ordered the original Act to be removed from the Rolls and burnt. Every person who possessed a copy or remembrance of it, was commanded to deliver up the same, under a penalty of fine and imprisonment at the tyrant's pleasure.[6] Henry granted a general pardon to Bishop Stillington in order to avoid prosecuting him for the offence of having borne witness to the illegitimacy. For he feared discussion. He then trumped up some other charge, threw the Bishop into prison, and that unfortunate prelate never came out alive.

But this was not enough. There was other work to be done from which Henry long recoiled. Yet without its perpetration he could not safely be married to Elizabeth, and there could be no security for his usurpation. Indeed, his position would be rendered even more precarious by the destruction of the evidence of illegitimacy. He had usurped a throne to retain which he saw that the committal of more than one crime was indispensable.

Meanwhile Henry had summoned the so-called Parliament of his outlawed adherents. He got his own attainder reversed. He then caused an act of attainder to be passed against the late King and many loyal noblemen and knights, whose property he seized. He had the effrontery to accuse them of treason to him, by dating the commencement of his reign from the day previous to the battle of Bosworth. No more shameless act of injustice is recorded in the annals of tyranny. The bit of legal chicanery by which an attempt was made to excuse it, shows the character of the man.

LOYAL MEN WITH THE KING AT BOSWORTH

ILLEGAL ATTAINDERS BY ORDER OF HENRY TUDOR PASSED IN THE SO-CALLED PARLIAMENT OF 1485

Richard III., King of England, K.G. }
John Howard, Duke of Norfolk, K.G. } Slain at Bosworth.
Thomas Howard, Earl of Surrey, K.G. Prisoner at Bosworth.
Francis Viscount Lovell, K.G. Slain at Stoke.
Walter Lord Ferrers, K.G. }
John Lord Zouch. } Slain at Bosworth.
Sir James Harington. (Clerk of the Council.) At Bosworth.
Sir Robert Harington. At Bosworth.
Sir Richard Charlton. At Bosworth.
Sir Richard Ratcliffe, K.G. Slain at Bosworth.
Sir William Berkeley, K.B. (Knight of the Bath at the Coronation.)
Sir Robert Brackenbury. (Constable of the Tower.) Slain at Bosworth.
Sir Thomas Pilkington. (Brother-in-law of the Haringtons.) Slain at Stoke.
Sir Robert Middleton.
Walter Hopton, Esq. (Treasurer of the Household.)
William Catesby, Esq. (Chancellor of the Exchequer.) Murdered at Leicester.
Roger Wake, Esq.
William Sapcote, Esq., of Huntingdonshire.
Humphrey Stafford, Esq. Put to death by Henry VII.
William Clarke, Esq., of Wenlock.
Walter St. Germain, Esq.
Walter Watkin, Esq. (Herald.)
Richard Revell, Esq., of Derbyshire.
Thomas Pulter, Esq., of Kent.
John Welch, Esq., otherwise Hastings.

John Kendall, Esq. (Secretary of State.) Slain at Bosworth.
John Buck, Esq. (Comptroller of the Household.) Murdered at Leicester.
John Batte, Esq.
William Brampton, Esq., of Burford.

(From the Plumpton Correspondence, p. 48.)

This odious measure outraged the feelings of all parties in the country. 'There was many gentlemen against it, but it would not be for it was the king's pleasure,' wrote Sir Robert Plumpton's correspondent from London.[7] The monk of Croyland wrote against the outrage, exclaiming 'O God! what security are our kings to have henceforth that in the day of battle they may not be deserted by their subjects who, acting on the awful summons of a king may, on the decline of that king's party, as is frequently the case, be bereft of life and fortune and all their inheritance.'[8] Nor was this insult to King Richard's memory, and the lawless robbery of his loyal subjects, forgotten by the people of England. They were resolved to secure themselves against a repetition of such proceedings. Ten years afterwards the tyrant had the mortification of being obliged to give his assent to an Act formally condemning the attainder of King Richard's officers.[9]

It is very significant that, although in the Act of Attainder King Richard is reviled for cruelty and tyranny, he is not accused of the murder of his nephews. This is most remarkable. Henry got possession of the Tower at once. He arrived in London on August 28. If the young princes were missing, it is certain that in the Act of Attainder the usurper would have promptly accused King Richard of having murdered them. But he did not do so. There can only be one explanation of this omission. The young princes were not missing.

Here then was Henry's great difficulty. This fully accounts for the long delay in marrying Elizabeth. He was afraid. He was ready to commit any crime with the forms of law. He did not hold with Lord Russell, that 'killing by forms of law was the worst kind of murder.' But a recourse to law was impossible in this case. Whatever he was to do, must be done in profound secrecy. Yet his timid and superstitious nature shrank from a crime the responsibility of which he could not share with others. Its perpetration had, he saw, become absolutely necessary for his security. He hesitated for months. All evidence of the illegitimacy had been hidden out of sight. No man dared to mention it. He long stood on the brink. At length he plunged into guilt. He married Elizabeth on January 18, 1486, nearly five months after his accession. The die was then cast. It became a matter of life and death to Henry VII. that the brothers of his wife should cease to exist.

We must now apply the same tests to Henry as we applied to Richard. Had Henry sufficient motive for the crime? It is impossible that a man in his position could have had a stronger motive. He had denied the illegitimacy, and had thus made his wife's brothers his most formidable rivals. He could not, he dared not let them live, unless he relinquished all he had gained. The second test we applied to Richard was his treatment of those persons who were in his power, and who were, as regards relationship, in the same position as the sons of Edward IV. Let us apply the same test to Henry. John of Gloucester, the illegitimate son of Richard III., fell into the hands of Henry. At first the boy received a maintenance allowance of 20l. a year.[10] But he was soon thrown into prison, on suspicion of an invitation having reached him to come to Ireland, and he never came out alive.[11] This 'active well-disposed boy,'[12] as he is described in the warrant in Rymer's 'Foedera,' fell a victim to the usurper's fears. His right to the crown was at least as good as that of Henry Tudor. He was the illegitimate son of a king. Henry was only the great-grandson of an illegitimate son of a younger son of a king. The Earl of Warwick, who was the rightful heir to the crown, was also in Henry's power. The tyrant hesitated for years before he made up his mind to commit another foul crime. But he finally slaughtered the unhappy youth under circumstances of exceptional baseness and infamy, to secure his own ends. His next supposed danger was caused by the Earl of Suffolk, another nephew of King Richard. The ill-fated prince was delivered into Henry's hands under a promise that his life should be spared. He evaded the promise by enjoining his son to kill the victim. That son promptly complied, and followed up the death of Suffolk by putting five other descendants of the Plantagenet royal family to death. These Tudor kings cannot stand the tests we applied to Richard III., which he passed unscathed. The conduct of Richard to the relations who were under his protection was that of a Christian king. The executions of which Henry VII. and his son were guilty were an imitation of the policy of Turkish sultans.

If the young princes were in the Tower when Henry succeeded, his conduct in analogous cases leaves no doubt of their fate. It was the fate of John of Gloucester, Warwick, Suffolk, Exeter, Montagu, Surrey, Buckingham, and the Countess of Salisbury.[13] They may not have been made away with before Henry's marriage, nor for some months afterwards. The tyrant had the will but not the courage. He hesitated long, as in the case of young Warwick. For reasons which will appear presently it is likely that the boys were murdered, by order of Henry VII., between June 16 and July 16, 1486, three years after the time alleged by the official Tudor historians.

Imprisonment of the Queen Dowager
Then, for the first time, the 'common fame' was ordered to spread the report that King Richard 'had put them under suer kepynge within the tower, in such wise that they never came abrode after,' and that 'King Richard put them unto secrete death.'[14] But Henry feared detection. The mother knew that this was false. If the boys were murdered in July 1486, that mother must soon have begun to feel uneasy.

She was at Winchester with her daughter when her grandchild Arthur was born on September 20, 1486, and was present at the baptism. But she was in London in the autumn, and before many months her suspicions must have been aroused. She must be silenced. Consequently, in February 1487 'it was resolved that the Lady Elizabeth, wife of King Edward IV., should lose and forfeit all her lands and possessions because she had voluntarily submitted herself and her daughters to the hands of King Richard. Whereat there was much wondering.'[15] She was ordered to reside in the nunnery of Bermondsey.[16] Once she was allowed to appear at Court on a State occasion.[17] The pretext for her detention was not the real motive, for Henry had made grants of manors and other property to his mother-in-law soon after his accession,[18] when her conduct with regard to King Richard was equally well known to him. The real reason was kept secret, as well it might be. Mr. Gairdner calls this proceeding 'a very mysterious decision taken about the Queen Dowager.'[19] Very mysterious, indeed, on the assumption of Henry's innocence. But not so if the mother knew that her sons were alive when Richard fell, and could now obtain no tidings of them. If the boys ceased to live in July 1486, it was high time for Henry to silence the awkward questions of their mother in the following February. He did so by condemning her to life-long seclusion in a nunnery. Henry was terrified that a lady who knew some of his secrets, and probably suspected more, should be at large. In the end of the following year, and not till then, Henry's wife Elizabeth was at length crowned on November 25, 1487. The King and his mother beheld the ceremony from a stage, but there is no mention of the poor Queen's mother.

Years passed on. Perkin Warbeck personated young Richard, and no one had such good reason as Henry for knowing that he was an impostor. But the tyrant dared not tell how he knew that Perkin was a 'feigned boy,' as he called him. At length, in 1502 or thereabouts, the first detailed story of the murder of the two princes was put forward, after the execution of Sir James Tyrrel. It may be considered as Henry's official statement, and was evidently communicated to his paid historian Polydore Virgil, in whose hands it took the following form:

'Richard lived in continual fear, for the expelling thereof by any kind of means, he determined by death to despatch his nephews, because so long as they lived he could never be out of hazard. Wherefore he sent warrant to Robert Brakenbury, Lieutenant of the Tower, to procure their death with all diligence by some means convenient. Then he departed to York. But the Lieutenant of the Tower of London, after he had received the King's horrible commission, was astonished with the cruelty of the fact, and fearing lest, if he should obey, the same might one time or other turn to his own harm, did therefore defer the doing thereof in hope that the King would spare his own blood, or their tender age, or alter that heavy determination. But any one of these points were so far from taking place, seeing that the mind therein remained immovable, as that when King Richard understood the Lieutenant to make delay of that which he had commanded, he anon committed the charge of hastening that slaughter unto another, that is to say James Tyrrel, who, being forced to do the King's commandment, rode sorrowfully to London, and to the worst example that hath been almost ever heard of, murdered those babes of the issue royal. This end had Prince Edward and Richard his brother, but with what kind of death these silly children were executed is not certainly known.'

This was the story put forward by Henry after Tyrrel's death. He may have added some other particulars afterwards.[20] It is indeed probable that he did. A much more detailed fable appeared in the history attributed to More, and in Grafton, both by the same hand. It has been seen already that the statements of this writer are unworthy of credit, and it is very difficult to distinguish what parts were authorised by Henry,[20] and what parts were fabricated by the writer himself. His story is as follows:

'At the time when Sir James Tyrrel and John Dighton were in prison for treason in 1502, they made the following confession. Taking his way to Gloucester in August 1483, King Richard sent one John Green with a letter to Sir Robert Brakenbury, Constable of the Tower, ordering him to put the children to death. Sir Robert plainly answered that he would not put them to death; with which answer John Green returning, recounted the same to King Richard at Warwick.

'The same night the King said to a secret page of his, "Who shall I trust to do my bidding?" "Sir," quoth the page, "there lieth one on your pallet without who I dare well say will do your Grace's pleasure, the things were right hard that he would refuse." This was Sir James Tyrrel, who saw with envy that Ratcliffe and Catesby were rising above him in his master's favour. Going out to Sir James, who was reposing with his brother Thomas, the King said "what Sirs are you abed so soon?" then, calling Sir James into his chamber, he brake to him secretly his mind in this mischievous matter. Tyrrel assented, and was despatched on the morrow with a letter to Brakenbury, to deliver to Sir James all the keys of the Tower for one night. After which letter delivered and the keys received, Sir James appointed the night next ensuing to destroy them, devising before and preparing the means. The princes were in charge of Will Slaughter (or Slater) called "Black Will," who was set to serve them and see them sure. Sir James Tyrrel devised that they should be murdered in their beds; to the execution whereof he appointed Miles Forest, one of the four who kept them, a fellow flesh-bred in murder before time. To him he joined his horse-keeper, John Dighton, a big, broad, square, strong knave. They smothered the children, and Tyrrel ordered the murderers to bury them at the stair foot, metely deep in the ground, under a great heap of stones. Then rode Sir James in great haste to King Richard, and shewed him all the manner of the murder, who gave him great thanks, and as some say, then made him knight. But the King allowed not their burial in so vile a corner, because they were King's sons. Whereupon a priest of Sir Robert Brakenbury took them and secretly interred them in such a place as, by the occasion of his death which only knew it the very truth could never yet be very well known. Very truth is it and well known that at such time as Sir James Tyrrel was in the Tower for treason, committed against King Henry VII., both he and Dighton were examined together of this point, and both they confessed the murder to be done in the same manner as you have heard. God never gave a more notable example of what wretched end ensueth such despiteous cruelty. Miles Forest at St. Martin-le-Grand piecemeal miserably rotted away. Sir James Tyrrel died on Tower Hill. Dighton, indeed, yet walketh alive, in good possibility to be hanged ere he die.' Grafton says: 'John Dighton lived at Calais long after, no less disdained and hated than pointed at, and there died in great misery.' The version in Kennet[21] makes both 'Dighton and Forest die in a most horrible manner, rotting away by degrees.' 'Thus, as I have learned of them that much knewe and little cause had to lye were these two princes murdered.' This last sentence is audacious. These informers, if they ever existed outside the writer's imagination, had very strong cause to lie. They thus complied with the wishes of the reigning powers, and furthered their own interests. The truth, if they knew it, would have been their ruin.

The story published by Rastell
Such is the detailed accusation which was finally put forward. It contradicts the story of Morton, in his alleged conversation with Buckingham, who says that the princes were murdered long before the King reached Warwick, and while Buckingham was still at Court. On the face of it there is no confession in this long story. It is a concocted tale, and, indeed, this is fully admitted. It is merely represented to be the most probable among several others which were based on various accounts of the alleged confession. If there ever was a confession why should there be various accounts of it? The silence of Fabyan, and of Polydore Virgil, who must have heard of the confession if it had been made, seems conclusive against the truth of the story of a confession.

Even this selected tale, as we have received it, is full of gross improbabilities and inaccuracies. For instance, Tyrrel, who is said to have been knighted for the murder, had been a knight for twelve years, and was also a Knight Banneret of some standing.[22] The first thing that strikes one is that, if the story had been true, Henry must have heard the main facts when he came to London, after the battle of Bosworth. For Sir Robert Brackenbury's supersession during one day, with the delivery of all the keys to Sir James Tyrrel, must inevitably have been known to his subordinates. All the officials of the Tower must have known it, and must also have known that the boys disappeared at the same time. Many persons must have been acquainted with what happened. Some of them would certainly have been eager to gain favour with Henry by telling him, when he enquired about the missing princes. Yet there is no accusation in the Act of Attainder against Richard or Tyrrel, and it is pretended that nothing was known until 1502. This proves that the story was a subsequent fabrication.

There is another proof that the tale was false. It is alleged that Tyrrel and Dighton both confessed. Yet Tyrrel was beheaded for another offence in defiance of Henry's plighted word, and Dighton was rewarded with a residence at Calais and, as will be seen presently, a sinecure in Lincolnshire. These are proofs that there was no such confession as was alleged and was embodied in the story which, as it now stands, must be a fabrication. For if the confessions were ever made, Tyrrel and Dighton must have been tried and convicted for these atrocious murders, and duly punished. It has been suggested that Tyrrel could not be proceeded against because his statement was under the seal of confession. It is clear from the story that this was not so. The story tells us that Tyrrel and Dighton were subjected to examination, and that it was in that way that their confessions were obtained. In point of fact Dighton does not appear to have been arrested at all. The names of those who were concerned in Tyrrel's business are given by the chroniclers, and Dighton is not one of them.[23]

It seems unnecessary to dwell on the absurdities and contradictions in the story itself. They have often been exposed, and indeed they are admitted by Mr. Gairdner, who merely contends that the story may be true in the main, although the details may not be correct. But it is worth while to refer to the contention of Sharon Turner, Lingard and others, that the story must be true, on the ground that the persons mentioned in it were rewarded by King Richard.

They maintain that 'Brakenbury and Tyrrel received several grants, Green was made receiver of the Isle of Wight and of the castle and lordship of Porchester, Dighton was appointed Bailiff of the manor of Ayton, Forest was keeper of the wardrobe at Barnard Castle.' But it is not pretended that 'Black Will' was rewarded by Richard. We shall presently see that he was by Henry. All this can easily be answered. Brackenbury and Tyrrel were Yorkist officers of rank, and such grants would have been made to them in any circumstances for their distinguished services. As regards the others, either the grants were made previous to the alleged date of the murders, or there is no evidence to show whether they were made before or after, or in any way to connect them with the crime. The statement that Green held the receiverships of the Isle of Wight and Porchester is derived from an entirely unsupported note by Strype.[24] There was a man named Green who was Comptroller of Customs at Boston, and another who was appointed to provide horse meat and litter for the King's stables. But the dates of these appointments were July 24 and 30, 1483, before the alleged date of the murders.

A man named Dighton was made Bailiff of the manor of Ayton[25]; but there is nothing to show that this appointment was after the murder, or that he was Tyrrel's horse keeper, or that Tyrrel ever had a groom of that name. It will presently be seen that the John Dighton of the murder was probably a clergyman and not a groom.

It is alleged of Miles Forest that he was one of four jailers in the Tower who had charge of the princes, that he was a professional murderer, and that he rotted away miserably, in sanctuary at St. Martin's-le-Grand. These assertions are certainly false. Miles Forest was keeper of the wardrobe at Barnard Castle[26] in the valley of the Tees in Durham, 244 miles from the Tower of London. There he lived with his wife Joan and his son Edward. A footman serving at Middleham Castle, named Henry Forest, was perhaps another son.[27] There is not the slightest reason for believing that Forest entered upon his appointment after the date of the alleged murders; but much to disprove this assumption. He died in September 1484, and, as his wife and son received a pension for their lives, he must have been an old and faithful servant who had held the office for many years.

Dr. Lingard suggests that the pension was granted because Forest held the post for such a short time, assuming that he was one of the murderers in the story. This is certainly a very odd reason for granting a pension![28] Some authors have thought that it was Baynard's Castle, the residence of the Duchess of York in London, where Forest was keeper of the wardrobe. But the names in the manuscript are quite clear.

Miles Forest was a responsible old official in a royal castle, living with his wife and grown-up sons in the far north of England; where he died and his family received a pension for his long service. We are asked to believe that he was, at the same time, a notorious murderer who was also a jailer in the Tower of London, and that he died in sanctuary at St. Martin's-le-Grand.

How Forest's name got into the story concocted from the pretended confession it is not possible, at this distance of time, to surmise. But the author of it was quite unscrupulous, and the above considerations justify the conclusion that Forest's name was used without any regard for truth. There was a desire to give names and other details in order to throw an air of verisimilitude over the fable. We see the same attempt in the use of the name of Dighton. He was not Tyrrel's horse-keeper, nor probably the actual murderer, but a different person, as will be seen presently. But there was a John Dighton living at Calais when the story was made up, who was known to be connected, in some mysterious way, with the disappearance of the princes. So the author of the story hit upon his name to do duty as a strong square knave who did the deed. The name of Forest was doubtless adopted owing to some similar chance. The name of neither Deighton nor Forest occurs in the authorised version as given by Polydore Virgil.

Henry at first only accused Tyrrel of the murders; but it seems likely that he subsequently put forward some further details. There is an indication of the Green episode in Polydore Virgil. It is therefore probable that it was sanctioned by Henry's authority, as well as the details respecting the interment of the bodies. All the rest about Dighton and Forest, and the mode in which their crime was committed, is an impudent fabrication, as regards Richard, based upon the authorised story which is given by Polydore Virgil. The Italian was supplied with the statement sanctioned by Henry, and he distinctly tells us that the mode of death was not divulged.

If the mode of death was not divulged, the alleged confession of Tyrrel and Dighton cannot have taken place. For this is the very thing they would have confessed.

There remains a circumstantial story which may really have been connected with a secret tragedy. It has a very suspicious look of having been parodied out of something which actually happened. It is unlikely to have been pure invention. The fear of detection must have been always haunting Henry's mind. He would be tortured with the apprehension that the vague rumours he had set afloat against Richard were not believed; and this would be an inducement to promulgate a more detailed and circumstantial story. He could not and dared not accuse Tyrrel while he was alive, for a reason which will appear directly, but as soon as he was dead it would be safe to do so. At the time when he got rid of Tyrrel his son Arthur had just died. The man's mind would be filled with fear of retributive justice. Then the terror of detection would increase upon him. He would long to throw off suspicion from himself, by something more decisive than vague rumour. The notion of imputing his own crime, in its real details, to his predecessor, is quite in keeping with the workings of a subtle and ingenious mind such as we know Henry's to have been. Hence, Tyrrel, Green, Dighton, Black Will, may have been the accomplices of Henry VII., not of Richard III. As soon as Tyrrel was disposed of, the circumstantial story might be divulged as his confession, merely substituting the name of Richard for that of Henry, and the name of Brackenbury for that of Daubeney.[29]

With this clue to guide us, let us see what light can still be thrown on the dark question of the murders. Sir James Tyrrel of Gipping had been a knight of some distinction. He had been on a commission for exercising the office of Lord High Constable under Edward IV. He had been Master of the Horse and was created a Knight Banneret at Berwick siege. King Richard made him Master of the Henchmen and conferred many favours on him. But he was not one of the good men and true who stood by their sovereign to the end. His name drops out of history during those last anxious months before Bosworth. He was no doubt a trimmer. But he could not escape the consequences of his long service under the Yorkist kings. Henry Tudor deprived him of his Chamberlainship of the Exchequer, and of his Constableship of Newport, in order to bestow those appointments on his own friends.[30] Tyrrel had to wait patiently in the cold shade. But he was ambitious, unscrupulous, and ready to do a great deal for the sake of the new King's favour. Here was a ready instrument for such a man as Henry Tudor.

The die had been cast. The usurper had married Elizabeth of York and entered upon the year 1486. There was a dark deed which must be done. Henry set out on a progress to York, leaving London in the middle of March. On the 11th of the same month, John Green received from the new King a grant of a third of the manor of Benyngton in Hertfordshire.[31] For this favour Green had, no doubt, to perform some secret service which, if satisfactorily executed, would be more fully rewarded. This grant was a small retaining fee. We know from the story what that service was. We also know from the story that Green did not succeed. Henry VII. returned from his progress in June, only to find that Green had failed him in his need. Then Henry (not Richard) may well have exclaimed 'Who shall I trust to do my bidding?' '"Sir," quoth a secret councillor'[32] (called a page in the story), '"there waiteth without one who I dare well say will do your Grace's pleasure." So Tyrrel was taken into favour, and undertook to perform Henry's work with the understanding that he was to receive a sufficient reward. He became a knight of the King's body.[33] On June 16, 1486, Sir James Tyrrel late of Gipping received a general pardon.[34] There is nothing extraordinary in this. It was an ordinary practice, in those days, to grant general pardons on various occasions. But it marks the date when Henry found 'one without' who was ready to do his pleasure. Tyrrel, as the story tells us, was given a warrant to the Lieutenant of the Tower, conferring on him the needful powers. The murders were then committed, as the story informs us, by William Slaughter or Slater, called 'Black Will,' with the aid of John Dighton. Slater was, no doubt, the jailer. Master Dighton, however, was not Tyrrel's groom. A John Dighton was a priest, and possibly a chaplain in the Tower. He may have been only an accessory after the fact, in connexion with the interments. The bodies, as we are told in the story, were buried at the stair foot, 'metely deep in the ground'; where they were discovered in July 1674,[35] 188 years afterwards. The tale about their removal,[36] and the death of the priest, was no doubt inserted by Henry, to prevent that discovery. On July 16, 1486, Sir James Tyrrel received a second general pardon.[37] This would be very singular under ordinary circumstances, the second pardon having been granted within a month of the first. But it is not so singular when we reflect on what probably took place in the interval. There was an offence to be condoned which must be kept a profound secret. Thus we are able to fix the time of the murder of the two young princes between June 16 and July 16, 1486. One was fifteen and a half, the other twelve years of age.

Henry had at length found courage to commit the crime. He may have excused it to himself from the absolute necessity of his position. It had been perpetrated in profound secrecy. If the mother, brother, or sisters suspected anything, they could be silenced. They were absolutely at his mercy. Henry caused the mother to be stripped of her property, immured in Bermondsey nunnery, and left dependent on him for subsistence. She was thus effectually silenced. The Marquis of Dorset, half brother of the murdered boys, was committed to the Tower during 1487; but he succeeded in convincing the tyrant that there was nothing to fear from him, and was eventually released. The eldest sister was Henry's wife and at his mercy—the wife of a man who, as his admirers mildly put it, 'was not uxorious.' She was within two months of her confinement. Doubtless for that reason her mother kept all misgivings to herself. Henry married the next sister, Cicely, to his old uncle Lord Welles,[38] who would ensure her silence. She was married in that very year, and sent off to Lincolnshire. The three youngest were children, and in due time could be married to his adherents, or shut up in a nunnery.[39] Others who knew much, and must have suspected more, were silent in public, for their fortunes, perhaps their lives, depended on their silence.

Yet the guilty tyrant could have known no peace. He must have been haunted by the fear of detection, however industriously he might cause reports to be spread and histories to be written, in which his predecessor was charged with his crimes. Then there was the horror of having to deal with his accomplices. Here fortune favoured him. Green died in the end of 1486[40]; though hush money seems to have been paid to 'Black Will' for some time longer.[41] John Dighton was presented by Henry VII. with the living of Fulbeck near Grantham, in Lincolnshire, on May 2, 1487.[42] But he was expected to live on the other side of the Channel. Sir James Tyrrel received ample recompense. He seems to have been appointed to the office of Constable of Guisnes immediately after the date of his second general pardon.[43] He was next sent as ambassador to Maximilian, King of the Romans, to conclude a perpetual league and treaty. In 1493 Tyrrel was one of the Commissioners for negotiating the Treaty of Etaples with France. In August 1487 he received a grant for life of the Stewardship of the King's Lordship of Ogmore in Wales. But Henry, although he was obliged to reward his accomplices, was anxious to keep them on the other side of the Channel as much as possible. Dighton had to reside at Calais. Tyrrel was required to make an exchange, giving up his estates in Wales to the King, and receiving revenues from the county of Guisnes of equal value.[44] In 1498 Henry still addressed him as his well-beloved and faithful councillor.

The long-sought pretext for getting rid of Tyrrel was found in 1502. The usurper dreaded the Earl of Suffolk, King Richard's nephew, as a claimant to the throne. He heard that Tyrrel had favoured the escape of the ill-fated young prince to Germany. Henry would be terrified at the idea of Tyrrel taking the side of another claimant, and publicly denouncing his misdeeds. He ordered the arrest of his accomplice, but Tyrrel refused to surrender the castle of Guisnes. He was besieged by the whole garrison of Calais. Henry then ordered Dr. Fox, the Bishop of Winchester and Lord Privy Seal, one of his most intimate associates, to send a promise under the privy seal, to the effect that Tyrrel should come and go in security if he would confer with Sir Thomas Lovell, Henry's Chancellor of the Exchequer, on board a ship at Calais. Tyrrel should have known his master by this time. But even he had not gauged the full depth of Tudor perfidy. He was deceived by the 'pulchris verbis' of Bishop Fox.[45] When he came on board he was told that he would be pitched overboard unless he sent a token to his son to deliver up the castle. The token was sent, and the King's promise under his privy seal was broken. Tyrrel was safely locked up in a dungeon of the Tower and beheaded without trial and in great haste on May 6, 1502.

At length Henry could breathe freely. Green and Tyrrel were dead. Slater does not appear again, so it may be assumed that he also had been got rid of. Only Dighton remained. He had to reside at Calais on the proceeds of his sinecure in Lincolnshire, and to be useful as a false witness. We know from Rastell and Grafton that he did live and die at Calais. The identity of names suggests the probability that he was a brother or son of the John Dighton who was Bailiff of Ayton Manor.

The story told in the publications of Grafton and Rastell was generally accepted as true; although, even after the lapse of so many years, there must have been many old people who knew it to be false. These people had the choice between silence and ruin. As they died off, the belief in the story became more and more universal. This fable, appearing first in Grafton, was the final touch to the hideous and grotesque caricature which was portrayed by the Tudor historians and dramatised by Shakespeare. The history of its reception in all its absurd and improbable details, of the ineradicable prejudice which could keep it alive for four centuries, and long after sound methods of criticism had begun to be applied to other historical questions, forms a curious chapter in the record of human credulity.

Henry Tudor suffered for his crimes. The secret removal of his wife's brothers and of her uncle's illegitimate son failed to complete the catalogue of them. Young Edward Earl of Warwick was another stumbling block in his way. But again his superstitious mind recoiled from guilt which his judgment recommended. If his wife had been legitimate, there would have been no danger to Henry from the Earl of Warwick; that young prince would have been far removed from the succession. His wife's illegitimacy made her cousin the rightful heir, and hence another crime seemed necessary. Henry put off the perpetration of this crime for years. Ferdinand of Spain refused to allow a marriage between his daughter and Henry's son Arthur, until the rightful heir to the crown of England had been put out of the way. This refusal at length gave Henry a motive for the crime which outweighed his superstitious fears. He committed it in a way which was thoroughly characteristic. He caused Perkin Warbeck to be given access to the Earl of Warwick in the Tower, and some of the jailers were told to suggest an attempt at escape. An informer, named Robert Cleymound, was employed to listen to the conversations of the two lads, and to report that an escape was meditated by them. This was made a capital charge against the young prince. He was subjected to a mock trial, so that Henry might indulge in his hope of limited liability for murder, and was then slaughtered on November 28, 1499. A man who was capable of committing such a cowardly murder in such a way was certainly as capable of the crime of which he falsely accused King Richard.

As soon as Richard III. was dead, Edward Earl of Warwick became de jure King of England, not only as the acknowledged heir to the dead King but also as the nearest in succession, and as the last male Plantagenet. His existence was, at that time, a serious danger to the usurper, who did not lose a day in securing the poor lad's person. If, as Henry afterwards caused it to be proclaimed, the declaration of the illegitimacy of the children of Edward IV. was false, then the Earl of Warwick ceased to be dangerous; and there was no object in condemning him to perpetual imprisonment. It was a useless act of injustice and cruelty. But if Henry knew that, in spite of his attempts to destroy all evidence of the illegitimacy, the awkward fact remained, his injustice and cruelty are explained. They afford one more proof of the truth of Dr. Stillington's evidence, which led to the accession of King Richard.

Warwick was now put out of the way, in obedience to the King of Spain. But remorse gnawed the tyrant's heart. His father confessor, though doubtless an astute courtier, failed to soothe his conscience. He sought the help of wizards and quacks. But his superstitions gave him little consolation. The Spanish Ambassador noticed the change that had taken place in Henry's appearance since the murder of young Warwick. Don Pedro de Ayala had been in Scotland during the interval. The King had come to look many years older in a single month. Dark thoughts were haunting his mind. His eldest son died, and an anonymous writer has recorded that he showed some feeling, and exchanged words of consolation with his wife.[46] This is quite in keeping with one side of his character. The other side is shown in his harsh treatment of Catharine of Aragon, in his monstrous proposal to marry her when his wife died, in his disgusting inquiries respecting the young Queen of Naples, and in his revolting offer for the hand of Juana (la loca). But the necessities of his position gave him little time for the indulgence either of such grief as he was capable of feeling or of the other less creditable sentiments that are revealed in his correspondence. His son's death must have seemed to him the Nemesis of his crimes. Yet within a month he was beheading Tyrrel, and fabricating a story to account for the disappearance of his wife's brothers.

We can never know how much that wife suffered. No doubt she was kept in ignorance of the fate of her brothers. But she knew they were not killed by her uncle. She saw her mother immured in a nunnery for life. She saw her brother, the Marquis of Dorset, committed to the Tower. She saw the sister, nearest to her in age, hurriedly married to old Lord Welles. She must have suspected much, even if she knew nothing. She could not have been kept in ignorance of the cruel imprisonment of her young cousin Warwick. She must have shuddered at his murder. She would have been less than human if she did not loathe the perpetrator of these deeds, even though he was the father of her children. The unhappy wife was released from companionship with the murderer of her relations on February 11, 1503.

Another crime was contemplated by the miserable usurper, to make his position safe. But he could not get the Earl of Suffolk into his clutches without giving a solemn promise to spare his life. He evaded the promise by advising his son to commit the crime after his death.[47] Murderous designs thus occupied his mind, even on his death-bed.

Yet one of Henry's last acts was an act of restitution. He restored in blood, and to all his estates, the son of his accomplice, Sir James Tyrrel, on April 6, 1507, feeling no doubt that the greater criminal of the two remained unpunished, except by his own remorseful conscience.

Henry became haggard and restless. Prosperous and successful as the world deemed him, we may rely upon it that his crimes were not unpunished. His cowardly nature was peculiarly susceptible to the torturing pangs of remorse. He died, full of terrors, prematurely old and worn out, at the early age of fifty-two, on April 21, 1509. He was successful as the world counts success. He accumulated riches by plunder and extortion. He established a despotic government. He cleared his path of rivals. We are told that he inaugurated a new era—era of 'benevolences' and Star Chamber prosecutions. In all these things he succeeded. He, and the writers he employed, were pre-eminently successful as slanderers. They succeeded in blackening for all time the fame of a far better man than Henry Tudor.

Hitherto we have been engaged in the investigation of positive evidence. There is, however, another side to the question—a negative side. We must now examine Henry's omissions. According to his story he found the two boys missing when he arrived in London after the battle of Bosworth. If Henry's story was true, it must have been well known to every official in the Tower that Sir Robert Brackenbury gave up charge to Sir James Tyrrel and that the boys had never been seen since. If Henry made any enquiries he must have heard this, and the whole story would have come out. Why were not Tyrrel, Dighton, Green, and Black Will arrested, tried, and hanged? Why was not King Richard accused of murdering his nephews in the Act of Attainder? It is very improbable, though just possible, that Henry might have failed to ascertain the details of the story, assuming it to have been true, when he first arrived. Still, if the boys were missing, it is certain that he would have accused Richard of their murder in the Act of Attainder. His omission to do so amounts to a strong presumption that they were not missing. According to the story, Tyrrel and Dighton confessed the murder in 1502. Why were they not tried and executed for it? This must have been done if there ever was a confession. It was clearly not made under the seal of confession, according to the story, but under the pressure of official examination. Tyrrel was actually beheaded, in great haste, on a frivolous charge, and his capture was a breach of a royal promise given under the privy seal. Surely this would have been avoided if there had been any other way, and there was another way. There was every possible reason for trying him for these horrible murders and executing him for them. Why was not this done? There can be only one answer. There was no confession. Henry's treatment of Dighton is still more extraordinary. It is alleged that he also confessed the murder. Yet he was not only unpunished, but allowed to live at large in Calais. When we find that Henry gave rewards to Tyrrel, Dighton, Green, and Black Will, the conclusion is inevitable that there was no confession to the King in 1502, because it was quite unnecessary. The confession was due from Henry himself.

Another omission in Henry's conduct is equally incriminating. If the children of Edward IV. were legitimate, why was not the Act of Richard III. published, which alleged their illegitimacy, and its falsehood fully exposed by evidence? Why was such extraordinary anxiety shown to conceal its contents, and violence threatened against anyone who preserved a record of them? Why were absurd, improbable, and contradictory tales invented, in substitution of the statements made in Richard's Act? There can be only one answer. The statements in the Act were true.

In no other way can Henry's cruel treatment of the young Earl of Warwick be accounted for. If Elizabeth was the legitimate heiress of York, then there could be no danger from Warwick, and no reason for molesting him. He was simply a harmless young prince, far removed from the succession. But if Elizabeth and her sisters were not legitimate, the case was very different. Warwick was then de jure Edward V. There was every reason for a usurper to imprison and kill him. The Lambert Simnel insurrection is explained in that case. It would have been without motive if Warwick came after five others in the succession to the crown. Here again Henry's conduct can only be explained in one way. Warwick was imprisoned and killed for the same reason that Richard's Act of Parliament, declaring his title, was destroyed.

The conduct of Henry adds weight to all the other evidence. It cannot be reconciled with his innocence. It can only be explained by his guilt.

[1] William Catesby was the son of Sir William Catesby of Ashby St. Leger in Northamptonshire, by Philippa, heiress of Sir William Bishopston. He was a learned man, well versed in the laws of his country. On June 30, 1483, he become Chancellor of the Exchequer, and was chosen Speaker of King Richard's Parliament. Lord Rivers had such confidence in his integrity that he nominated him executor of his will. His wife was Margaret, daughter of William Lord Zouch. He made his own will on August 25, 1485, leaving his wife sole executrix and dividing his property among his children. His unjust attainder was afterwards reversed in favour of his son George.

[2] Yet Dr. Lingard tells us that 'Henry was careful not to stain his triumph with blood.' This is a strange assertion, when it is directly followed by the admission that he did stain his triumph with blood. Of all his prisoners,' he continues, 'three only suffered death, the notorious [why notorious?] Catesby and two persons of the name of Brecher, who probably had merited that distinction by their crimes' (iv. p. 260). This is a pure assumption, unwarranted by any evidence whatever. If the word 'loyalty' had been substituted for 'crimes,' Dr. Lingard would have been nearer the truth. All that this historian's praise amounts to is that Henry refrained from committing a massacre, such as he caused to be perpetrated on a subsequent occasion, when Warbeck's followers landed in Kent.

Mr. Gairdner says: 'Whether these executions were just is another question, save that the ministers of a bad king must take the responsibility even of his worst deeds' (p. 311). He evidently sees that Henry's conduct is indefensible; and he has elsewhere admitted that Richard was not a bad King.

The more impartial Hutton says: 'Thus the first regal act performed by Henry was an act of tyranny' (Bosworth, p. 148).

[3] 'For men remember not any King of England before that tyme which used such a furniture of daily soldiers.'—Hall, p. 425.

[4] Gairdner.

[5] 'De jure belli et de jure Lancastriæ.'

[6] Rot. Parl. vi. 289a. The monk of Croyland had a copy, but luckily for him, he was not found out.

[7] Plumpton Correspondence. Letter dated December 13, 1485 (p. 49).

[8] Translation by Mr. Gairdner in his Henry VII. (p. 38).

[9] 11 Henry VII. cap. 1 (1496). It was enacted that no person serving the King and Sovereign Lord of the land for the time being shall be convicted of high treason, nor suffer any forfeiture or imprisonment. In the previous year the usurper, also no doubt from fear of public opinion, had paid 10l. 1s. to James Keyley for King Richard's tomb (Excerp. Hist. p. 105).

[10] Grant to John of Gloucester of an annual rent of 20l. during the King's pleasure, from the revenues of the manor of Kingston Lacey, parcel of the Duchy of Lancaster in the county of Dorset. March 1 1486.—Materials for a History of the Reign of Henry VII. i.

[11] 'About the same time there was a base-born son of King Richard III. made away, having been kept long in

prison.'—Buck, p. 105, from Chron. MS. in 4to. apud Dr. Rob. Cotton.

[12] Rymer, xii. p. 265.

[13] A critic, after reading this work, objected that partiality was shown by the fact that while the older writers are blamed for blackening Richard's character in other ways, in order to make the charge of murdering the princes more plausible, precisely the same thing is done with Henry VII. But the other charges against Henry are proved and acknowledged facts. Those against Richard have been disproved. The older writers are justly blamed for inventing calumnies.

[14] Fabyan.

[15] Polydore Virgil. Lord Bacon observes, in his Life of Henry VII., 'which proceeding, being even at that time taxed for rigorous and undue makes it probable there was some greater matter against her, which the King, upon reason of policy, would not publish.' Undoubtedly, there was; she knew too much.

[16] Dr. Lingard (iv. 279 and 286n) and Nicolas (p. lxxviii) bring forward a negotiation with the King of Scots, in November 1487, in which Henry proposed that James III. should marry the Queen Dowager, as a proof that he never deprived her of liberty. If he suspected her, they argue, he would not have given her the opportunity of plotting against him, which her situation as Queen of Scotland would have afforded her. Although Henry may have momentarily entertained the idea of getting rid of a woman who knew too much by this expatriation, he soon changed his mind. She was safer in his power. The negotiations

were broken off, and James was killed in the following year.

[17] She was present when her daughter gave audience to the French Ambassador in November 1489 (Leland Coll. iv. 249). Henry allowed her a pension of 400l. a year from February 19, 1490. Her will, dated April 10, 1492, is witnessed by the Abbot of Bermondsey. She here confirms the fact of the seizure of her property by her son-in-law. Her words are decisive on that point. 'Whereas I have no worldly goods.' Sir H. Nicolas tried to account for this by suggesting that she only had a life interest in her income. But this will not explain so sweeping a statement as that she had no worldly goods at all (p. lxxx).

Mr. Gairdner says: 'Henry VII. found it advisable to shut up his mother-in-law in a monastery, and had not the slightest scruple in taking her property away from her' (Richard III. p. 88).

[18] Letters Patent, March 4, 1486.

[19] Gairdner's Henry VII.

[20] 'The King's manner of showing things by pieces and side lights hath so muffled it that it hath left it almost a mystery to this day.'—Lord Bacon.

[21] i. 501.

[22] He was made a Knight Banneret at the taking of Berwick, in 1482.

[23] They were Sir William Courtenay, one Welborne, and Tyrrel's son, who were pardoned; Sir Walter Tyrrel and Sir John Wyndham beheaded; a Ship-master hanged at Tyburn,

a Poursuivant named Curson, and a Yeoman named Matthew Jones executed at Guisnes; all on suspicion of having aided the Earl of Suffolk to escape.

[24] In Rennet's England, i. p. 552. Mr. Gairdner, referring to this note by Strype, says: 'I own I cannot find his authority.'—Richard III. p. 164.

[25] Harl. MS. 433, fol. 55.

[26] Harl. MS. 433, fol. 78 and 187.

[27] Ibid. 433, fol. 118.

[28] v. 577.

[29] The Earl of Oxford was appointed Constable of the Tower for life, on September 22, 1485. We may hope that Oxford, who did not reside, had no guilty knowledge.

[30] Memorials of Henry VII. i. pp. 41, 95.

[31] Memorials of Henry VII. i. p. 384.

[32] Was this Morton? Buck had heard so.

[33] Memorials of Henry VII. ii. p. 251.

[34] Ibid. i. p. 460.

[35] Sandford, v. p. 404.

[36] 'The latter part of the tale, which declares their interment by the priest and their removal by Richard's order, was evidently fabricated by Henry, to prevent the hazard of a search.'—Hutton's Bosworth, p. 169.

[37] Memorials of Henry VII. i. p. 486.

[38] Lord Welles was a half brother, on the mother's side, of Henry's mother.

[39] Anne was eleven. In due time she was married to the son of the Earl of Surrey. Katherine was only seven. When she was twenty she became the wife of the Lancastrian Earl of Devonshire. Bridget, the youngest, was five. She was immured in a nunnery at Dartford, as soon as she was old enough.

[40] Memorials of Henry VII. i. p. 617.

[41] As late as 1488 there is a grant of five marks, at Easter, 'by way of reward,' to William Slater. If this was the jailer, he received hush money for two years after the perpetration of the murders. He is not heard of again. Memorials of Henry VII. ('Writs under the Privy Seal. Easter Term 3 Hen. VII.'), ii. p. 298.

[42] Memorials of Henry VII. ii. p. 148.

[43] This appears from general pardons having been granted to the former Constable, to the Chaplain, and to twenty-four soldiers of the garrison of Guisnes on the same date, July 16. No doubt these pardons were on the occasion of the appointment of a new Constable, and the return of part of the garrison to England.

[44] Memorials of Henry VII. ii. pp. 188, 251.

[45] This is an ugly story. Dr. Richard Fox was originally an agent of Morton and other conspirators abroad. This discreditable work brought him to Paris early in 1485, where he became known to Henry Tudor. A man so

employed could not have been a good priest. He came with Henry to England as his Secretary, and was of course well rewarded. He became Bishop of Winchester and Lord Privy Seal; and appears to have been munificent and diligent as a prelate. By his 'pulchris verbis' he treacherously drew Tyrrel into the clutches of Sir Thomas Lovell. This appears from a letter of the Earl of Suffolk to the Emperor Maximilian dated at Aix-la-Chapelle on May 12, 1502. So hurried were the proceedings against Tyrrel that he was actually beheaded six days before the date of Suffolk's letter announcing his treacherous capture. Bishop Fox has been much eulogised. But no one could be for years in the inner counsels of such a man as Henry VII. without being in sympathy with his ways, which certainly do not deserve eulogy.

[46] Leland's Coll. v. p. 373. From an anonymous manuscript. Letters of Richard III. and Henry VII., B. P. i. Pref. p. 29.

[47] Lord Herbert of Cherbury, Life of Henry VIII. p. 36. 'Our King executing what his father at his departure out of the world commanded, as Bellay hath it.'

CHAPTER VI MR. GAIRDNER'S RICHARD III

It will be interesting, in conclusion, to examine the critical treatment of these questions by the latest historian who has written on the subject.[1] Mr. Gairdner argues in favour of the Tudor portrait of the last Plantagenet King, but only to a limited extent.

The thick and thin believers in the Tudor caricature, such as Hume and Lingard, aroused doubts in many minds. Mr. Gairdner is the most formidable enemy to the memory of the gallant young King that has yet appeared, because he is, beyond comparison, the best informed author that has ever treated of this part of history, has conscientiously striven to be fair and impartial, and has stated both sides of the question, while retaining a belief in Richard's worst crimes. His predecessors, who have taken his view, simply adopted all the statements of Tudor writers as facts, and have depicted a cool, calculating, scheming, cruel, and most revolting villain without a redeeming feature. They thus portrayed at least a possible monster. But Mr. Gairdner, while striving to be fair and just, still clings to what he calls 'tradition,' that is to the Tudor stories of crimes, told many years after the time. The two things are incompatible, so that he produces a monster which would be impossible anywhere. His Richard III. is a prince, headlong and reckless as to consequences, but of rare gifts and with many redeeming qualities. He was wise and able, brave, generous, religious, fascinating, and yet had committed two very cowardly assassinations before he was nineteen, murdered his defenceless nephews, and gratuitously slandered his mother. Such a monster is an impossibility in real life. Even Dr. Jekyll and Mr. Hyde are nothing to it.

Let us see how Mr. Gairdner arrived at his two-sided monster. He explains his method in his preface. He demurs to the view of the late Mr. Buckle that commonly received opinions should be doubted until they are found to stand the test of argument.[2] He lays it down that no attempt to set aside traditional views can be successful until the history of the particular epoch has been re-written, and the new version exhibits a moral harmony with the facts of subsequent times and of times preceding.[3]

'Tradition,' Mr. Gairdner tells us, is an interpreter and nothing more, and seldom supplies anything material in the way of facts.[4] Yet he adds that the attempt to discard it is like an attempt to learn a language without a master, and he thinks that a sceptical spirit is a most fatal one in history. It is difficult to follow him when he announces that, in spite of this view of tradition, his plan is to place the chief reliance on contemporary information, and that this treatment of history should be adhered to.[5]

'Tradition,' in Richard's case, means the embellishments of later chroniclers writing long after the events, in the interests of another dynasty. Unfortunately Mr. Gairdner does not always adhere to contemporary evidence, but prefers 'tradition.'

In the case of Richard III. Mr. Gairdner thinks that it is not clearly shown that the story would be more intelligible without 'tradition,' and that the said 'tradition' is not well accounted for.

Let us endeavour to test these two propositions by the light of Mr. Gairdner's own admissions.

His Richard stood high in general estimation when Duke of Gloucester.[6] As King the people showed him marks of loyalty.[7] In the north undoubtedly, and perhaps with the common people generally, he was highly popular, and there was every evidence of devoted loyalty and personal popularity at the time of Buckingham's rising.[8] He was an able ruler,[9] he had the confidence even of his enemies in his justice and integrity,[10] he was generous not only to the widows and children of fallen enemies, but even to the wives of rebels in open revolt,[11] his generous acts were done graciously and in no grudging spirit,[12] there was nothing mean or paltry in his character,[13] his manners were ingratiating, and he had great influence over others.

A person so described is very unintelligible if the assassinations and infamies of 'tradition' have to be added. Richard's character is far more intelligible without them; and 'tradition' is perfectly accounted for by the necessities of the new dynasty, whose well-paid writers created it.

Mr. Gairdner acknowledges that 'tradition' seldom supplies anything material in the way of facts. Yet he maintains that traditional views cannot be set aside unless the history of the particular epoch is re-written, and the new version exhibits a moral harmony with the facts of subsequent times and times preceding.

Of course certain passages in history would have to be re-written when they were found to be erroneous. But the truth or falsehood of a particular accusation cannot be affected by facts of subsequent times or times preceding. Its truth or falsehood is not established by moral harmony with something else, but by contemporary evidence.

My detailed remarks on Mr. Gairdner's views respecting Richard's alleged crimes are intended to show that his conclusions are mistaken when they deviate from his own plan of placing the chief reliance on contemporary evidence; and that a sceptical spirit, in the special case of

Richard, is absolutely necessary if the truth is to be reached.

Mr. Gairdner assumes that Richard murdered his nephews, and, on the strength of his guilt in committing that crime, he argues that the criminal was capable of anything during his former life, and on this ground believes in some of the other alleged crimes. The earlier accusers appear to argue in the reverse way. They accumulated every accusation they could think of, with reference to Richard's former life, in order to make the main crime more probable.

Though Mr. Gairdner's sense of justice obliges him to make so many admissions that the revolting monster of earlier histories almost disappears in his hands, yet in some respects he goes backwards. For he still clings to the assassinations of young Edward and of Henry VI., two horrible stories invented by later chroniclers. Surely the sound arguments of Sharon Turner and others ought to have been allowed finally to expunge these revolting fables from our history.

However, in Mr. Gairdner's book the venomous hunchback, born with teeth, entirely disappears. He gives us, in his place, a prince 'whose bodily deformity, though perceptible, was probably not conspicuous.' In his latest version, he abandons the assassination in the King's tent by his chief nobles. He thinks that Richard is unduly blamed about the murder of Henry VI. because it was probably sanctioned by others. He pronounces Richard to be guiltless of the death of Clarence. He admits that Anne was not married to young Edward, and that there is some reason to believe that she regarded Richard with favour. He gives no countenance to the insinuation that Anne was poisoned by her husband. He is inclined to credit the pre-contract of Edward IV. with Lady Eleanor Butler, and admits the strength of the evidence for its truth. He considers it remarkable that a man (Lord Rivers) who suffered by the Protector's order could appeal to him to be supervisor of his will. This would certainly be very remarkable if Gloucester and Rivers had been accomplices in two cowardly murders. Such monsters do not usually place confidence in each other. But the simple truth is not remarkable. Rivers felt that he had failed and must pay the penalty, but he placed full and deserved confidence in Richard's honour and integrity, as well as in his generosity.

Mr. Gairdner has thus removed much of the Tudor garbage from the picture of King Richard, but he will not sweep off the rest. His researches show him that the accusations of the Tudor writers are irreconcilable with the results of modern investigations. But his preconceived convictions, although much shaken, are not yet swept away. The inevitable result is that the life and character of Richard become a puzzle to him. Generous, kind, and patriotic acts continue to be recorded of the young King throughout his life, which are certainly not the acts of an habitual assassin. Those who are forced to acknowledge the facts, and yet cling to a belief in the fictions, find themselves in a tight place. This is Mr. Gairdner's position. He will not give up all the Tudor fables, and clings to such shreds of them as it seems to him possible to retain. Yet his own researches force him to abandon much and to apologize for the rest. The man's acts cannot be made to harmonize with the Tudor calumnies. The consequent contradictions necessitate the explanation that 'Richard was not yet even a hardened criminal' (p. 46); while some of the events which cannot be disputed are 'certainly remarkable' (p. 91), and others 'almost inconceivable' (p. 214).

Mr. Gairdner cannot quite give up the fable of the murder of young Edward at Tewkesbury. He admits that it was not countenanced by any contemporary writer, that it was first told by Fabyan many years after the event, and that the final embellishment, according to which young Gloucester was a participator in the crime, was a tradition of later times. Yet in his history, he preferred the tradition of later times to the story of Fabyan, although he thought the latter had every appearance of probability, and he preferred both to the unanimous testimony of contemporaries.[14] There is no reason for this topsy-turvy criticism, except that what Mr. Gairdner calls a 'tradition' accuses Richard, while Fabyan and the contemporaries do not.

His arguments in favour of the murder given in his 'Life of Richard III.' were that Richard may very probably have been a murderer at nineteen, if any one of his other alleged murders be admitted; and that he was capable of a cowardly assassination because he condemned prisoners to death in his judicial capacity. On these grounds alone he urged that the accusation is not to be rejected. He did not maintain that it is true, but that it cannot safely be pronounced apocryphal. He also admitted that Richard ought not to bear the whole responsibility, as he was only an accessory. This is very different from the downright condemnation of Hume and Lingard.[15] The fable is evidently doomed. But there can be no sharing of responsibility. If Richard stabbed his young cousin he was a cowardly ruffian, whether other ruffians did the same or not. If he did not, no words can be strong enough to express the infamy of his Italian slanderer.

Mr. Gairdner has since shifted his ground,[16] and, adopting Warkworth's version, has admitted that young Edward was slain in the field, calling for succour to the Duke of Clarence; but he cannot bring himself to acquit Richard altogether, and suggests that he was the slayer, because no meaner person would have taken the responsibility of slaying so valuable a prisoner. As if these fine-drawn distinctions were made in the heat of a desperate mêlée. But even so, the two boys being about the same age and weight, it was a fair fight. There was no crime. Yet Mr. Gairdner still calls it a 'murder'! Of course there is no authority or ground whatever for bringing Richard in at all, if Warkworth's version is adopted. Verily the fiction is dying hard!

There is no reason for considering the Duke of Gloucester to have been capable of assassinating his cousin because it was his duty to sit in judgment on prisoners as Lord Constable. The trial of rebels before a court consisting of the Earl Marshal and the Lord Constable was perfectly legal and constitutional. Speaking of trial by jury, Chief Justice Fortescue laid it down that in England 'some cases might be proved before two only, such as facts occurring on the high seas, and proceedings before the Earl Marshal and the Lord Constable.' It was a constitutional tribunal, and, although very young, his office of Constable made it incumbent on Gloucester to sit in judgment. The Earl Marshal, being an older man, would probably take the leading part. Mr. Gairdner says that it was a summary tribunal and that all who were brought before it were beheaded. It was a constitutional tribunal, and only thirteen prisoners were condemned to death. As many as twelve of the leaders were pardoned, if not more, and all the subordinate officers and soldiers. In comparison with Lancaster and Tudor proceedings under similar circumstances,[17] the tribunal at Tewkesbury was lenient.[18]

Although it does not affect Richard, a serious accusation against Edward IV. should here receive attention, namely, that his enemies who had taken refuge in Tewkesbury Abbey might, in Mr. Gairdner's words, 'have saved themselves by flight if Edward had not sworn in church upon the sacraments to pardon them. As to the executions being vindictive, I should very much like to know what other character they can possibly bear except that they were perfidious also.' They may be called vindictive if all executions for treason in a civil war are to be so called, but not, as Mr. Gairdner evidently intends, in any special sense. The sting of the accusation, however, is in the alleged perfidy.

Here is Habington's version of the accusation referred to by Mr. Gairdner. 'King Edward with his sword drawn would have entered the church and forced the fugitives thence. But a priest with the eucharist in his hand would not let him until he had granted to all a free pardon. But this pardon betrayed them, for on the Monday after they were taken out of the church and all beheaded.'

There are some assertions so contrary to all reasonable probability that they cannot be accepted, after having been examined with any care. This is one. The fugitives had taken refuge in the abbey because they were too closely pursued, and escape was not possible. How could they have saved themselves by flight when Tewkesbury was occupied, and the abbey surrounded by Edward's army? We are asked to believe that the King swore on the sacrament to pardon all, and next day beheaded all. Why should he commit this wholly useless act of perjury? There was no object, nothing to gain by it. Even if he refrained from taking the fugitives out of the church, which the story has it that he did do next day, he could soon have starved them out. It is untrue that all were beheaded. The story that he took such an unnecessary oath, intending to break it next day, is too absurd for acceptance. As the result proved, the King intended to have the prisoners tried before the Earl Marshal's Court, to cause some of the condemned to undergo their sentence, and to pardon others. He may possibly have told a priest that some would be pardoned. This would soon be turned, by partisans, into all being pardoned. In point of fact many were pardoned.

In discussing the alleged murder of Henry VI., Mr. Gairdner admits that 'an after age has been a little unjust to Richard in throwing upon him the whole responsibility of acts in which others perhaps participated.' But this amounts to a surrender of the whole point at issue. Richard either stabbed Henry VI. without his brother's knowledge, as the story attributed to Sir Thomas More tells us, or he did nothing. The boy of eighteen either obtained the custody of the Tower from his political enemy Lord Rivers, without the King's knowledge and consent, went to Henry's room, and stabbed the unarmed feeble invalid with a dagger, or he did not. Assuming the murder, Mr. Gairdner appears to mean by saying that others participated in it, that it was committed by Edward IV. and his Council, with the complicity of Rivers the Constable of the Tower. It is difficult to see what else he can mean. In that case the statement of the historian whom Mr. Gairdner believes to be Sir Thomas More, that Gloucester committed the murder without his brother's knowledge, is false.

Mr. Gairdner is mistaken about the household accounts. He thinks they only refer to the expenses and diet of Henry's servants. But the statement is clear and distinct that the expenses and diet for fourteen days after May 11, that is until May 24, are for Henry himself as well as his attendants. The only contemporary writer gives the same date, and Polydore Virgil, the official writer employed by Henry VII., tells us that his death was long after May 21, the day when Richard was in the Tower. Fabyan and Warkworth's informant give this date of May 21, in contradiction to the above conclusive evidence for the 24th or night of the 23rd. First they assumed the murder, and then they fixed the date of it on the only day when Gloucester was there to commit it. The household accounts expose this fabrication of dates.

Mr. Gairdner settles the difference between these authorities in a very summary fashion. 'Considering the source from which this statement comes' (for the 23rd) 'and its total disagreement with the accounts of almost all other writers in or near the time, it is impossible to attach any weight to it whatever.' The answer to the last part of this sentence is that the writer in question was the only one who wrote at the time; and that Warkworth and Fabyan, who wrote afterwards, are the only authorities for the 21st. Moreover Polydore Virgil, who had access to all official records, directly contradicts Warkworth and Fabyan, giving a much later date for the death of Henry VI.

Mr. Gairdner's other reason for rejecting the evidence of the writer in Fleetwood is that his report was official, and that consequently 'it is impossible to attach any weight to his statement whatever.' But on this principle Mr. Gairdner ought to sweep away all the accusations against Richard made by Tudor writers; for they are almost all the work of official partisans engaged, some of them paid to vilify the predecessor of their employer. Official chroniclers should be held in suspicion, and their narratives call for strict scrutiny. But there ought to be discrimination. If a document is official, it is not ipso facto false. There must be some evidence against it besides its official character. The writer who sent a narrative of the restoration of Edward IV. to the citizens of Bruges has not been detected in any misrepresentations. He gave a plain statement of the course of events, with no other object than to convey to the generous Flemings a knowledge of what had befallen the gallant young King whom they had befriended. He gave the 23rd as the date of the death of Henry VI. because the fact was within his own personal knowledge. This was not the case with any writer who has given a different date. According to the story the murder was committed in profound secrecy. The most virulent Tudor chroniclers only mention it as a suspicion. There was no ground whatever for the accusation, or they would have stated it. This suspicion, as regards Gloucester, was never whispered until the Tudor King was in power. It is, therefore, to the last degree improbable that, assuming there was a crime, it should have been needlessly divulged to the author of the letter to Bruges with orders that he should falsify the date. If the murder was a secret, as the Tudor chroniclers affirm, and if, as two of them assert, the date of Henry's death was known, it would have been useless to falsify a date which was known, to conceal an unknown deed. The inevitable conclusion is that the date was not falsified in the letter to Bruges; and that the 23rd was the day of Henry's death. The suggested falsification would be such an act of folly as no writer, even if he wrote officially, would be at all likely to commit; for it would be uselessly raising a suspicion where none existed. If anything of the kind had been attempted, the date of Richard's presence, not of Henry's death, would have been altered. But there is really nothing to raise a suspicion of the author's good faith.

Very different are the authorities who contradict him. Warkworth's story contains a statement that the Duke of Gloucester was present in the Tower at the time of Henry's death, and then the date is given with that excessive minuteness of day and hour which is characteristic of the lie circumstantial. The whole story is dished up with a miracle or two. It is not necessary to suppose that Dr. Warkworth was himself guilty of misrepresentation. He was evidently very credulous, and he was deceived by his informer. As for Fabyan, he wrote in the days of Henry VII. and was desirous of suiting his tales to the wishes of that jealous tyrant. Apart from the undesigned evidence of the household accounts, the letter to the citizens of Bruges must, on every principle of historical criticism, be accepted as a more reliable authority, on this point, than the miracle-monger Warkworth or the unscrupulous time-server Fabyan. The whole story about Henry VI. having been murdered by Gloucester is palpably a Tudor calumny invented long afterwards, and told so clumsily that it certainly did not deserve the success which has attended it.[19]

Mr. Gairdner acquits Richard of responsibility for the death of Clarence, as was inevitable. For he would not be supported even by the most unscrupulous enemy of Richard's memory if he refused to acquit him. Clearly there was no belief among his contemporaries that Richard was in any way to blame. Yet Mr. Gairdner cannot let the matter rest. He suggests that Richard's foundation of colleges at Middleham and Barnard Castle, with provision for masses for the souls of his father, brothers, and sisters, betokens remorse for the death of Clarence, because the licences to found these colleges were granted soon after his brother's death. Clarence is not specially mentioned, only brothers and sisters. This pious act might betoken regret, but it cannot be supposed to betoken remorse. The man's conscience must indeed have been morbidly sensitive if it caused remorse for that which the King and the Parliament had done, but which he had opposed. It was quite natural that Richard should have provided for these masses from ordinary feelings of regret and affection for all the deceased members of his family. The idea of remorse is gratuitous and very far-fetched; for Richard had arranged for the foundation of these colleges before the death of Clarence. Mr. Gairdner further remarks that Richard gained by his brother's death, his son being created Earl of Salisbury and he himself receiving the whole of a lordship of which he previously owned half. Richard certainly would not have compassed his brother's death, even assuming him to have been the monster of 'tradition,' for the sake of an earldom for his son, seeing that the father had two earldoms already, scarcely for the other half of the Barnard Castle estate. Mr. Gairdner cannot surely think that Richard had some hand in his brother's death for the sake of such very small gains. For he has told us that there was nothing mean or paltry in Richard's character, and he acquits him of the death of Clarence. King Edward, naturally enough, gave the vacant earldoms of Warwick and Salisbury to the infant sons of his two brothers.

Mr. Gairdner has nothing to say against the young prince with regard to his marriage. We, therefore, come to our historian's treatment of the events which led to Richard's accession. Mr. Gairdner dismisses the accusations against the Duke of Gloucester, that he was carrying on intrigues with Buckingham and other members of the Council, between the date of his brother's death and that of his arrival in London.[20] He also considers the arrest and execution of Lord Rivers and his companions to have been justifiable. He believes that the Woodville party intended to keep the government in their own hands by main force,[21] that the generality of the people were convinced that Rivers and Grey had entertained designs distinctly treasonable,[22] and he mentions the fact that their baggage contained large quantities of armour and implements of war. This is a proof that they contemplated the raising and arming of a large force. Mr. Gairdner even goes so far as to admit that the retribution dealt out to Rivers and his companions was 'not more severe than perhaps law itself might have authorised.' As we know from Rous that the law was invoked, these admissions amount to an exculpation of King Richard, as regards his treatment of Rivers, Vaughan, and Grey.

Mr. Gairdner's position with regard to Richard's title to the crown is curious. That title was based on the fact that Edward IV. had entered into a marriage contract with Lady Eleanor Butler before he went through the ceremony with the widow of Sir J. Grey. The Tudor King attempted to destroy all record of this event, and his official writers then put forward two other statements, which they alleged to have been made as justifications of Richard's claim to the crown. One of these was that Richard's elder brothers were illegitimate, the other that the previous marriage was with a woman named Lucy. The name of Lady Eleanor is carefully suppressed. Long afterwards the official document was discovered in which the title is based solely on the previous contract with Lady Eleanor Butler.

Such is the case very briefly stated. Mr. Gairdner believes that the story of the pre-contract with Lady Eleanor may be true. He considers that the care taken by the Tudor writers to suppress and pervert it is evidence of its truth. He even suggests that the death of Clarence was due to the fact that he had got possession of the secret. But he fails to see that the truth of this pre-contract not only invalidates the other stories invented by the Tudor writers to conceal it, but entirely destroys their credibility. Morton's statement that it was alleged by Richard's supporters that the pre-contract was with Lucy must be false, as well as the assertion that a calumny was promulgated against the Duchess of York; if the pre-contract with Lady Eleanor is true. Surely Mr. Gairdner must see that the statement of a title made in an officially inspired sermon or speech must have been made to agree with that in the document which Henry VII. attempted to destroy. Having made away with the document, so that they could mis-state its contents, Henry's chroniclers put what inventions they pleased into the mouths of preachers and orators. But the document has since been found. Its real contents are known. Men who would deliberately make this elaborate series of false statements are utterly unworthy of credit. Yet Mr. Gairdner still clings to the belief that the odious slander about the Duchess of York was promulgated, and continues to quote Morton's story as if it were authentic and reliable history.

The sole ground put forward for still believing that the slander was uttered against the Duchess of York is that one of these authorities alleges that the people were scandalised at the sermon, and another that the Duchess complained of the dishonour done her. These additions to the fable, from the same suspicious sources, can in no conceivable way strengthen its credibility.[23]

We now come to the main stronghold of Tudor calumny—the story of the smothering of the little princes in the Tower. Mr. Gairdner makes a hesitating defence. He cannot doubt that the dreadful deed was done. But he admits that the story, as told in the narrative attributed to Sir Thomas More, is full of inaccuracies and improbabilities. He contends, however, that it is not necessary for it to be true in all its details, in order to give credence to the main allegation. He also admits that the crime imputed to Richard rests upon the assertions of only a few, and that two of these mention it merely as a report. He denies that Richard was the cold scheming calculating villain of previous histories; and apparently thinks that, if this had been his character, he would not have acted in the way alleged in the story. Consequently the story could not be true. For a cold calculating villain would not have been so foolish as to leave London, and then send his orders to the Tower, without having previously ascertained that they would be obeyed. Mr. Gairdner's theory is that Richard was headstrong and reckless as to consequences, a man of violent and impatient temper. Such a man, Mr. Gairdner thinks, might act in the way described in the story; if a strong motive was suddenly supplied to him. Mr. Gairdner looks round for such a motive, and thinks he has found it in the alleged contemplated rising in favour of the two young princes. But no such motive existed. The date given for the alleged murders was August 1483. The rising, even if it had been in favour of the boys and not of Buckingham, was in October. Mr. Davies has shown that the first tidings reached the king at Lincoln on October 11,[24] and Mr. Gairdner fully admits that Richard was taken completely by surprise. This proves that no motive for the crime was supplied in August, calculated to make a violent and reckless man take sudden action. If there was no motive there was no murder. Thus Mr. Gairdner's explanation fails, while the improbabilities remain as strong as ever. The difficulties disappear as soon as Richard is acquitted, and his astute successor is placed in the dock.

With reference to this horrible accusation against King Richard, Mr. Gairdner had opened his work with the dictum that 'it is vain to deny that Richard had long lost the hearts of his subjects.' But Mr. Gairdner himself has supplied some of the proofs that the King never lost the hearts of his subjects. Mr. Gairdner acknowledges that up to September 1483, 'in the north undoubtedly, and perhaps with the common people generally, Richard was highly popular' (p. 147). In November 1484, when, on the young King's return to London he was received with demonstrations of loyalty, Mr. Gairdner says that 'perhaps he had to some extent recovered the good will of the people' (p. 243). But, in the meanwhile, we are not supplied with a shadow of a proof that he had ever lost it. He was the victim of the perfidy of a few traitors. There was no national movement against him in favour of Henry Tudor. Sharon Turner truly remarked that 'the nation had no share in the conflict. It was an ambush of a few perfidious and disaffected noblemen against the crown. Richard was overwhelmed by the explosion of a new mine, which he had not suspected to be forming beneath him, because it was prepared and fired by those whom gratitude, honour and conscience ought to have made faithful.' The city of York recorded the grief of the people at King Richard's death. He was popular to the end.

Mr. Gairdner fully explains the causes of Richard's popularity (p. 313). 'His taste in building was magnificent and princely. There was nothing mean or paltry in his character (p. 318). Many of his acts were dictated by charitable feelings or a sense of justice. He had in him a great deal of native religious sentiment (p. 47). He made it his endeavour, so far as it lay in his power, to prevent tyranny for the future (p. 205), and as king he really studied his country's welfare (p. 313). No wonder that such a King, who was also renowned for his valour in the field and his wisdom in council, should have been popular among his subjects! But it is wonderful that thoughtful and accomplished men, who admit all this, should cling to the vile and wretched calumnies, the discredited tatters of which still partly obscure the truth.

The work of Mr. Gairdner is of great value owing to its conscientious attempt to be judicially impartial, to the learning and research that are apparent in every page, and to the considerable number of errors it exposes, and of mistakes that are finally cleared up by it. The good points in the character of King Richard III. are prominently brought forward. The excellence of his government and the generosity of his character are made so apparent, that one is surprised, in the midst of this goodly record, to come suddenly on such epithets as 'usurper,' 'tyrant,' 'inhuman King.' Mr. Gairdner's learning and critical insight have so weakened the traditional fables, a half belief in which he cannot quite shake off, that they are not likely to retain a place much longer in serious history.

[1] History of the Life and Reign of Richard III., by James Gairdner (1878), 1st ed. History of the Life and Reign of Richard III., by James Gairdner (1898), 2nd ed. Henry the Seventh, by James Gairdner (1889). Article in the English Historical Review, 1891.

[2] Preface to Gairdner's Life of Richard III. p. x.

[3] Ibid. p. x.

[4] Ibid. p. xii.

[5] Ibid. p. xii.

[6] Gairdner's Richard III. p. 38.

[7] Ibid. p. 112.

[8] Ibid. pp. 115, 131.

[9] Ibid. p. 247.

[10] Ibid. p. 73.

[11] Ibid. p. 250.

[12] Ibid. p. 251.

[13] Ibid. p. 251.

[14] Stow set a better example. He adopted the 'probable story' of Fabyan, and rejected the 'tradition of later times,' as Mr. Gairdner calls the unsupported calumny of Polydore Virgil.

[15] Dr. Lingard says that 'Clarence and Gloucester, perhaps the Knights in their retinue, despatched young Edward with their swords' (iv. p. 189). In a foot-note he sees no good reason to doubt Stow. But Stow says nothing of the kind. He merely adopts Fabyan's tale that King Edward's servants despatched the prince. He does not even mention either Clarence or Gloucester. The accusation against the knights in the retinue of those princes is Lingard's own, unsupported by any evidence whatever.

[16] English Historical Review, 1891 (July), p. 448.

[17] The Lancastrians gave no quarter at Wakefield, slaughtering all prisoners high and low. At the second battle ol St. Albans their cruelty was deepened by bad faith. After Bosworth, Henry Tudor ordered four executions which, in his outlawed condition, were lawless murders. The atrocious conduct of his son, in suppressing the Pilgrimage of Grace, was still more horrible. Executions went on, long after all resistance had ceased, with unrelenting cruelty.

The tribunal at Tewkesbury is unjustly arraigned by modern historians, while the barbarities of Lancastrians and Tudors are slurred over or ignored.

[18] 'I am struck with the singular leniency of Edward IV. towards his political enemies. The rolls of Parliament are full of petitions for the reversal of attainders. I do not recollect a single instance in which the petition was refused.'—Thorold Rogers, Agriculture and Prices, iv. p. 180.

[19] Dr. Lingard's chief reason for believing that Gloucester murdered Henry VI. is that 'writers who lived under the next dynasty attributed the black deed to Richard'

(iv. p. 192). Of course they did. They were well paid to do so.

[20] P. 61. He considers it more probable that Gloucester was ignorant of what had been going on in London.

[21] P. 62.

[22] P. 66.

[23] Dr. Lingard's argument in favour of the calumny against the Duchess of York is that a man who would shed the blood of his nephews would not refuse to allow his mother to be slandered. Doubtless the Doctor would have been equally ready with the reversed argument. A man who would slander his mother would not refuse to allow his nephews to be murdered (iv. p. 232 n).

[24] York Records, p. 181 n.

Printed in Great Britain
by Amazon.co.uk, Ltd.,
Marston Gate.